Architectural Design
July/August 2006

Programming Cultures:
Art and Architecture in the Age of Software

Guest-edited by
Mike Silver

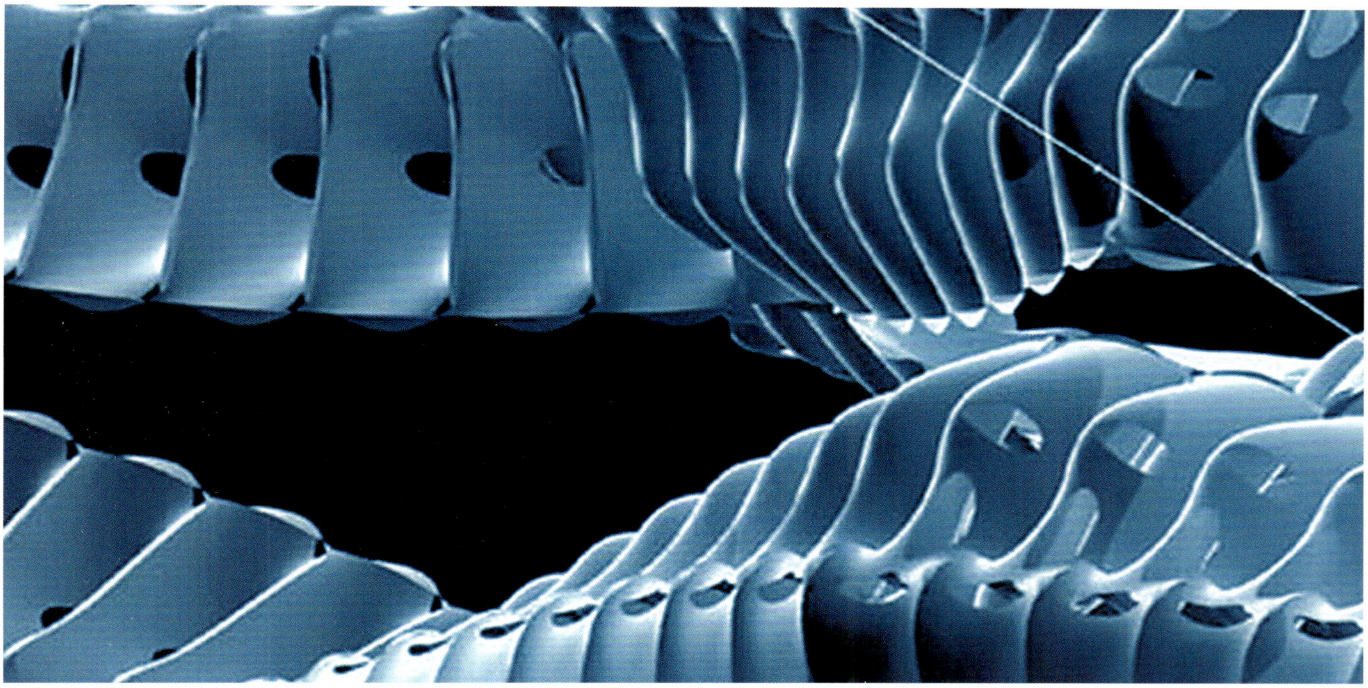

WILEY-ACADEMY

ISBN-13 9780470025857
ISBN-10 0470025859
Profile No 182
Vol 76 No 4

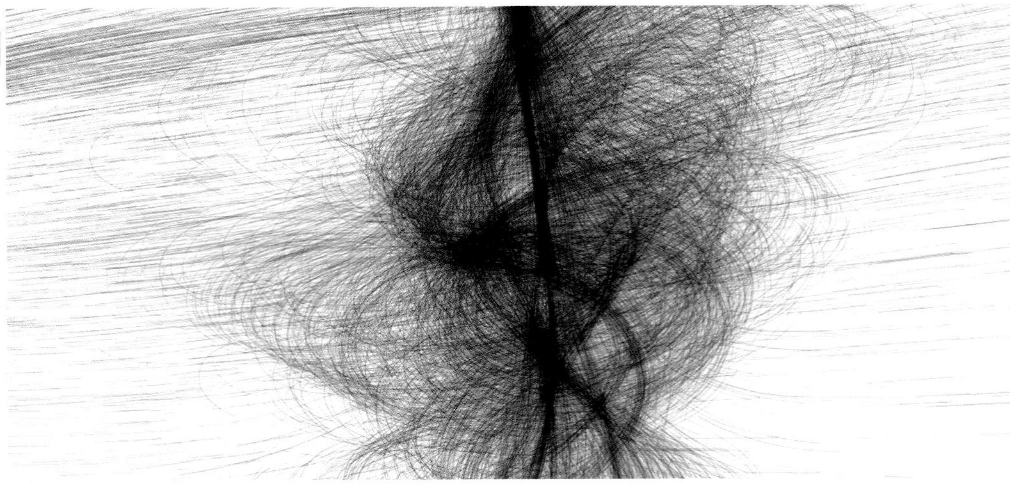

26

AD

Editorial Offices
International House
Ealing Broadway Centre
London W5 5DB

T: +44 (0)20 8326 3800
F: +44 (0)20 8326 3801
E: architecturaldesign@wiley.co.uk

Printed in Italy by Conti Tipicolor

Abbreviated positions
b = bottom, c = centre, l = left, r = right

Front cover: Process 6 (Image 4), 28" x 28" inkjet print, 2005. Print derived from Process 6 (see 'Process/Drawing', pp 26–33). A dense surface of circles emanate from fixed points. The forms emerge as lines are drawn between their centre points as they expand outwards. Each circular element is the same software run with a different configuration. Each grows differently in response to its simulated environment. © CEB Reas.

AD
p 4 courtesy Greg Lynn FORM; pp 5-11, 13 & 46-51 © Mike Silver; pp 16-17, 19 & 23-5 © Ingeborg Rocker; p 18 © Stephen Wolfram LLC; p 20(t) © From *Alan Turing, The Enigma*, by Andrew Hodges, published by Hutchinson. Reprinted by permission of The Random House Group Ltd; p 20(b) courtesy Arthur W Burks, from John von Neumann, *Essays on Cellular Automata*; p 21 © Kevin Lindsey www.kevlindev.com; p 22(t) © Reprinted from Aristid Lindenmayer, 'Mathematical models of cellular interactions in development: I. Filaments with one-sided inputs', Journal for Theoretical Biology, Vol 18, 1968, figs 1 &2 (p 286), figs 4 & 5 (p 310) & figs 6 & 7 (p 312); p 22(b) © Allen Bernholtz, FRAIC; pp 26-33 © CEB Reas, courtesy of bitforms gallery, New York; pp 34-37 © Stephen Wolfram LLC; pp 38 & 43-44 © Karl Chu; p 41 courtesy Karl Chu; pp 52, 56(bl), 57 & 59-60 © Lalvani Studio; p 53 © Milgo/Bufkin; pp 54-55 & 56(br) © Milgo-Lalvani; pp 62-71 © Evan Douglis; pp 72-81 © Alisa Andrasek; pp 82-87 © Gehry Technologies; pp 88-95 courtesy Greg Lynn FORM.

AD+
pp 98, 99 & 100 © Arup Associates; p 101 © Christian Richters; pp 102-103 © Arup Associates/Oaker; p 104(t) © Peter Cook; p 104(b) © Arup Associates/Roland Reinardy; pp 106–109 © Dine Murphy Wood; p 110 © David Clifton; pp 113, 115(b) & 117(t) © Jordan Mozer and Associates; p 114 © Kingmond Young; pp 115 (tl, tr & c), 116 & 117(b) © Doug Snower Photography; pp 118-119, 120(c&b), 121 © Philip Ruault; p 120(t) © Lacaton Vassal; pp 122 & 128 © FAT; pp 123-24 &126-127 © Len Grant; p 129 © NASA; pp 130-131 © Will McLean; pp 132-134 © Helen Peyton.

Published in Great Britain in 2006 by Wiley-Academy, a division of John Wiley & Sons Ltd

Telephone +44 (0)1243 779777
Email (for orders and customer service enquiries): cs-books@wiley.co.uk
Visit our Home Page on wileyeurope.com or wiley.com

Subscription Offices UK
John Wiley & Sons Ltd
Journals Administration Department
1 Oldlands Way, Bognor Regis
West Sussex, PO22 9SA
T: +44 (0)1243 843272
F: +44 (0)1243 843232
E: cs-journals@wiley.co.uk

[ISSN: 0003-8504]

AD is published bimonthly and is available to purchase on both a subscription basis and as individual volumes at the following prices.

Single Issues
Single issues UK: £22.99
Single issues outside UK: US$45.00
Details of postage and packing charges available on request.

Annual Subscription Rates 2006
Institutional Rate
Print only or Online only: UK£175/US$290
Combined Print and Online: UK£193/US$320
Personal Rate
Print only: UK£99/US$155
Student Rate
Print only: UK£70/US$110
Prices are for six issues and include postage and handling charges. Periodicals postage paid at Jamaica, NY 11431. Air freight and mailing in the USA by Publications Expediting Services Inc, 200 Meacham Avenue, Elmont, NY 11003
Individual rate subscriptions must be paid by personal cheque or credit card. Individual rate subscriptions may not be resold or used as library copies.

All prices are subject to change without notice.

Postmaster
Send address changes to 3 Publications Expediting Services, 200 Meacham Avenue, Elmont, NY 11003

Contents

52

62

Editorial

Despite AD's long-standing association with the digital in design, this is the first issue with any reference to programming or software in the title. This says much about architecture's previous relationship with the computer. At the end of the 1990s when I first started editing AD, I was often confounded by the gap between design process and text. Why was everyone generating amorphous Maya-inspired blobs, but talking about Derrida? *Programming Cultures* hails the way for a new generation of work that comes out of a pure, unadulterated passion for software. For a young designer like CEB Reas, who has been playing with script since childhood, it is an entirely natural creative impulse. For experienced designers like Malcolm McCullough and Greg Lynn, it has come out of decades of pioneering work on computer-aided design. McCullough, one of the first architecture managers for Autodesk, exhorts us that 'all you need is the will to improvise'; Lynn enthuses 'I love the moment when I discover some new potential in software.' This is all constructive play which, as described by Ingeborg M Rocker in her interview with Lynn, adds up to 'exhaustive exploration'. It is a not insignificant shift, which moves architects away from being mere consumers of software towards becoming knowledgeable adapters, crafters and, ultimately, producers. So much more than a development of architects' technical skill bases, it is set to have a huge impact on the culture of architecture. Could the deftness with scripting that educators and designers like Mike Silver, the guest-editor of this issue, is encouraging in his students at New York's Pratt Institute of Architecture become commonplace? Could scripting become the new drawing? The potential aesthetic impact of this way of working is anticipated by Pia Ednie-Brown's discussion of the new compositional principles spearheaded in the work of Alisa Andrasek of biothing. For, as Ednie-Brown points out: 'Working with computational algorithms as primary generative material offers a different bent to, for example, the mathematical ratios of the Renaissance or the flow diagrams of Modernism.' At such a nascent stage, the ultimate cultural repercussions of a new programming era are only to be guessed at. The implications are that we could be at the brink of an entirely new period of culture and knowledge; if so, could Stephen Wolfram be set to become the next Isaac Newton, and Gehry Technologies' software be about to eclipse the pattern-books of Palladio?

Helen Castle

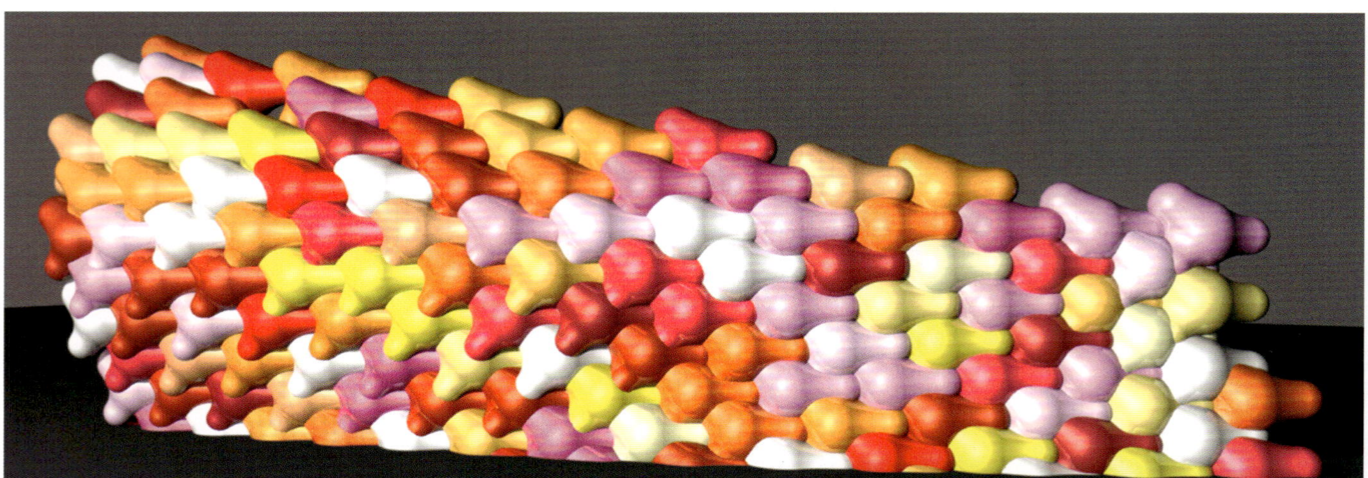

Greg Lynn, Slavin House, Venice, California, due for completion 2007
In this project, Lynn is testing the limits of Gehry Technologies' software. As Lynn states in his interview with Ingeborg M Rocker (page 88), the use of the software is 'provocative at many levels and is having a pretty significant effect on my work'.

Towards a Programming Culture in the Design Arts

In his introduction to this issue of *AD*, guest-editor **Mike Silver** celebrates 'the flexible language of commands and logical procedures' of computers whose creative potential has until now been undervalued in architecture. He explains how the 'happy accident' of late 1990s blob architecture is now giving way to a focus on programming and composing new code, which promises 'to generate new and unprecedented modes of expression'.

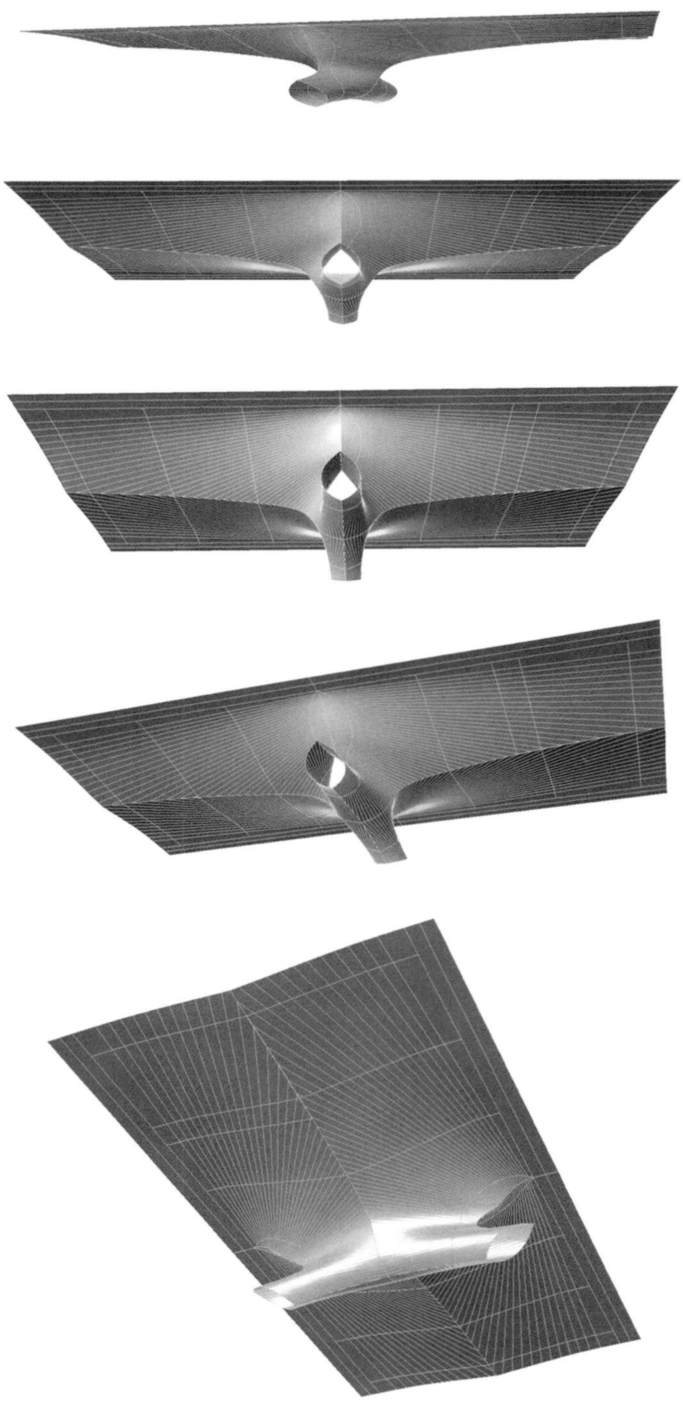

Pratt Institute School of Architecture, Carbon-fibre chandelier studio project, autumn 2006
In this studio led by Professor Mike Silver, students' bent for scripting was applied in a project that developed new software to coordinate the movement of a CNC machine's rotating bed with the controlled trajectory of its servo-controlled hotwire. Here, foam shapes cut on a CNC hotwire foam-cutter were used as moulds for hand-laid carbon-fibre panels.

Chandelier fabrication process using epoxy resin, carbon-fibre and Nomex drapes over a CNC foam-cut mandrel.

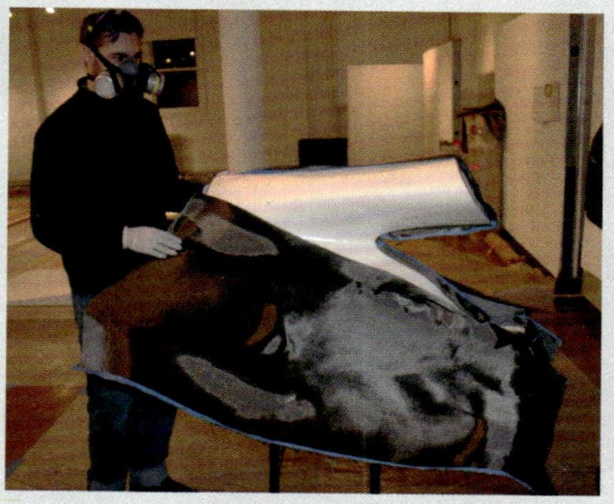

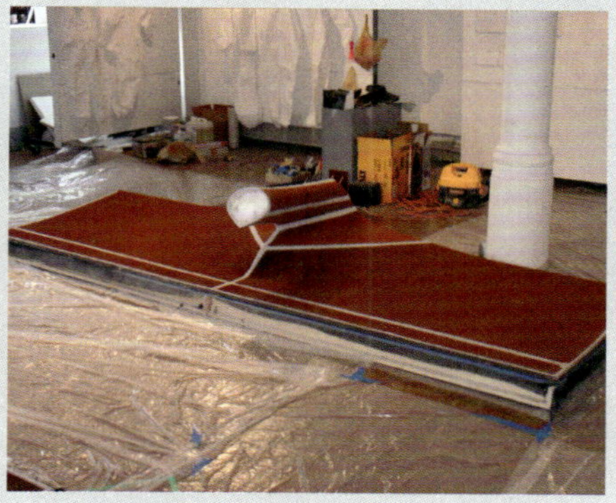

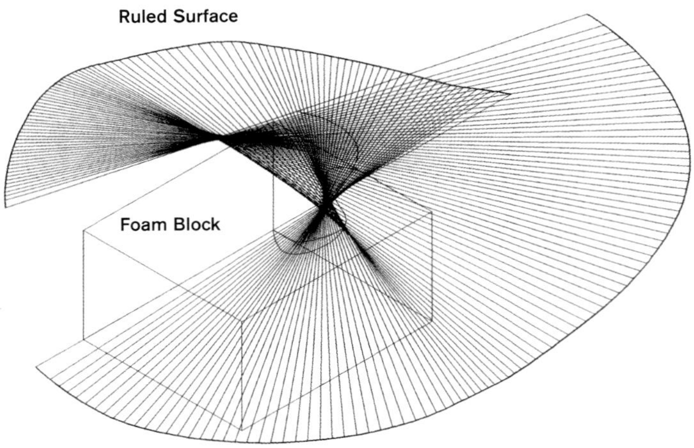

Ruled surface.

```
Sub Cutsurface
Dim strCutpath, strAngle, strBound, arrCenterpt
Dim arrStartpts, arrEndpts, arrTemp, strTemp, arrTemp2, strStartPt,
strEndPt

Dim strStartLineID, strEndLineID
Dim strDetail
Dim strStartpts, strEndpts

Dim strTheta, PI, arrMatrix, arrOrigin, strOrigin

Dim arrEdgesrfs

strOrigin = "0,0,0"

arrOrigin = Rhino.Str2Pt(strOrigin)

PI = 3.141592653589793

strCutpath = Rhino.GetObject("Curve of cut path (This should be in
the XZ Plane)")
If IsNull(strCutpath) Then
Exit Sub
End If
```

Proprietary script for generating ruled surfaces.

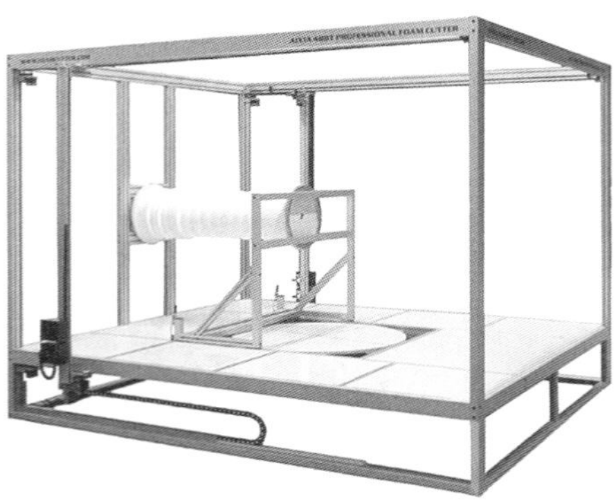

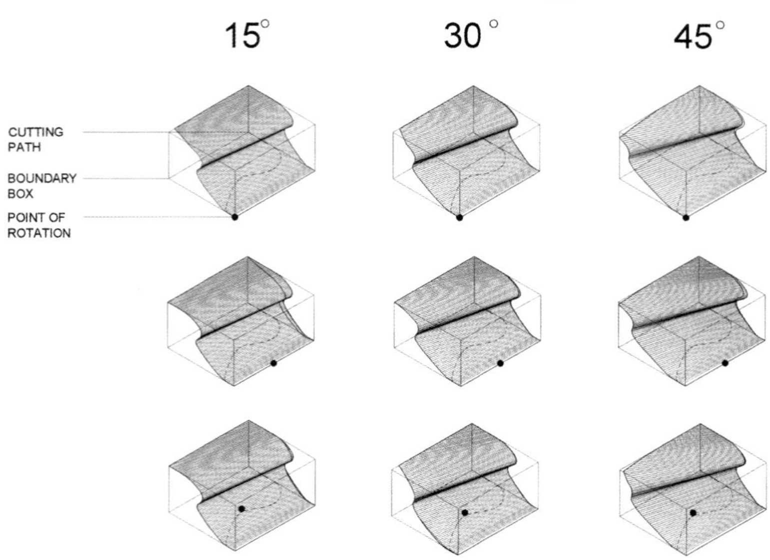

Ruled surface generated from proprietary script by Japhy Bartlett.

'You write a few lines of code and suddenly life is better for a hundred million people.'

Charles Simonyi, inventor of Microsoft Word[1]

The first architects to use computers were interested primarily in maximising the efficiency of conventional modes of production. Designers working on the World's Fair in 1964 used a primitive calculating machine to build the Unisphere, and around the same time Eero Saarinen engineered the complex reinforced-concrete shells of his TWA terminal using early structural-analysis software. During the 1980s many architectural practices employed the first automated systems for drafting construction documents, as computers became cheaper and more readily available. In the 1990s the buzz surrounding blob architecture embodied design's obsession with digital media at the brink of a new millennium. This trend has now given way to the more urgent problem of process and code. Many of the contributors to this issue have expanded on a programming paradigm originally explored at MIT by the artist and graphic designer John Maeda, whose protégé, CEB Reas is featured in this issue.

Not surprisingly, architecture has lagged far behind these pioneers with creativity and experimentation taking a back seat to the priorities of disciplinary continuity, history and function. At MIT, architecture's foray into programming was mostly restricted to the computer replication of known forms and building types exemplified in the work of William Mitchell and Richard Freeman, and the shape grammars of George Stiny. As Greg Lynn has pointed out, these systems were 'merely an extension of a previously delineated and closed set of potential

Finished panels for the Carbon-fibre chandelier project.

forms whose characteristics can be stated in advance by an ideal mathematics'.[2] Today, programming in architecture has become a much more open process, one that is inspired by the capacity to generate new and unprecedented modes of expression (see Malcolm McCullough's essay on scripted space). For many architects coding has become the formal and operative focus of building itself.

Universality = Difference

In the 1990s, the association between computers and architecture was marked by the proliferation of amorphous, curvilinear forms. But this link is far from necessary or inevitable. It is, in fact, a happy accident precipitated by pre-computational experiments based on 'folding' and the subsequent appropriation of operationally specific modelling software. How, then, do we determine the relationship between computing and architecture? What forms, practices and techniques will seem most relevant if the internal structure of software and the theories that drive its development are changed at the same time? Can we even define computational architecture? The answer to this last question is that we cannot. As Ingeborg M Rocker's essay on page 16 shows, computers are universal machines. Unlike classical machines (clocks, steam engines and tin-openers) they can perform a wide variety of tasks without significant changes to their physical design. Through the writing of new programs, very different operations can be executed on a single device.

Where the information theorist defines universality through the production of difference, for architects it holds exactly the opposite meaning. The stripped-down and monolithic style of international Modernism was thought to be universal for all places and times. Miesian 'universal space' was constrained by a homogeneous and infinitely extended grid, very much unlike the complex, convoluted matrix of interconnected microcircuitry that constitutes today's digital networks. The universality of a programmable computer is therefore measured by its degrees of freedom. What makes it unique, as a device, is the flexible language of commands and logical procedures that can instantly transform it from one function to another. With existing software, designers are often forced to conduct experimental work using fixed protocols originally developed to solve the visualisation problems faced by aircraft designers and Hollywood film-makers. Even in these disciplines, staff programmers are busy creating new codes for challenges that are beyond the scope of a particular product. Not surprisingly, this has also become true for the early advocates of software appropriation in architecture. Faced with increasingly complex commissions and a growing practice, many designers have turned to the in-house creation of proprietary code. Here, one immediately thinks of Dennis Shelden's redevelopment of CATIA at Gehry Systems, and Greg Lynn's collaboration with Microstation.

Both examples suggest the possibility of freeing computer-aided design (CAD) from any one particular concept of form rooted in any one particular software. If indeed codes can be changed to fit specific needs or developed from scratch, then there can be no such thing as a 'computational architecture'; only possible architectures actualised by new programs. These programs can be both simple, generative codes that

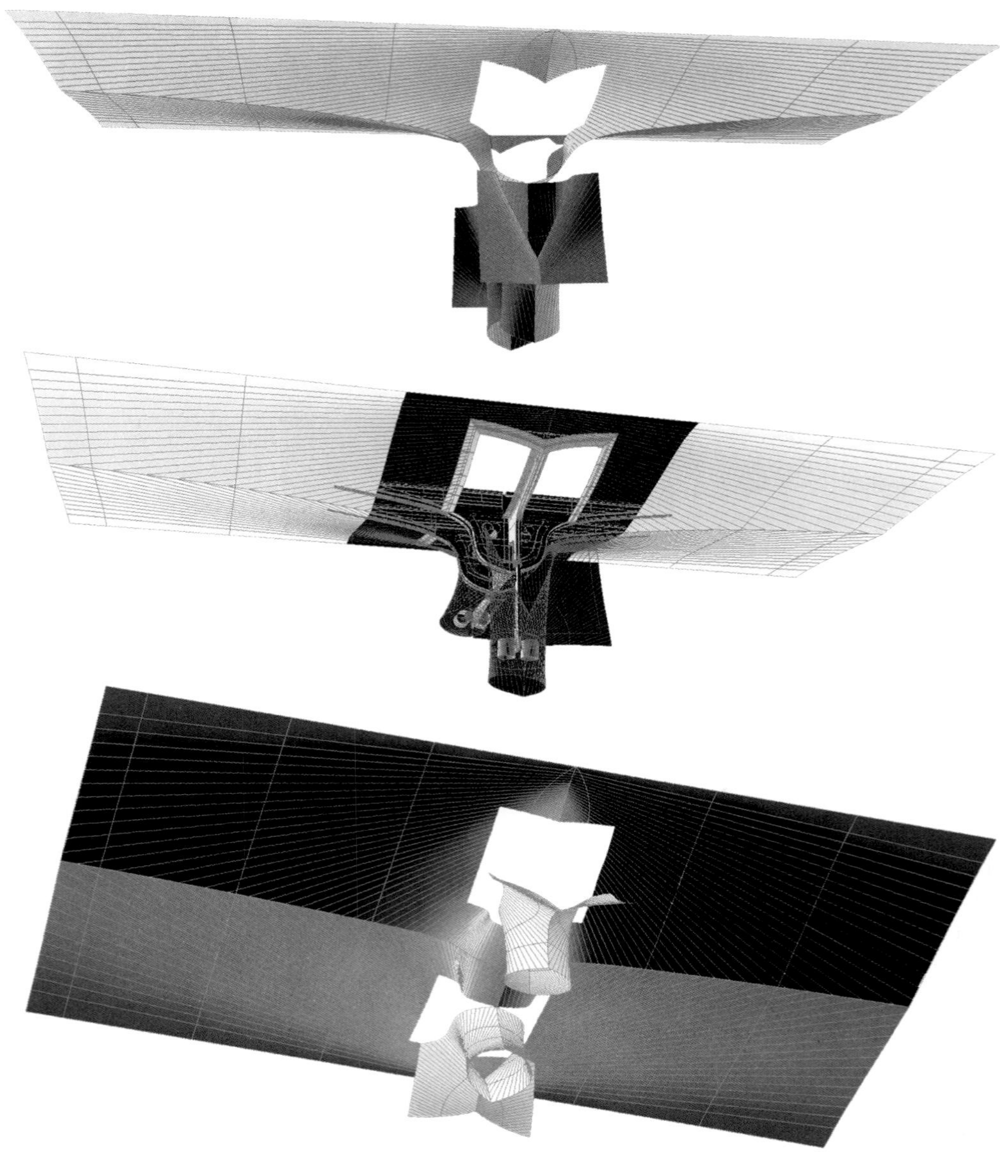

Carbon-fibre chandelier project showing the movable light-reflecting ceiling shroud and retractable downlights.

produce complexity (see, for example, the articles by Stephen Wolfram and Karl Chu),[3] or complex programs that help make difficult tasks easy. Programs have become pervasive mainly because their instructions can be applied to so many diverse problems (for example, one piece of software in the stealth bomber actually counteracts the plane's poor aerodynamics and prevents it falling from the sky even when the pilot deliberately initiates a stall). New systems of feedback and control, database-management protocols, genetic design algorithms and a whole universe of scripting systems now drive everything from a simple electric toothbrush to the Internet.

Building Programs and Programs for Building

The ability to craft tools that address both the practical challenges of building design and the human capacity to imagine new forms is a fairly recent development. As specific programming languages become less mysterious and easier to master, 'home-made' software will most likely become a familiar part of design culture. This move by the design community to take an active role in the production of code transcends the limitations of prefabricated software tools.

To a great extent this shift is becoming a necessity. Large, unanticipated gaps in the computer-aided design and construction process can only be bridged by the creation of special software. Many of these tools cannot be anticipated in advance by outside developers since the most imaginative projects begin with ideas that exceed ordinary expectations. In order to connect different production processes, materials and fabrication devices, new tools are required. In fact, as architect Haresh Lalvani has demonstrated in his collaboration with Milgo/Bufkin (see his interview with John Lobell), unexpected functions for standard digital-fabrication equipment can be created simply by writing code.

In academia, students and teachers have been increasingly drawn to the possibilities of proprietary software development. For many architects programming has become the new drawing. In the carbon-fibre chandelier project designed for the lobby of Pratt Institute's new School of Architecture,[4] complex EPS moulds for hand-laid composites were produced using a large-scale computer-numerically controlled (CNC) foam-cutter. In order to precisely construct the necessary 3-D shapes, new software was developed to coordinate the movement of the machine's rotating bed with the controlled trajectory of its servo-controlled hotwire. The ability to link disparate material practices (foam-cutting and advanced composite construction) would not have been possible without the new scripts.

With these examples in mind, *Programming Cultures* explores the power of code by encouraging artists and architects to become more involved in the creation of home-made, task-specific tools. Through individual labour or by collaborating with skilled developers, designers can harness the power of universality. In this way universality supports difference in opposition to the sterile homogeneity commonly associated with rigid protocols and fixed procedures. What computation must now serve (as the work of Evan Douglis aptly demonstrates) are the founding concepts, intuitions and desires that can only emerge from a varied and creative practice. Rather than working through algorithms imposed on the architect by an external agent or product philosophy, intuition and desire motivate artistic production while encouraging the spread of individual creativity.

As the projects in this book suggest, it is only a question of time before software development becomes an integral part of the building design process. Certainly, this will be an unprecedented moment in the history of architecture. AD

Mike Silver

Thank you to Evan Douglis and Dean Thomas Hanrahan at the Pratt Institute School of Architecture for their support of the Universal Machines symposium held during the spring of 2005, which provided the original impetus for this issue. Malcolm McCullough, John Lobell and Yee Peng Chia were especially instrumental in provoking questions and inspiring discussion. *Programming Cultures: Architecture, Art and Science in the Age of Software Development* would not have been possible if it were not for the support provided by Helen Castle, the staff of John Wiley & Sons and a generous grant from the Graham Foundation.

Notes

1 Steve Lohr, *Go To*, Perseus Books (New York), 2001, p 2.
2 Greg Lynn, 'Variations on the Rowe Complex', from *Folds, Bodies and Blobs: Collected Essays*, Books-by Architects Series, Bibliotheque de Belgique, 1998, p 212.
3 Where Wolfram defines 'code' as a generative abstraction that emulates pattern formation at a multitude of spatial dimensions within the universe (analytic) for Chu 'codes' are used for the construction of possible worlds (synthetic).
4 Carbon-fibre chandelier. Critic: Professor Mike Silver. Advisers: Mark Parsons, Evan Douglis, Rob Langoni. Programming: Japhy Bartlett. Design and Construction: Patrick Weise, Hanna Meeran, Felice Basti, Jakie Nguyen, Milton Hernandez, Genoveva Alvarez, Jonathan Lee, Julie Camfrancq, Michael Chase, Jean Keesler, Eddy Adu, Jong Kim, Tomoko Miyazaki. Research: Mel Sakor, Arta Yazdansets, Hasti Valipour, Kenneth Chong, Caitlin Duffy.

The Universal Machines Symposium

This issue of AD developed out of the Universal Machines symposium held at the School of Architecture at the Pratt Institute in February 2005. The symposium continued a long tradition at Pratt of combining interests in theory and practice, thereby allowing students, teachers and practitioners to address emerging technological and social issues in architecture.

It is therefore satisfying to see that while several of the articles here address highly theoretical issues on computation and architecture, just as many bring that interest into new forms of material practice.

The faculty and programmes at Pratt are diverse and address a wide range of interests, all of which combine to create Pratt's unique strength. With the Universal Machines symposium and this issue of AD we are continuing a long-standing commitment to design excellence.

Thomas Hanrahan,
Dean, School of Architecture, Pratt Institute

20 Years of Scripted Space

Malcolm McCullough is an advocate of the importance of play and manipulation within the parameters of established software. As he asserts, 'Once the design world has been set up, it still needs to be explored, played and mastered with finesse'. A veteran of architectural programming (he was the first architecture product manager for Autodesk, from 1985 to 1986), he reflects on the last two decades of development.

The Invitation: Rules and Two-Part Design

You have to get free of the grind. It is just too much work to construct every design element uniquely, directly and without regard for what knowledge it represents. Now that technology lets us treat abstract schemas as objects for manipulation, it makes no more sense to design by drawing each line and modelling every surface than it does to drive an aeroplane down a highway. The more kinds of representation that software lets us manipulate, the more opportunity we have to take design to a higher level. After all, the very essence of software is to represent problems abstractly, through the use of variables, conditionals, iterations and procedures. All of this has now been made accessible to nonspecialists via user-friendly, shrink-wrapped design software. The disciplined programming work has been done by the professionals behind all this gear: all you need is the will to improvise.

Indeed you must. For as the coders in Silicon Valley would be the first to admit, while their knowledge of shapes and data structures and usable interfaces naturally surpasses anything some casual tinkerer (or headstrong academic) could come up with on his or her own, such knowledge stops at the border between the theory and the application of form. They know how to process forms, but only the design professional knows which forms, when, where and why. Thus every discipline must bring its domain knowledge to the question of software representation. The software part has been made as easy as possible by new scripting languages. Architects, engineers, fabricators – any domain whose knowledge depends on form – have all begun to adapt and extend generic software tools to the specifics of their disciplines. It is no longer so rare for a design firm to have a few people writing code – not the kind of code that requires a degree in computer science to get right, but the kind that can be crafted one line at a time on top of commercial software while working on form. No need to learn how to link headers or throw exceptions. This kind of code is by you, for you – and it is fun.

This is because it lets you game the rules of play. The amazing part of scripting is how it adds a whole extra level to design thinking. First you set up some rules for generating forms, then you play them to see what kind of design world they create, and then you go back and tweak the rules. With a bit of interface technology, even just a few simple buttons sliders, you can tweak almost as quickly as you play.

This does require some change in outlook. Many designers, or at least most design students, believe that any constraints on the character and construction of form will just hamper their creativity. This is wrong as wrong can be. Any expressive medium has its idioms, types and genres, and the better established of those are often where the richest expressions occur. Meanwhile, many technologists and managers also believe that computer usage is serious work, and that play is just distraction or, worse, entertainment. This too is wrong. Even before computers, tangible speculation was the heart of design work. Software just articulates and accelerates that conjecture. We can ask 'What if?' more often, and about more abstract kinds of assumptions.

But consider one last misconception, namely the old ambition (especially prevalent in the 1980s) towards the computability of all knowledge. To understand the limits of this, it is a degree not in computer science but in philosophy that is necessary. Any sage should know that some things are easier done than said, that an approximation is almost always enough, that convenience of measurement should not be mistaken for completeness of truth, that logic is so cumbersome that humans seldom use it, and so on. Therefore the role of computers in design is seldom one of automation. There are few sets of design rules that can be set up to be

There are few sets of design rules that can be set up to be interesting enough to run on their own. Once the design world has been set up, it still needs to be explored, played and mastered with finesse.

interesting enough to run on their own. Once the design world has been set up, it still needs to be explored, played and mastered with finesse.

At least that is what they were saying in the 1980s. I'm old enough, and fortunate enough, to report some of this first-hand.

Some Basic History and Theory of Design Computing

Twenty years ago, in 1986, you couldn't just noodle with spline surface models all day. No online chat idled in some nearby window – nor shopping nor shooter game. No gargantuan operating system was there to interrupt you with security alerts, nor to push you unwanted software, nor to cram your 'personal' computer with 10,000 needless things. Back then there was no presumption that anyone but the computer was dumb. You could almost still hear yourself think.

That year is significant in terms of today's interest in scripting because it was the year Autodesk took over the personal computer design-software market – mainly, I still think, because of its new advantages in scripting language. When a desktop PC was the world's idea of a 'microcomputer', the field was still wide open: and while the big architecture firms were still breaking the bank on a Vax or a Prime, something had to give. The company's AutoCAD was the first of the PC computer-aided design (CAD) programs to record command-line sequences of its drawing operations (which remains essential to the craft aspect of this culture) within the variable structures and flow constructs of an interpreted programming language. And even if the vast majority of its users never fully rose to this, there was remarkable promise in that this language was Lisp, the usual preference among the artificial intelligence (AI) community of the day. If we define 'scripting' as coding one line at a time on an interpreter that belongs to a powerful host program, then it is difficult to find an earlier popular instance in design graphics, nor one that expanded the constituency for design computing so far, so rapidly. (Among my own responsibilities as the company's architecture product manager in 1986 was reviewing proposals from dozens of new businesses to be included in Autodesk's catalogue of such scripted 'third party' software.)

The universities were aiming much higher, of course. Also coming of age in the 1980s was a knowledge representation that has long remained an academic focus in architectural computing: shape grammars. (At Autodesk we read all the papers of the theory's inventor, George Stiny, with whom I had just studied briefly at UCLA.) Everyone knew that the discrete entity-and-layer structure of early CAD systems was not enough. Theoretically, grammars were a powerful way beyond this towards substitutions and subdivisions in articulating form. It was expected that these could become very practical expert assistants on well-formed classes of design problems. Unfortunately, the level of codification was high. Early applications operated within very specific architectural motifs, the most famous example of which was Wrightian Prairie-style houses. Even for applications in rote architectural production – say, laying out a set of hotel rooms – these better formal structures had less ready application to everyday architectural problem-solving.

The more accessible next step in knowledge representation was instead a dimensionally driven approach that became known simply as 'parametrics'. This is mainly a matter of expressing design problems or, more specifically, formal types, computationally in terms of a short set of independent design variables, especially dimensions. From the values of these few independent dimensions, software can derive a particular instance in that type of form. The essence of the type is implied in the parameterisation, the circumstances of the instance are specified in the arguments given to the dimensional variable, and the two-level process of design begins. Although some classes of form can be codified to a single size variable, such as is designated for a hat or a pair of shoes, most cannot. Although many more arbitrary classes of form can be constructed if the number of independent

Recalling AutoLisp, the earliest generative scripting language to be used widely in giving architectural form.

Tool-like operations modified visual objects of design in real time onscreen. Dense continuous notation became available for modelling, illustrating and orchestrating in time. Density was a matter of response time and resolution. Between any two states of a digital artefact, there was effectively another. This made it much easier to achieve design states by discovery through manipulation rather than derivation through formulas.

variables is sufficiently large, the parametric process is more valuable if that set of variables is kept manageably low. The value is in the use of dependent variables to generate relatively detailed instances from relatively few inputs. This is especially true if those inputs can couple the generation of form to the ranges and constraints of the machine processes by which they are to be fabricated.

'The essence of the architectural type' quickly became good subject matter in design education using the new computational medium. In 1989, a healthy few years in advance of the wave that would reduce us all to teaching freeform direct manipulation with the latest spline surface modeller, Harvard introduced what may have been the first programming course required for all professional degree candidates in a leading school of architecture. The software basis for this initiative was a program called TopDown, written mainly at UCLA, by Robin Liggett and William Mitchell. This had been inspired in part by shape grammars, and in part by the existing pedagogy of teaching design theory through programming, and in part by recent improvements in ready-made interface widgets. TopDown provided a visual and dynamic way to combine substitution and dimensional variations on a compositional motif. To make a beginning artefact in it involved in the order of 20 lines of Pascal code. Even this was alien, however.

A self-conscious and sleep-deprived Harvard architecture student was often not the best casual coder. Furthermore, much of the faculty then still believed that gentlemen did not operate machinery. It is an understatement to say that this course met with resentment.

The Direct Manipulation Boom

As the 1990s wore on, the graphical user interface did so much to make computing accessible to nonspecialists that it quickly became the only form of computer use that most people had ever known. Perhaps the most essential principle of this interface remained that 1980s breakthrough of 'direct manipulation'. Tool-like operations modified visual objects of design in real time onscreen. Dense continuous notation became available for modelling, illustrating and orchestrating in time. Density was a matter of response time and resolution. Between any two states of a digital artefact, there was effectively another. This made it much easier to achieve design states by discovery through manipulation rather than derivation through formulas. Nevertheless, a notation was effectively kept in software standard file formats. In other words, unlike any previous medium that was dense and fluid enough to allow continuous coaxing into conformity with whatever was held in the designer's mind's eye, this new medium had reproducible documentation. It also allowed a proliferation and management of versions without loss of quality. No longer 'just a tool' (in the apologetic sense of not influencing one's intentions), design computing rapidly matured as a medium in which bias, appreciation, expression and new genres were inevitable.

Alas the great rush to the seductions of all this new technical possibility effectively drowned most existing agendas in designers' programming culture. For the first time, the majority of computer users were noncoders. Improvisation prevailed over composition.

The theoretical prospects raised were of an open and bottom-up morphology rather than closed and top-down. Deleuzian difference-and-repetition spread through the discipline like an invasive species. So by 1996, not only did noodling with spline surfaces all day work comfortably in practice: it also worked in theory.

Of course there were other, more fundamental reasons why programming played out better in other form-giving disciplines than in architecture. The course of parametrics seems significant in this regard. Parametrics work better in domains whose subject matter is engineered form itself – especially in mechanical components for complex assemblies such as vehicles. Parametric design works less well where physical configuration and performance are just the means, and a more emergent usage pattern is the end. Or, to put it the other way round, when the subject matter of design is more the social arrangements and less the mechanical assemblies used to house them. Parameterisation breaks down when the design problems are wickedly under- or overconstrained, or where the design variables are less obvious. Compared to an aeroplane part, even the aforementioned rote hotel room is less computable.

Then, of course, the spirit of casual improvisation in code moved on – and struck gold with the World Wide Web. Accomplishments in scripting interactivity (for example using Java, Lingo and Perl) at least temporarily drew attention away from the prospect of scripting pure form. Indeed, it could make a million for you overnight.

Among those who did not abandon built form for more visual pursuits, code seemed unnecessary. Especially among architects preoccupied with radical novelty in autographic form – a pursuit now made so accessible by software that any fool could do it – the more immediate technical possibilities of direct manipulation were the order of the day. The most favoured genre of improvised objects became known as 'blobs'.

Nevertheless, the flame continued to burn for design education through programming. In 1996, John Maeda launched a Java-based design fundamentals pedagogy amid the gizmo-centrism of MIT, and the results were instantly stunning. As documented in *Design By Numbers*,[1] *Creative Code*[2] and the former's progeny online at dbn.media.met.edu, there is a lot to be said for the role of simple algorithmic beauty in aesthetic education. It is beyond the scope of this essay to document this landmark work, which is mentioned here mainly to set the historical context.

For one thing, the purity of Maeda's approach let aspiring designers step right outside the increasingly bloated commercial software standards. In the 1980s, the PC had been hailed as the first machine that someone might look forward to using, but by the late 1990s it was no longer so personal, nor pleasant, due to the disfiguring bloat of its operating system. Where any theory of abstract craft broke down was on the stability of the personal tools and medium. There wasn't any.

Even in the most delusional hours of the blobmeisters' boom, not all was the vagaries of fashion. And as the smoke cleared from the dotcom crash, many transformations in design work remained. Seemingly on the basis of such advances, programming culture has been rediscovered in architecture. Consider some reasons why.

Architecture Rediscovers Programming

Even in the most delusional hours of the blobmeisters' boom, not all was the vagaries of fashion. And as the smoke cleared from the dotcom crash, many transformations in design work remained. Seemingly on the basis of such advances, programming culture has been rediscovered in architecture. Consider some reasons why.

Advances in digital fabrication must be first among these motives. Simply put, there is now far more incentive to express design in terms of a few variables based on the machining process. Whether in the schools, design-build practices or new niches in the just-in-time supply chain for a rapidly building world, rapid prototyping and computer-numerically controlled (CNC) machining have become competitive necessities.

Second, the theoretical basis of cultural expression in form is increasingly informed by a domain of knowledge that appears relatively comfortable with notions of generative algorithmic beauty: namely biology. Especially with respect to growth and emergence, but also with respect to the harmonies and recursions of static biomorphic objects, this present fashion in architecture has a greater need for coded formulations.

In addition, more people (and most management gurus) know that information technology and organisational change are just two sides of the same coin. Task automation gives way to strategic reconfiguration that legitimises creative work in more circles, and creates niches for new kinds of practice in the delivery of customisable design.

And finally, and perhaps most widespread culturally, the crafts of personalising one's workspace and scripting one's intellectual pleasures have become far more distinct in the generation of designers who grew up with computing. The bloat does not seem to bother so many of them, and the interruptions and multitask, fragmented attention may actually be felt as an advantage. Some of these designers have excellent training in algorithmic structures, even.

Given the visual interfaces of better software today, with the right process mindset, you might not even know when you are coding. The trick is to see patterns, and then to find the free play within the structures of them. Surely this is a form of intelligence. AD

Notes

1 John Maeda, *Design By Numbers*, MIT Press (Cambridge, MA), 1999.
2 John Maeda, *Creative Code: Aesthetics and Computation*, Thames and Hudson (New York), 2004.

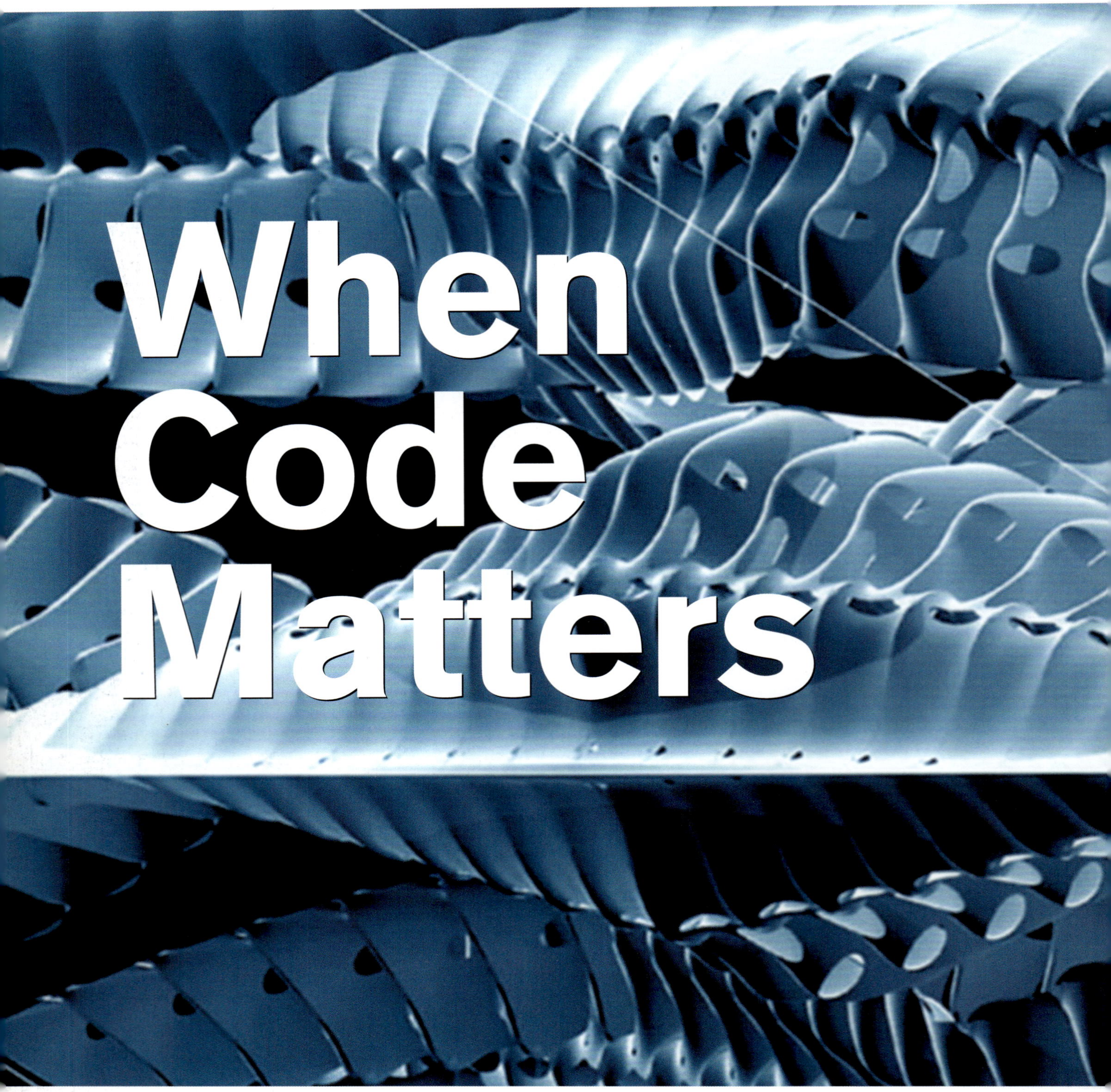

When Code Matters

'Architecture has been bound and shaped by changing code and constraints throughout its history.' **Ingeborg M Rocker** traces, in turn, first the development of calculus into computation and, then, the introduction of computers into architecture. In so doing, she asks what will be the potential effects of computation on the recoding of architecture.

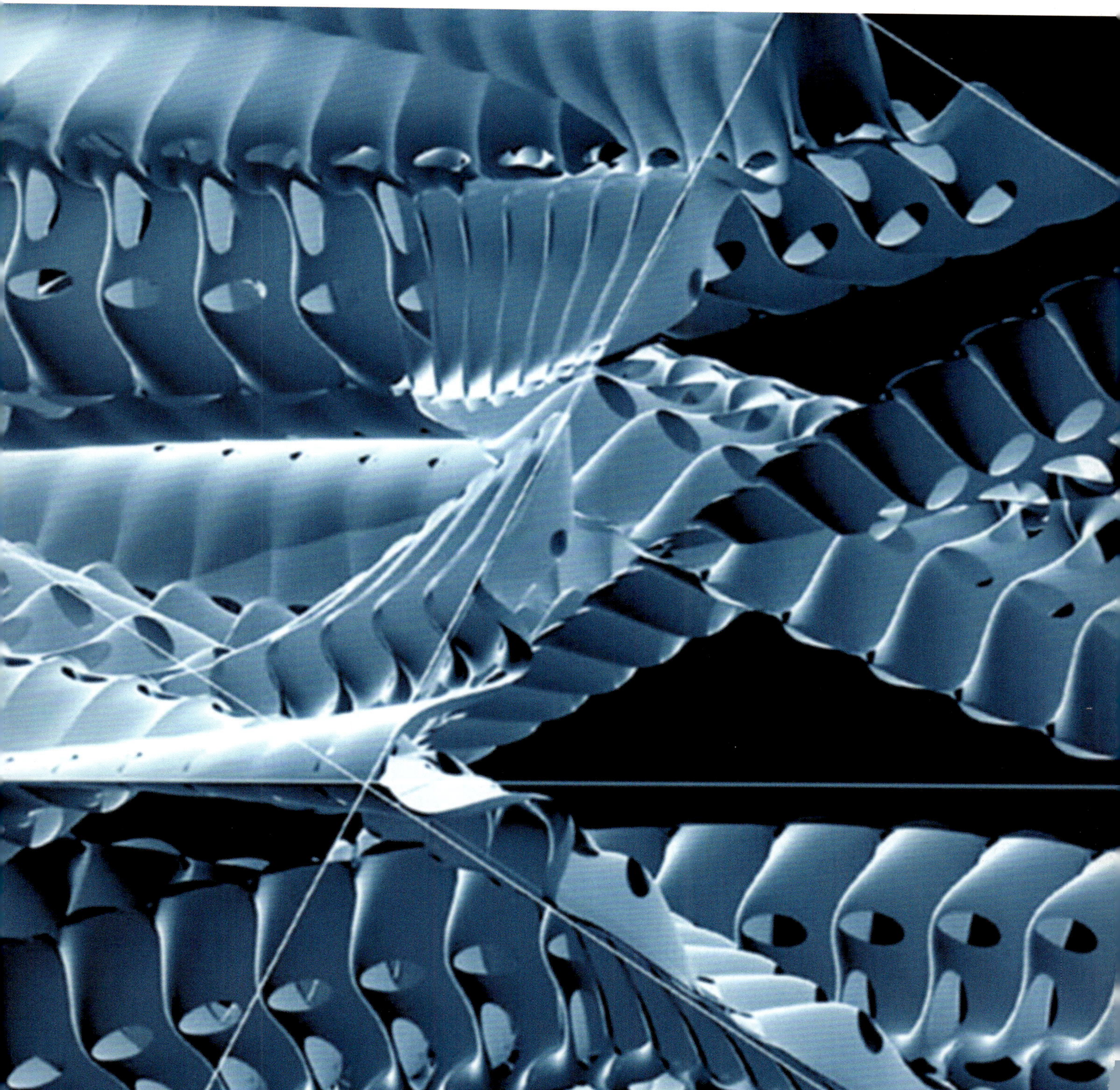

Brandon Williams/Studio Rocker, Expression of Code, 2004
When code matters previously unseen structures begin to emerge. The initiated code may be expressed in different variations ranging from straight walls to twisting columns. At this point performance-based generative systems could, and should, have been applied.

'When God calculates and exercises his thought, the world is created.'

Leibniz,1677

Today, when architects calculate and exercise their thoughts, everything turns into algorithms! Computation,[1] the writing and rewriting of code through simple rules, plays an ever-increasing role in architecture.

This article explores the role of computation in the discourse and praxis of architecture, and addresses the central question of when code matters: when it gains importance in architecture, and when it, literally, materialises. It looks at historical computational models and concepts – research independent of traditional mathematics and the computer – and hopes to contribute to a critical assessment of architecture based on code.

From Traditional Mathematics to Computation

With the introduction of calculus[2] in the late 17th century, abstract rules became increasingly successful in describing and explaining natural phenomena. An abstract mathematical framework then developed from which scientific conclusions could be drawn without direct reference to physical reality. Eventually, physical phenomena became reproducible. Calculus could be applied to a broad range of scientific problems as long they were describable using mathematical equations. Nevertheless, many problems – in particular those of complexity – remained unaddressed.

In the early 1980s, the mathematician Stephen Wolfram began to explore problems of complexity in computer experiments based on cellular automata,[3] and 20 years on his *A New Kind of Science*[4] hoped to initiate a further transformation of the sciences – comparable to that which resulted from the introduction of calculus – this time based on computation.

Wolfram criticised the traditional sciences for relying mainly on mathematical formalism and predictions that often proved incapable of anticipating the complex behaviour of a system. His research suggested that computation, rather than

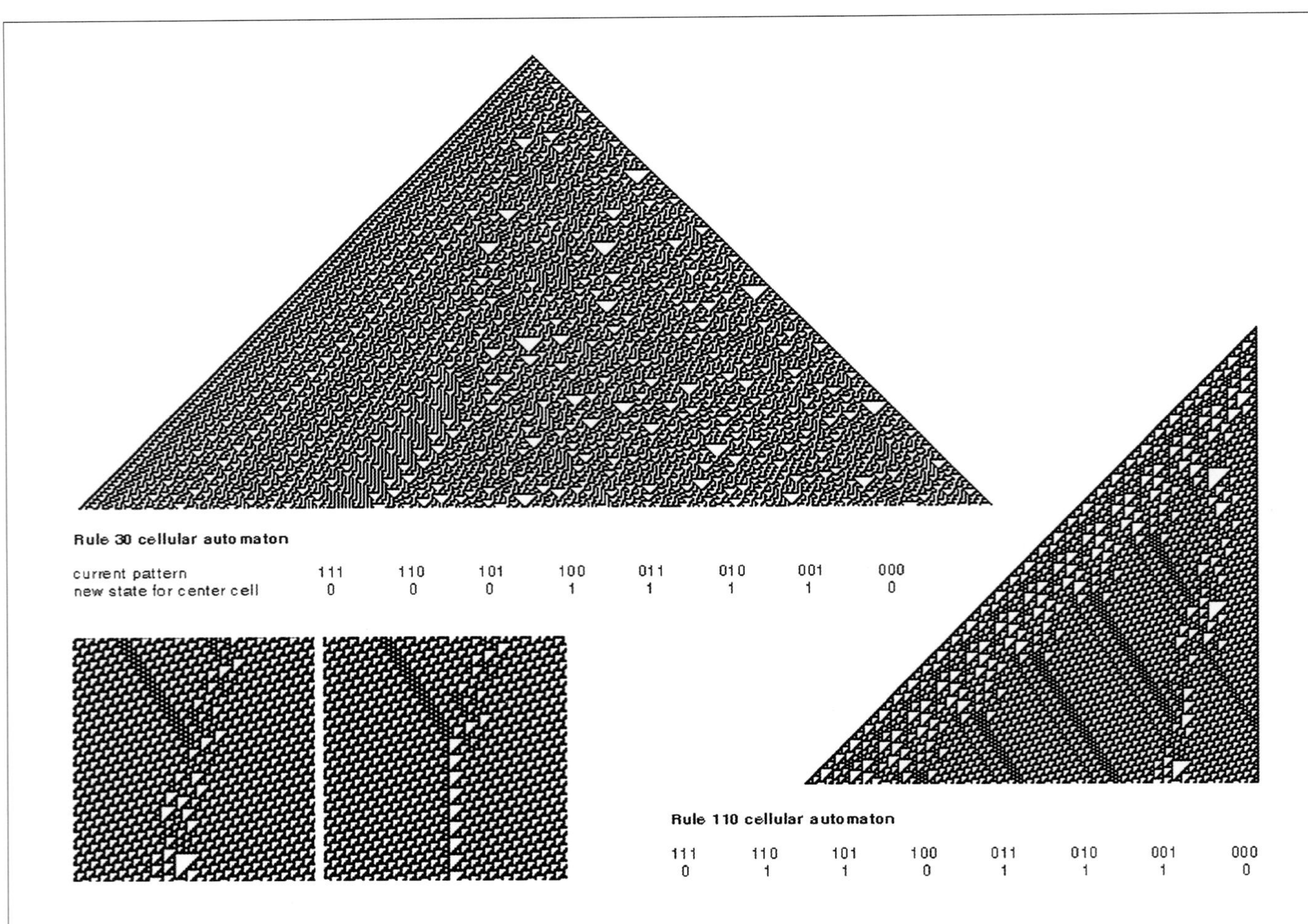

Stephen Wolfram, Cellular automata, 2002
Here, simple rules generate complexity. Images from Stephen Wolfram, *A New Kind of Science*, Wolfram Media (Champaign, IL), 2002.

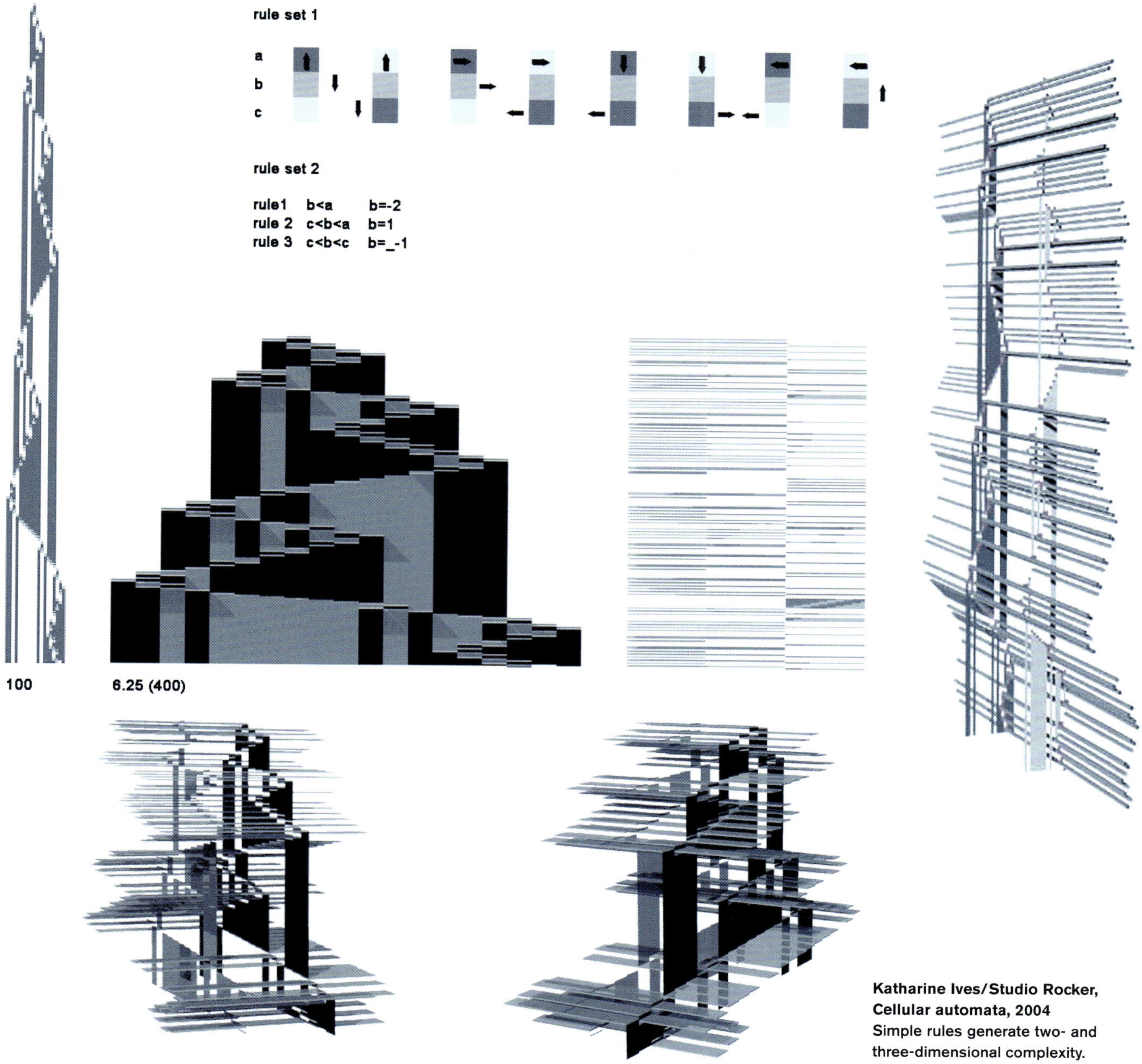

Katharine Ives/Studio Rocker, Cellular automata, 2004
Simple rules generate two- and three-dimensional complexity.

mathematics, was the proper means of realising[5] complex natural and artificial processes. Counter to the prevailing belief that complexity is either the product of complex processes or complex formal arrangements, Wolfram suggested that simple rules can produce great complexities. In computation – rather than traditional mathematics – simple rules were sufficient to generate, approximate and explain complex phenomena:

'There are many systems in nature that show highly complex behavior. But there are also many systems, which rather show simple behavior – most often either complete uniformity, or repetition. ... Programs are very much the same: some show highly complex behavior, while others show rather only simple behavior. Traditional intuition might have made one assume that there must be a direct correspondence between the complexity of observed behavior and the complexity of underlying rules. But one of [my] central discoveries ... is that in fact there is not. For even programs with some of the very simplest possible rules yield highly complex behavior.'[6]

Using computer experiments, Wolfram not only explored complex phenomena, but also their self-organisation over time. Such phenomena and their behaviours could not be anticipated prior to their computation. Only by successive, step-by-step computations is the system of complexities realised and thus becomes realisable. Consequently, only actual computational experiments – rather than a priori determined models of classical mathematics – are sufficient to capture both complex phenomena and their self-organisation.

Wolfram calls his computational methods 'a new kind of science', suggesting a dramatic shift in the sciences away from the mathematical to the computational. Computation will, as Wolfram expects, change our intuition regarding simplicity and complexity.

Universal Machines

Wolfram's research in the field of computation builds on earlier models such as Alan Turing's Machine (1936) and Aristid Lindenmayer's L-systems (1968). The main features of such models are explained below, as they are increasingly gaining relevance in contemporary discussions on algorithmic architecture.

The Turing Dimension[7]

In 1936, the model for the Turing Machine, developed by English mathematician Alan Turing, laid the theoretical foundation for computing.[8] Turing did not envision his machine as a practical computing technology, but rather as a thought experiment that could provide – independent of the formalism of traditional mathematics – a precise definition of a mechanical procedure – an algorithm.[9] In principle, the machine could be physically assembled out of a few components: a table of contents that held the rules for its operations, a reading and writing head that operated along the lines of those rules, writing 0s or 1s – the code – on a presumably infinitely long tape. The moving head followed three modes of operation: writing, scanning, erasing.

Though basic, this design was sufficient for Turing to prove that a certain set of mathematical problems were fundamentally noncomputable. Nevertheless, his machine, based on a finite set of rules and symbols, was able to compute every problem outside of this set. Turing consequently considered his machine universal in the sense that it could simulate all other (calculable) machines. It had the unprecedented ability to emulate divergent and multivalent processes.

Inspired partly by the Turing Machine model, in the 1940s John von Neumann, a member of the Manhattan Project Team, began work on self-replicating systems at the Los Alamos National Laboratory.[10]

'Von Neumann's initial design was founded upon the notion of one robot building another robot. This design is known as the kinematic model. As he developed this design, von Neumann came to realise the great difficulty of building a self-replicating robot, and of the great cost in providing the robot with a "sea of parts" from which to build its replicant.'[11]

At the suggestion of his colleague Stanislaw Ulam, who at the time was studying the growth of crystals using simple two-dimensional lattice networks as his abstract models, von

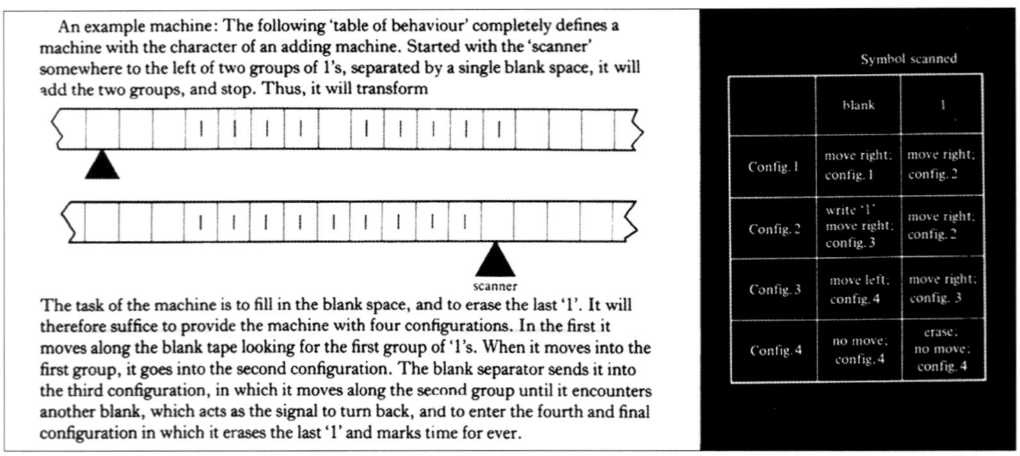

An example machine: The following 'table of behaviour' completely defines a machine with the character of an adding machine. Started with the 'scanner' somewhere to the left of two groups of 1's, separated by a single blank space, it will add the two groups, and stop. Thus, it will transform

The task of the machine is to fill in the blank space, and to erase the last '1'. It will therefore suffice to provide the machine with four configurations. In the first it moves along the blank tape looking for the first group of '1's. When it moves into the first group, it goes into the second configuration. The blank separator sends it into the third configuration, in which it moves along the second group until it encounters another blank, which acts as the signal to turn back, and to enter the fourth and final configuration in which it erases the last '1' and marks time for ever.

	Symbol scanned	
	blank	1
Config. 1	move right; config. 1	move right; config. 2
Config. 2	write '1' move right; config. 3	move right; config. 2
Config. 3	move left; config. 4	move right; config. 3
Config. 4	no move; config. 4	erase, no move; config. 4

Alan Turing, Turing Machine, 1936
The Turing Machine consists of a head reading and writing on a tape according to a set of rules. The operation of the machine depends on the rules provided – and thus changes as the rules change. It is for this reason that the machine can emulate the operation of various machines. Images from Andrew Hodges, *Alan Turing: The Enigma*, Simon and Schuster (New York), 1983, pp 98–9.

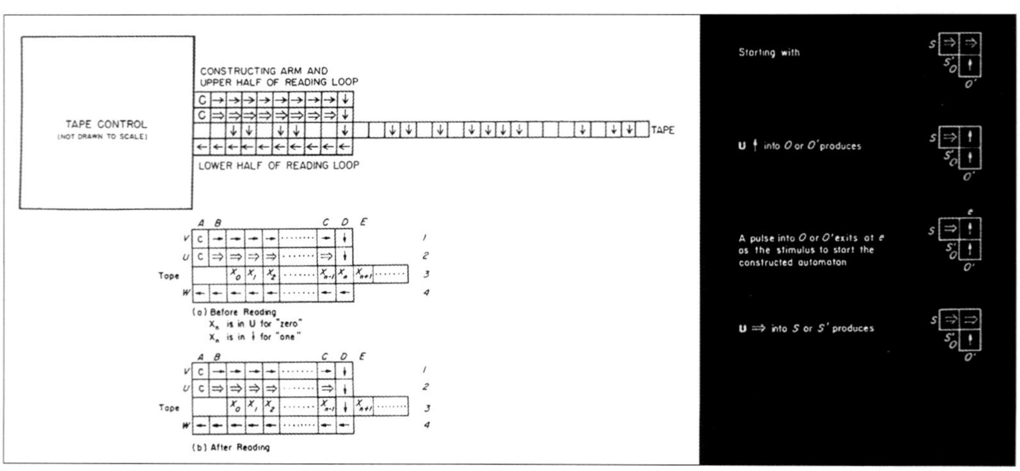

John von Neumann, Universal Copier and Constructor, 1940s
Von Neumann's hypothetical machine for self-replication proved that theoretically a cellular automaton consisting of orthogonal cells could make endless copies of itself. Images from John von Neumann, *Essays on Cellular Automata*, ed Arthur W Burks, University of Illinois Press (Urbana, IL), 1970, pp 37, 41.

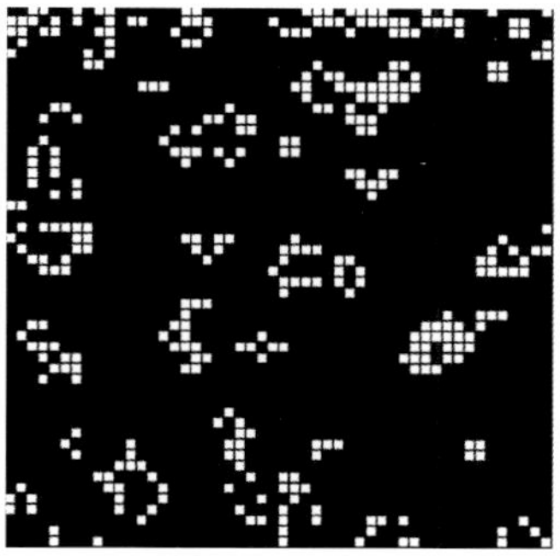

John Conway, Game of Life, 1970
The image shows Kevin Lindsey's implementation of Conway's Game of Life using JavaScript and SVG. The rules (algorithms) of the game are very simple: if a black cell has two or three black neighbours, it stays black; if a white cell has three black neighbours, it becomes black. In all other cases, the cell stays or becomes white.

Neumann developed the first two-dimensional self-replicating automaton, called the 'Universal Copier and Constructor' (UCC), which at once seemed to reference and at the same time extend Turing's Machine. Here, the process of self-replication was described through simple rules: 'The result of the construction is a copy of the universal constructor together with an input tape which contains its own description, which then can go on to construct a copy of itself, together with a copy of its own description, and so on indefinitely.'[12]

In the open system of the UCC, the machines operated upon one another, constantly modifying each other's configurations (code) and operations (rules): 'The machines were made sustainable by modifying themselves within the inter-textual context of other Universal Turing Machines.'[13]

The system's most important function was the self-replication of its process, which resulted in a successive iteration of each system-cell's state, manifesting itself in evolving and dissolving patterns. Patterns became the visual indicator of an otherwise invisible algorithmic operation. The interactions of the different machines thus opened up a new dimension, the Turing Dimension. This differs from the spatial dimensions commonly used in architecture as it is an operational dimension, where one programmatic dimension is linked with another. Small local changes of the Turing Dimension may resonate in global changes to the entire system.

In 1970, another type of cellular automaton was popularised as the Game of Life through an article in *Scientific American*.[14] The two-state, two-dimensional cellular automaton developed by the British mathematician John Conway operated according to carefully chosen rules.[15] It consisted of two-dimensional fields of cells, with the state of each system-cell determined through the state of its neighbours. All cells are directly or indirectly related to each other, rendering visible, via changes in colour, the process of computation. The player-less game was solely determined by its initial state (code) and rules (algorithms). Similar to the Universal Turing Machine, the game computed anything that was computable algorithmically. Despite its simplicity, the system achieved an impressive diversity of behaviour, fluctuating between apparent randomness and order. The changing patterns directly reflected how the machine's operation writes and rewrites its code over time. Thus with Conway's Game of Life, a new field of research on cellular automata was born.[16]

L-systems

Cellular automata were tested across the sciences. In 1968, the theoretical biologist and botanist Aristid Lindenmayer devised – based on Chomsky's grammars – L-systems for modelling the growth of plants.[17] L-systems consist of four elements: a starting point, a set of rules or syntax, constants and variables. Diversity can be achieved by specifying varying starting points and different growth times.[18] L-systems grow by writing and rewriting the code, and expression of the code depends on the graphical command selected. They are still used to model plant systems, and to explore the capabilities of computation.

Regardless of which of the models of computation described above is applied, anything that surfaces on the screen is visualised and materialised by one and the same: the digital medium, the alteration of 0s and 1s.

Code in Architecture

Turning the focus of this discussion on computation to architecture, and to the question of when code matters in architecture, it is necessary to look at the role of codes in the past and how they have changed since the introduction of the digital medium in architecture. The use of code has a long tradition dating back to the Latin term *codex* that refers to documents formed originally from wooden tablets. The Romans used such documents to distribute a system of principles and rules throughout their empire. In architecture, systems and rules have dominated, and still dominate, all stages of architectural production, in the form of drawing and design conventions. Throughout its history, architecture has been bound and shaped by changing codes and constraints, and neither architecture nor its media (from pencil drawings to physical models, computer renderings to the built projects) will ever be free of codes. Architecture is, and always has been, coded.

The arrival of computers extended understanding of code in architecture. Code was now understood as a set of instructions written in a programming language. It stood for 'source code', a series of statements written in some human-readable computer programming language, or 'machine code', instruction patterns of bits (0s and 1s) corresponding to different machine commands.

Writing code, writing a set of instructions, with the aim of generating architecture, forced the architect of the past to formalise both the design process and the design. In contrast to many scientific procedures, which could quite easily be expressed through mathematical equations, the often intuitive and even unconscious use of design rules could not. Perhaps it was for this reason that previously many algorithms were invented and implemented in planning,

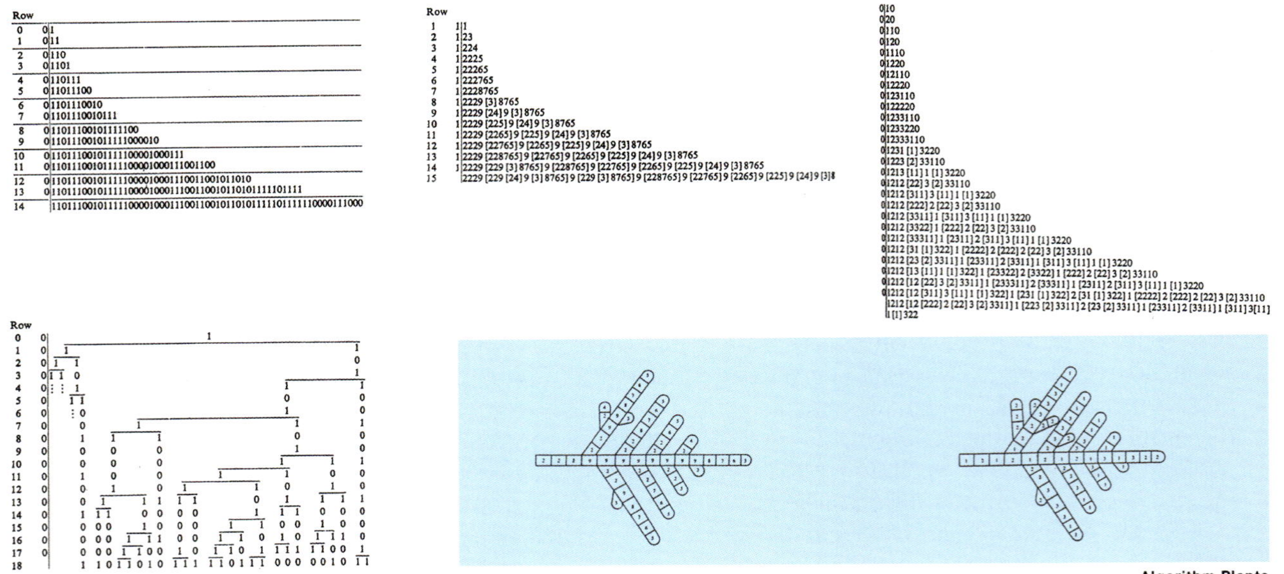

Algorithm Plants

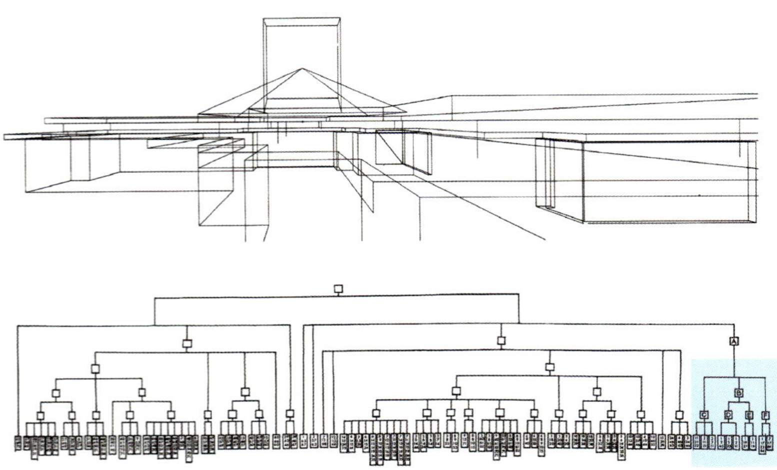

Algorithm House

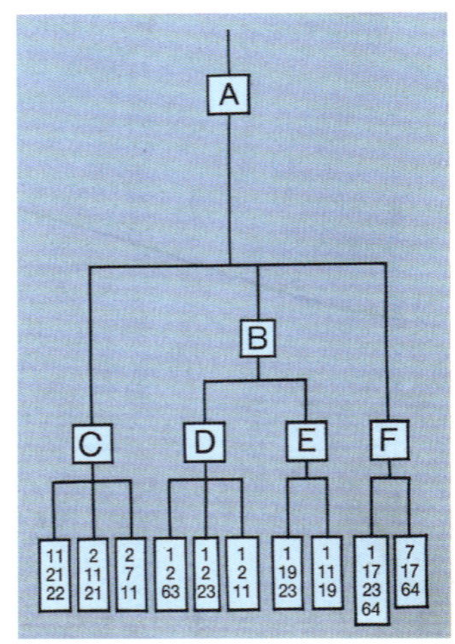

Algorithm Garage

Aristid Lindenmayer, L-system generating algorithmic plants, 1968

Top: Lindenmayer studied mathematical models of cellular interactions in development and their simple and branching elements. Images from: Aristid Lindenmayer, 'Mathematical models of cellular interactions in development: I. Filaments with one-sided inputs', *Journal for Theoretical Biology*, Vol 18, 1968, figs 1 and 2 (p 286), figs 4 and 5 (p 310), and figs 6 and 7 (p 312).

Allen Bernholtz and Edward Bierstone, Algorithmic de- and recomposition of design problem, 1967

Above: Bernholtz, of Harvard University, and Bierstone, of the University of Toronto, adopted Christopher Alexander's and Marvin L Manheimer's computer program HIDECS3 (1963) for hierarchical de- and recomposition to first decompose a complex design problem into its sub-problems and then to recompose a solution. The marked area addresses the design of the garage for which 31 out of 72 possible 'misfit factors' were held characteristic and needed to be excluded in order to arrive at the most appropriate design. Images from Martin Krampen and Peter Seitz (eds), *Design and Planning 2: Computers in Design and Communication*, Hastings House, (New York), 1967, pp 47, 51.

rather than in architectural design. An exception to this was Christopher Alexander's HIDECS3 (1963), a program that decomposed algorithmically complex design tasks into simple sub-problems in order to then recompose them to the 'fittest design'. However, in the end Alexander's algorithms served only to force architectural design into an overly structured rational corset.

The Computational Turn

Regardless of the absurdity of the planning mania of the past, architects are now once again devoted to code, this time in the form of scripting algorithms. While previously architects were obsessed with the reduction of complexity through algorithms, today they are invested in exploring complexities based on the generative power of algorithms and computation.

We are now witnessing a 'computational turn' – a timely turn that countermands the reduction of architectural praxis to the mindless perfection of modelling and rendering techniques.

For many of the architects featured in this issue, the prepackaged design environments with their inscribed limitations – regardless of all the rhetoric associated with them – never really addressed the genuine operations of the digital medium: 'The dominant mode of utilizing computers in architecture today is that of computerization.'[19]

Most architects now use computers and interactive software programs as exploratory tools. All their work is informed by, and thus dependent on the software they are using, which inscribes its logic, perhaps even unnoticed, onto their everyday routines. Such users of software packages have little or no knowledge of the algorithms powering the programs they employ. Most of the interactivity is reduced to a manipulation of displayed forms on the screen, neglecting the underlying mathematical calculations behind them. All of this – even though implemented on computers – has little to do with the logics of computation.

For architects and artists like Karl Chu, Kostas Terzidis, George Liaropoulos-Legendre, Mike Silver and CEB Reas, scripting is the means to develop their own design tools and environments. According to Kostas Terzidis: 'By using scripting languages designers can ... transcend the factory set limitations of current 3-D software. Algorithmic design does not eradicate differences but incorporates both computational complexity and creative use of computers.'[20]

In writing algorithms, design intentions or parameters become encoded. Terzidis and Chu base most of their explorations on simple, clearly defined rules capable of computing a priori indeterminable complexities. As such, alternative modes of architectural production are developed: 'Unlikely computerization and digitization, the extraction of algorithmic processes is an act of high-level abstraction. ... Algorithmic structures represent abstract patterns that are not necessarily associated with experience or perception. ... In

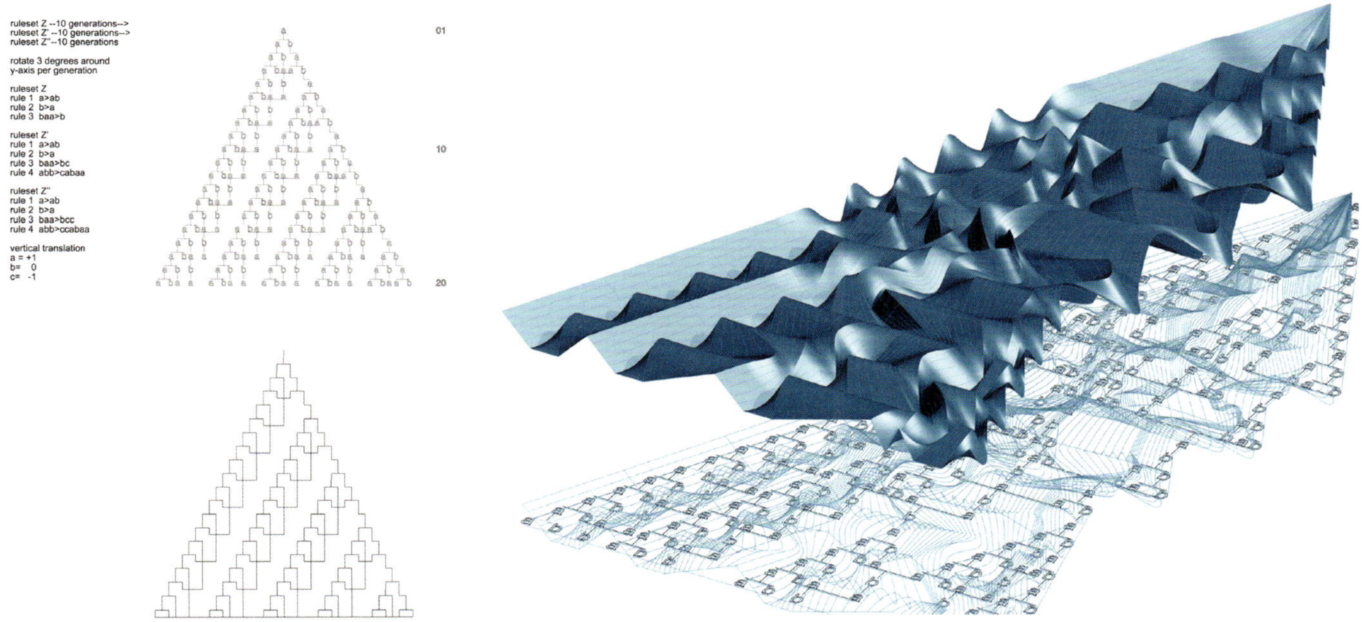

Brandon Williams/Studio Rocker, Recursions, 2004
Recursive procedures that repeat indefinitely are reading and writing code according to preset rules: line by line, generation by generation. Hereby, each generation impacts the next generation and consequently all following ones. Patterns of code appear and disappear.

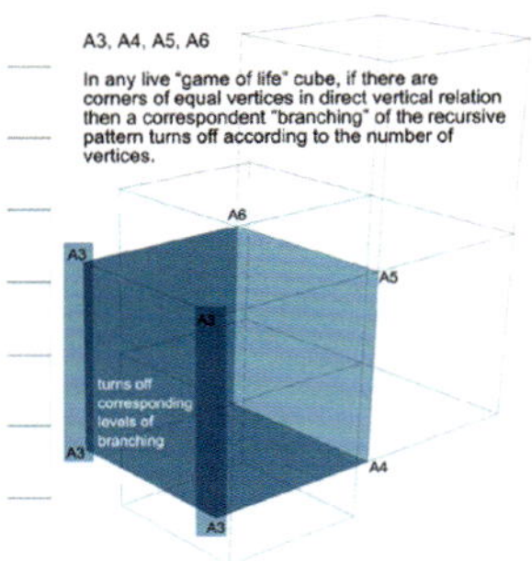

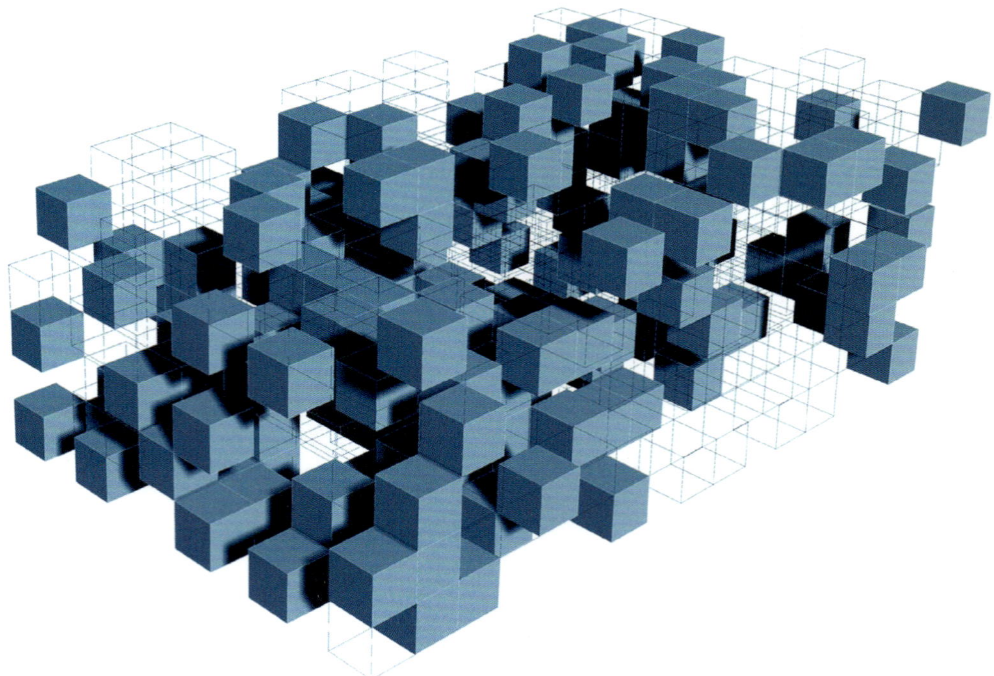

Brandon Williams/Studio Rocker, 3-D Game of Life, 2004
Cellular automata and the Game of Life became the architect's basis for experimentation. The moment a cell turns active, the project code is realised, and thus becomes realisable.

this sense algorithmic processes become a vehicle for exploration that extends beyond the limits of perception.'[21]

The computer is no longer used as a tool for representation, but as a medium to conduct computations. Architecture emerges as a trace of algorithmic operations. Surprisingly enough, algorithms – deterministic in their form and abstract in their operations – challenge both design conventions and, perhaps even more surprisingly, some of our basic intuitions.

For the supporters of algorithmic architecture, a new field of explorations has opened up, one that aims at a better understanding and exploration of computation's genuine processes and their potential for the production of architecture. They are fascinated by how complex architectures emerge from simple rules and models like the Turing Machine and the cellular automaton, in the moment of their computation, as exemplified here by some of the work produced by Studio Rocker[22] in spring 2004.

The promises and limits of such explorations are diverse. The use of genetic algorithms has been traditionally driven by the desire to generate novel forms yet without a deeper consideration of their physical actualisation and performance. Most, if not all, explorations into algorithmic process- and form-generation generally neglect the structural and material integrity of architecture. Nevertheless, some projects do present a significant development within the production and discussion of design, and many have recast the authorial role of the architect, upsetting the guardians of the humanist school.

The projects presented in this issue attempt to counter the neglect referred to above by exploring specific links between

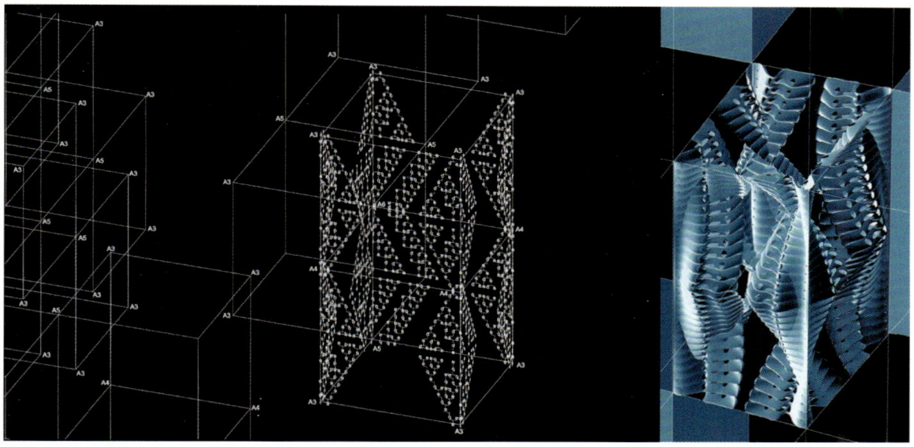

Brandon Williams/Studio Rocker, Expression of code, 2004
Quite different to the Turing Machine, which only uses a one-dimensional tape, Brandon Williams's design is a two-dimensional surface. Modes of transposition determine how the abstract code, consisting of As and Bs, realises and thus becomes realisable as surface and structure. Obviously, the chosen mode of transposing code into its expression is just one of many possibles. Any code's expression is thus always just one of an infinite set of possible realisations. We just have realised the incompleteness of realisation.

computation and material praxis. They therefore represent an important development within the production and discourse of design. The question remains open as to whether the turn to computation will reconfigure architecture to such an extent that a new kind of architecture will emerge.

Coding a Strategy for Alteration

This article presents code as a technical and discursive construct. Code is hereby not considered a normalising restriction of architecture, but rather as a site where a recoding of architecture may occur. The strategy of coding and recoding embraces the free play of symbolic code, as it impacts on architecture's traditional coding systems and their standardised, prototypical material realisation. Computation allows for the emergence of form and space independent of such traditional constraints, and thus allows us to arrive at alternative formal and spatial conceptions, which decode and, at the same time, recode architecture.

Here code matters. ⌂

Notes

1 Emphasis in this article is given to computation. The logic of computation, not the literal use of computers, is relevant for the argument.
2 The word 'calculus' originated from the development of mathematics: the early Greeks used pebbles arranged in patterns to learn arithmetic and geometry, and the Latin word for 'pebble' is *calculus*, a diminutive of *calx* (genitive *calcis*) meaning 'limestone'.
3 Stephen Wolfram, *Cellular Automata and Complexity: Collected Papers*, Addison-Wesley (Reading, MA), 1994.
4 Stephen Wolfram, *A New Kind of Science*, Wolfram Media (Champaign, IL), 2002.
5 'Realisation' is in this context used in the double sense of the word, suggesting something that becomes real and graspable, intelligible.
6 Wolfram, *A New Kind of Science*, p 351.
7 A term I owe to Karl Chu. For further reference see Karl Chu, *Turing Dimension*, X Kavya (Los Angeles, CA), 1999.
8 Alan M Turing, 'On computable numbers, with an application to the Entscheidungsproblem 1936–37', in *Proceedings of the London Mathematical Society*, Ser 2, 42, pp 230–65.
9 The word 'algorithm' etymologically derives from the name of the 9th-century Persian mathematician Abu Abdullah Muhammad bin Musa al-Khwarizmi. The word 'algorism' originally referred only to the rules of performing arithmetic using Hindu-Arabic numerals, but evolved via the European-Latin translation of al-Khwarizmi's name into 'algorithm' by the 18th century. The word came to include all definite procedures for solving problems or performing tasks. An algorithm is a finite set of well-defined instructions for accomplishing some task. A computer program is essentially an algorithm that determines and organises the computer's sequence of operations. For any computational process, the algorithm must be rigorously defined through a series of precise steps that determine the order of computation.
10 The Los Alamos National Laboratory, officially known only as Project Y, was launched as a secret centralised facility in New Mexico in 1943 solely to design and build an atomic bomb. Scientists from all over the world and from different fields of study came together to make Los Alamos one of the US's premier scientific research facilities.
11 Source: http://en.wikipedia.org.
12 Christopher G Langton, 'Cellular automata', in *Proceedings of an Interdisciplinary Workshop*, Los Alamos, New Mexico, US, 7–11 March 1983. See also John von Neumann, *Theory of Self-Reproducing Automata*, edited and completed by Arthur W Burks, University of Illinois Press (Urbana, IL), 1966.
13 See also Karl Chu, op cit.
14 Martin Gardner, 'Mathematical Games: The fantastic combinations of John Conway's new solitaire game "life"', *Scientific American* 223, October 1970, pp 120–3.
15 Ibid. 'Conway chose his rules ... after a long period of experimentation, to meet three desiderata: 1. There should be no initial pattern for which there is a simple proof that the population can grow without limit; 2. There should be initial patterns that apparently do grow without limit; 3. There should be simple initial patterns that grow and change for a considerable period of time before coming to end in three possible ways: fading away completely (from overcrowding or becoming too sparse), settling into a stable configuration that remains unchanged thereafter, or entering an oscillating phase in which they repeat an endless cycle of two or more periods.'
16 Ibid.
17 Aristid Lindenmayer, 'Mathematical models for cellular interaction in development: Parts I and II', *Journal of Theoretical Biology*, 18 (1968), pp 280–315.
18 The working of L-systems is here exemplified through a simple one-dimensional system consisting of variables (AB), constants (none), a start point (A) and rules (A -> B and B -> AB). With each pass through the system the rules are applied. The rule B -> AB replaces a B with AB. Consequently, stage after stage the system's pattern alternates.
Stage 0: A
Stage 1: B
Stage 2: AB
Stage 3: BAB
Stage 4: ABBAB
Stage 5: BABABBAB
Stage 6: ABBABBABABBAB
Stage 7: BABABBABABBABBABABBAB
Any letter combination can also be used to introduce another set of rules.
19 Kostas Terzidis, *Expressive Form: A Conceptual Approach to Computational Design*, Spon Press (London and New York), 2003, p 71.
20 Ibid, p 72.
21 Ibid, p 73.
22 Strategies for coding and re-coding were explored in my design studio 'Re-coded' at the University of Pennsylvania School of Design, Graduate Program for Architecture, in spring 2004. The work was shown at the 'Re-coded: Studio Rocker' exhibition at the Aedes Gallery East in Berlin during July and September 2005. See also Ingeborg M Rocker, *Re-coded: Studio Rocker*, Aedes East (Berlin), 2005.

Process/Drawing

Writing software is at the core of **CEB Reas**'s artistic practice. The digital is his medium of choice rather than a means of manipulation. He reflects on the evolution of his work in software and why the history of using computers to produce visual images is largely an unrecorded one in the history of art, but why this might all be set to change as scripting takes on a new primacy in contemporary art.

I started playing with computers as a child. Our family's Apple IIe machine was a toy for playing video games and writing simple programs in BASIC and Logo.[1] I spent years exploring and testing it, but I preferred drawing and my interest in computers slowly dissipated. In 1997 I was introduced to John Maeda and the work of his students in the Aesthetics and Computation Group at MIT. They were creating a unique software by fusing traditional arts knowledge with ideas from computer science. Experiencing their explorations revealed a new direction for my work and I started programming computers in earnest in 1998. I began my graduate studies at MIT the following year. My time there was personally transforming and I shifted from being a software consumer to a producer. I expanded my views of technology in relation to culture and the history of art, and my current ideas emanate from this experience.

Writing software is now the core of my artistic practice. Many artists use software as a tool to support their work, but few are using it as a unique medium. It is now very common for photographers to manipulate their images digitally, for painters to construct sketches and preparatory drawings with software, and for video artists to edit their work on computers. However, it is far less common for artists like myself to write their own software and to run and operate this software for their performances and installations.

For the past four years, my principal interest in software has been in exploring the phenomena of emergence. Emergence refers to the generation of structures that are not directly defined or controlled. Instead of overtly determining the entire structure, I write simple programs that define interactions between elements. Structure emerges from the discrete movements of each element as it modifies itself in relation to its environment. The structures generated through these processes cannot be anticipated, and develop through continual iterations involving alterations to the programs and exploring changes through interacting with the software. The works Tissue (2002) and MicroImage (2003) are among the results of this exploration.

In 2003 I became obsessed with the work of Sol LeWitt, and exploring his work had a clear impact on my recent software.

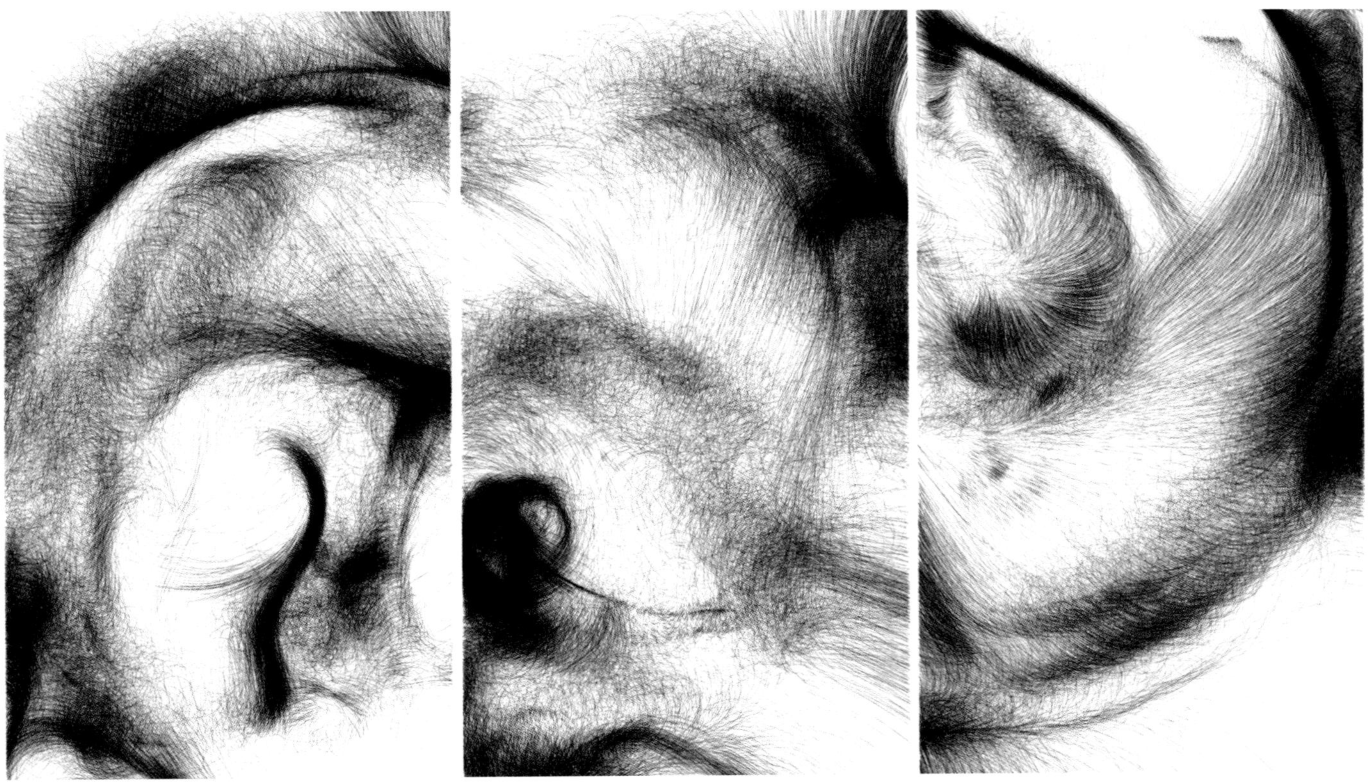

MicroImage, 24in x 34in inkjet prints, 2003
Above: Three prints derived from the MicroImage software. The MicroImage software is an exploration into emergent form. Autonomous software elements interact with their continually changing environment to create a kinetic field.

Tissue Type B-06, 11in x 14in inkjet print, 2002
Opposite: One of 28 prints derived from the Tissue software. The Tissue software exposes the movements of synthetic neural systems. People interact with the software by positioning a group of points on the screen. An understanding of the total system emerges from the relations between the positional input and the visual output.

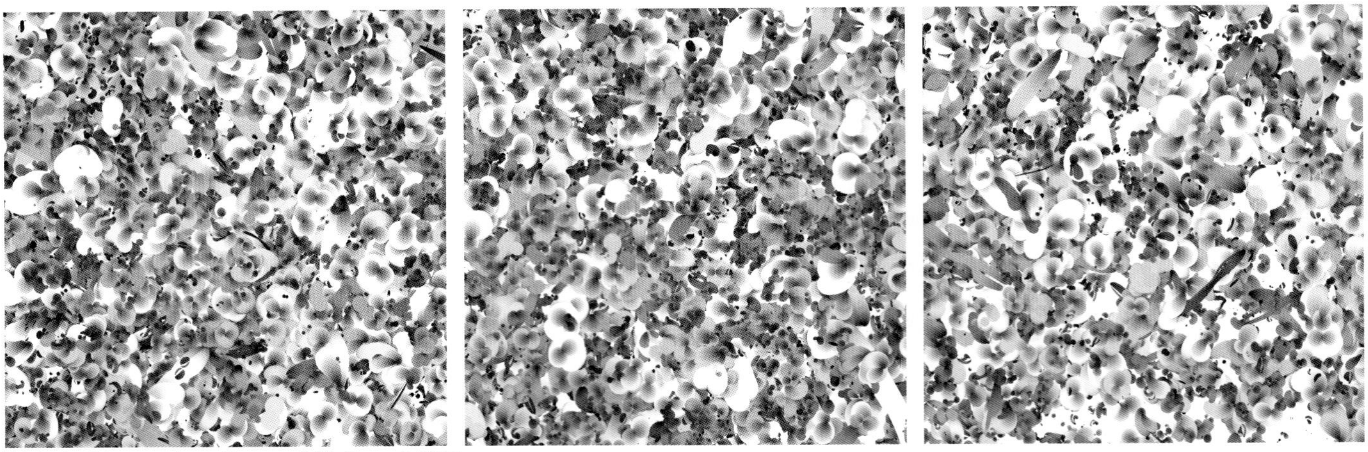

Triptych of images from Process 8 (Software), 2005
A rectangular surface densely filled with instances of Element 2, each with a different size and speed. Display the intersections by drawing a circle at each point of contact. Set the size of each circle relative to the distance between the centres of the overlapping elements. Draw the smallest possible circle as black and largest as white, with varying greys between.

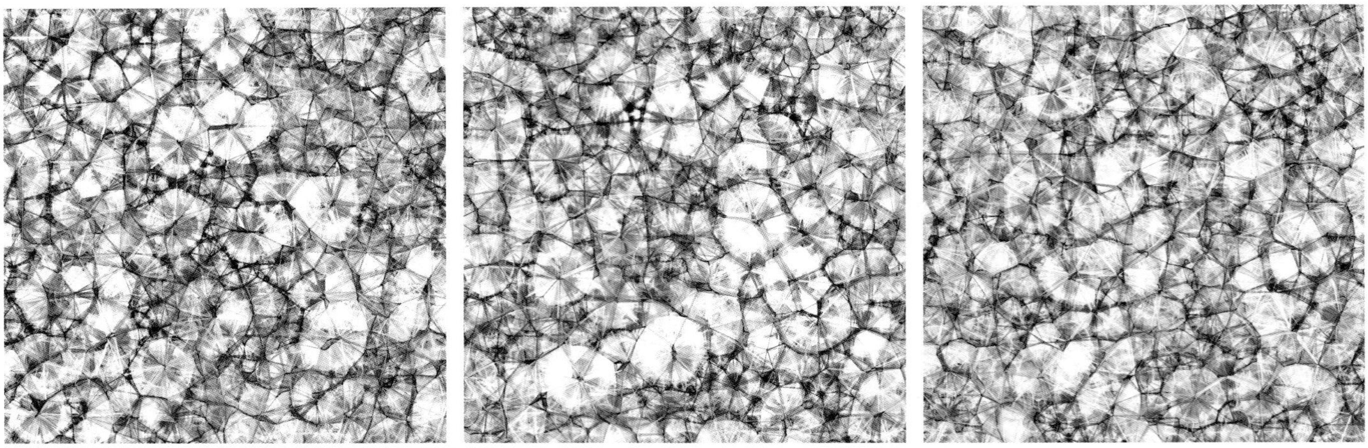

Triptych of images from Process 7 (Software), 2005
A rectangular surface filled with varying sizes of Element 1. Draw a line from the centres of elements that are touching. Set the value of the shortest possible line to black and the longest to white, with varying greys between. Draw the perimeter of each element as a white line and the centre as a black dot.

Triptych of images from Process 6 (Software), 2005
Position three large circles on a rectangular surface. Set the centre of each circle as the origin for a large group of Element 1. When each element moves beyond the edge of the circle, move its position back to the origin. Draw a line from the centres of elements that are touching. Set the value of the shortest possible line to white and the longest to black, with varying greys between.

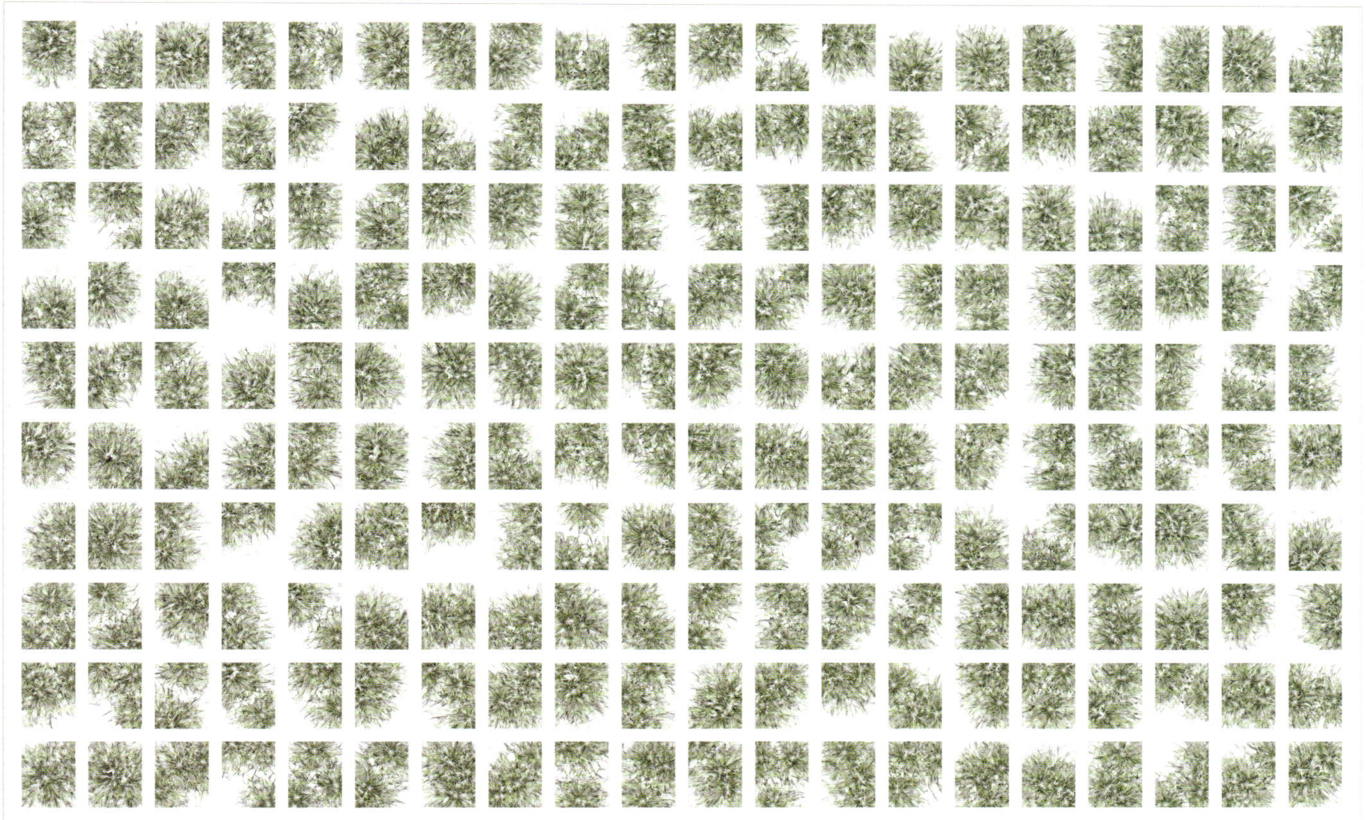

Process 6 (Image 2), 36in x 22in inkjet print, 2005
Print derived from Process 6. Each grid unit is the same software run 400 iterations. Each unit was given a different initial position to create the visual diversity.

In spring 2004 I completed the Software {Structures}2 project for the Whitney Museum of American Art's Artport. I started with a simple question: 'Is the history of conceptual art relevant to the idea of software as art?' I began to answer the question by implementing three of LeWitt's drawings in software and then making modifications. After working with the LeWitt plans, I created three new structures unique to software. These software structures are text descriptions outlining dynamic relations between elements. They develop in the vague domain of thought and then mature in the more defined structures of human language before any consideration is given to a specific machine implementation. Twenty-six pieces of software derived from these structures were written to isolate different components of software structures including interpretation, material and process.

My work in the past year has synthesised ideas explored in Software {Structures} with my previous explorations of emergence. Each new work is called a 'process' and defines rules and instructions that describe a relation between 'elements' outside of a specific physical medium. Different manifestations of the process in diverse media such as software, print and installation give a more complete view of the concept. The software implementation is closest to the actual concept, but the other media provide additional perspectives. Working in software allows me to engage the live process and to change its parameters to affect the way it behaves, and working in print gives me the opportunity to examine the state of the process at a precise time with extremely high fidelity.

The most important element of each process is the text. The text is the process described in English, written with the intention of translating its content into software. Each process defines the relationships of software elements to their environment and to each other. Each element is comprised of a visual form and one or more behaviours. Element 2, for example, is defined as Form 1 with Behaviours 1 and 4 applied. This means Form 1 is a circle with a constant linear motion, and when it moves off the edge of the screen, it moves to the opposing side of the screen. The remarkable aspect of each process is the relationship between the simple instructions and the density and sensitivity of the images and movements they create. Each text is translated from natural language into a machine language to create the software.

The elements used in the process texts are currently limited to two configurations, one form and four behaviours. This list will expand in time to increase the dynamic range of the processes:

TI installation at the BANK Art Gallery, Los Angeles, 2004–05
Nineteen white discs hover above the floor, each containing a projected, kinetic image of expansion and decay. Aggregate layers of abstraction remove every trace of systemic complexity, revealing a living surface. Structured form emerges from the results of thousands of local interactions between autonomous elements.

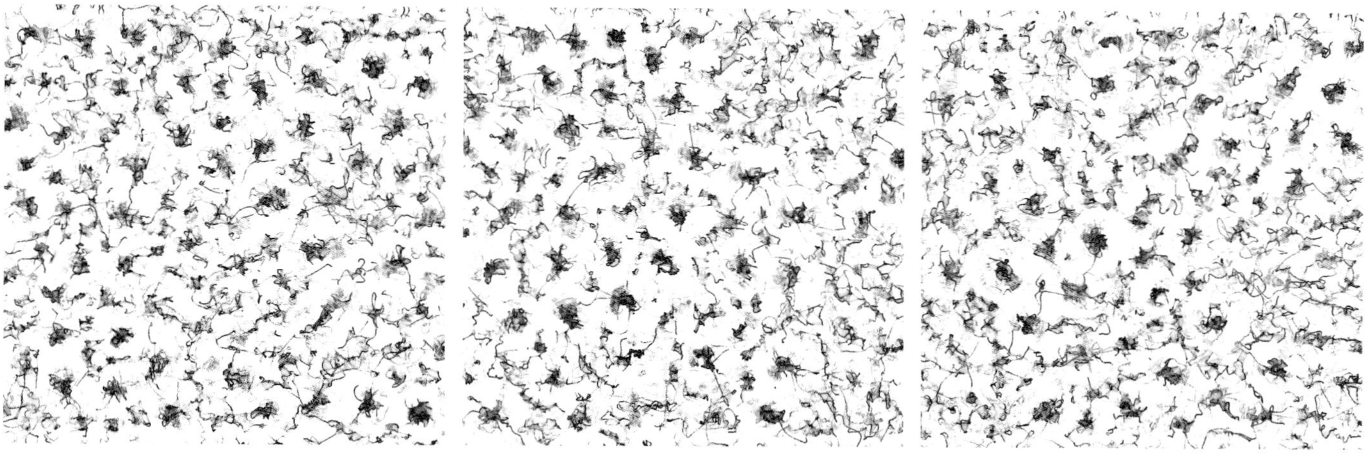

Triptych of images from Process 5 (Software), 2005
A rectangular surface filled with varying sizes of Element 1. Draw the perimeter of each element as a white line and the centre as a black dot. If two small elements are touching, draw a grey line between their centres.

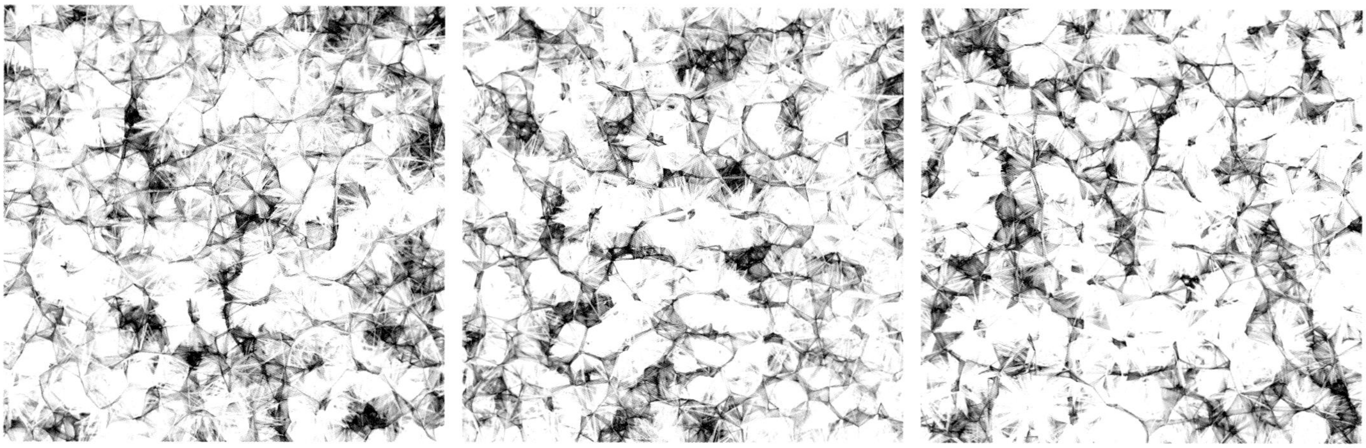

Triptych of images from Process 4 (Software), 2005
A rectangular surface filled with varying sizes of Element 1. Draw a line from the centres of elements that are touching. Set the value of the shortest possible line to black and the longest to white, with varying greys between.

Element 1: Form 1 + Behaviour 1 + Behaviour 2 + Behaviour 3
Element 2: Form 1 + Behaviour 1 + Behaviour 4

Form 1: Circle

Behaviour 1: Constant linear motion
Behaviour 2: Constrain to surface
Behaviour 3: When touching another, change direction
Behaviour 4: After moving off the surface, enter from the opposing edge

The texts for Processes 4 to 8 are reproduced below. Processes 1 to 3 were defined during the Software {Structures} project and additional processes are continuously in development. Processes 4 to 8 were implemented by the author using the C++ programming language and the OpenGL graphics library. Future processes will be implemented using different programming languages and may be implemented by people other than the author. The process descriptions refer to the elements listed above.

Process 8: A rectangular surface densely filled with instances of Element 2, each with a different size and speed. Display the intersections by drawing a circle at each point of contact. Set the size of each circle relative to the distance between the centres of the overlapping elements. Draw the smallest possible circle as black and largest as white, with varying greys between.

Process 7: A rectangular surface filled with varying sizes of Element 1. Draw a line from the centres of elements that are touching. Set the value of the shortest possible line to black

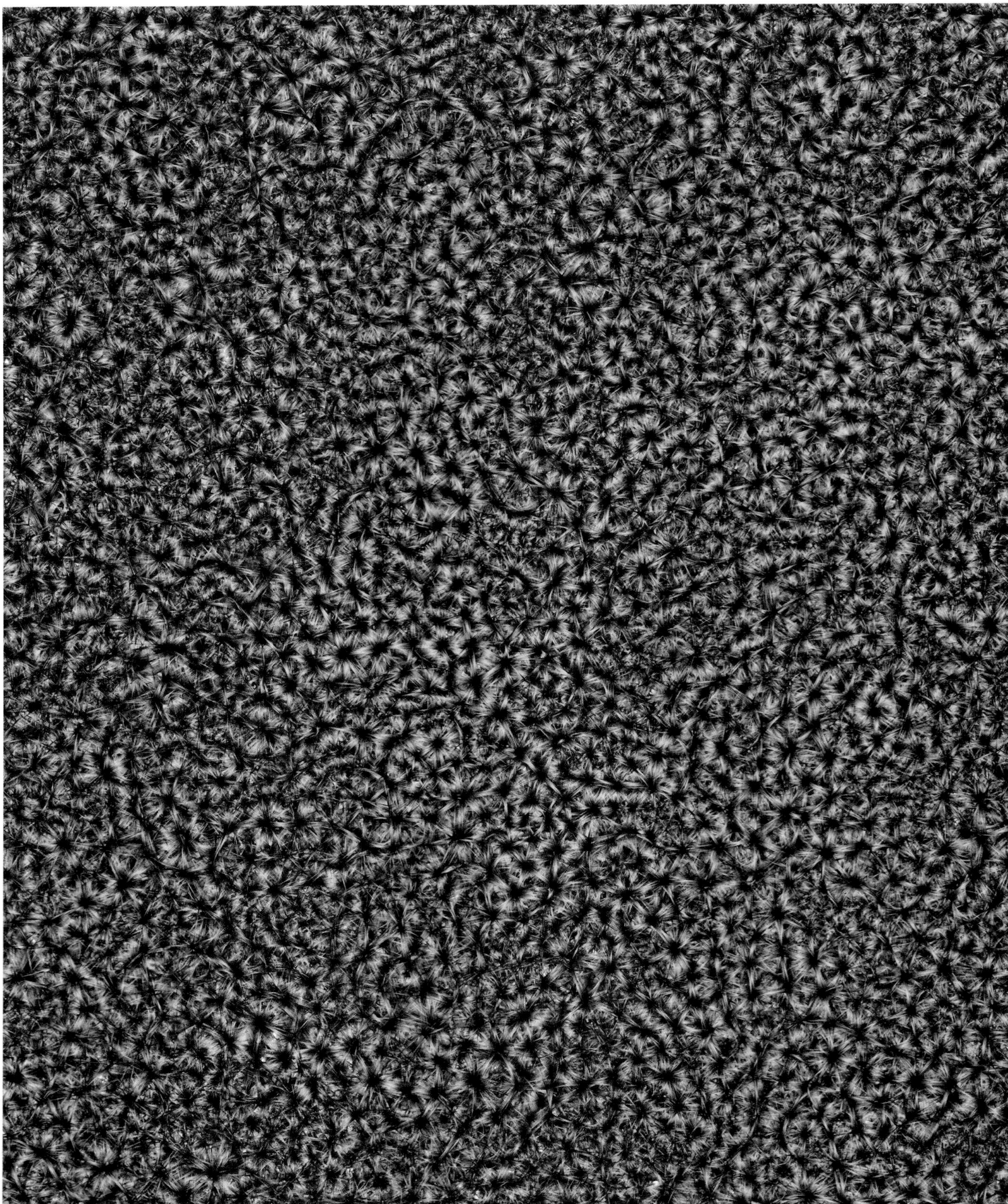

Process 4 (Image 1), 28.625in x 28.625in inkjet print, 2005
Print derived from Process 4. The Process 4 software was modified to create this dense network diagram.

and the longest to white, with varying greys between. Draw the perimeter of each element as a white line and the centre as a black dot.

Process 6: Position three large circles on a rectangular surface. Set the centre of each circle as the origin for a large group of Element 1. When each element moves beyond the edge of the circle, move its position back to the origin. Draw a line from the centres of elements that are touching. Set the value of the shortest possible line to white and the longest to black, with varying greys between.

Process 5: A rectangular surface filled with varying sizes of Element 1. Draw the perimeter of each element as a white line and the centre as a black dot. If two small elements are touching, draw a grey line between their centres.

Process 4: A rectangular surface filled with varying sizes of Element 1. Draw a line from the centres of elements that are touching. Set the value of the shortest possible line to black and the longest to white, with varying greys between.

The hardware running this software is inconsequential. In time, it will inevitably fail. It was selected to be as robust as possible with current technology, but contemporary electronics are fragile. If an element of the hardware fails, it can be replaced without diminishing the work. Eventually, compatible components will no longer be available because computing technology is continually shifting. When hardware failure inevitably occurs, a new hardware system will need to be acquired and the software should be rewritten for the new hardware to take advantage of the technical advances since the inception of the process.

Software as Art

Searching for the history of software as an art medium reveals two distinct groups of progenitors that emerged in the 1960s. There is one category of artists who used early digital computers for the production of their work, and another of artists who explored ideas now associated with the synthesis of software and art, but did so without working directly with the technology. The history of using computers to produce visual images is a largely unrecorded one that is rapidly coming into focus through recent publications and exhibitions. As a result of its obscurity, this work has had little impact on contemporary artists working in software.[3] Alternatively, we can look at the work of artists in the critical groupings of conceptual art and Fluxus. These artists, including Sol LeWitt, Yoko Ono, La Monte Young, Hans Haacke and John Baldessari, have all influenced the way contemporary artists think about software. Software is an immaterial medium, much like thought, and the work of these artists is extremely relevant to the idea of software as art.

In the 1950s the first images created using computers were generated by scientists and engineers who had access to the scarce, expensive and complex technology. Even in 1969, Jasia Reichardt, then a curator at the Institute for Contemporary Art in London, wrote: 'So far only three artists that I know have actually produced computer graphics, the rest to date having been made by scientists.'[4] The works created during this time were typically made as collaborations between technicians at research labs and invited artists. Organisations such as Experiments in Art and Technology (EAT) and the Los Angeles County Museum of Art's Art and Technology programme facilitated these collaborations. A Michael Noll, a pioneer of computer images, is quoted in Gene Youngblood's 1970 book *Expanded Cinema* as contradicting this strategy: 'A lot has been made of the desirability of collaborative efforts between artists and technologists. I, however, disagree with many of the assumptions upon which this desirability supposedly is founded. First of all, artists in general find it extremely difficult to verbalize the images and ideas they have in their minds. Hence the communication of the artist's ideas to the technologist is very poor indeed. What I do envision is a new breed of artist ... a man who is extremely competent in both technology and the arts.'[5]

Every artist must decide whether he or she will work collaboratively or directly with software, and this has a major impact on his or her work. Working directly with code leads to a deeper understanding of the conceptual potential of the medium. The number of artists writing their own software has increased significantly in the last 35 years, especially since the introduction of the personal computer. Another increase in software literacy occurred with the rapid adoption of the Internet in the mid-1990s.

However, while the communities of artists writing software continues to grow, there are many remaining cultural and technical barriers to be removed. One of the largest obstructions is the lack of tools for writing software for artists. Existing programming languages and environments have been written by software engineers to meet their specific needs, which have always been different from the needs of artists. The open-source software movement has provided a way for artists to collaborate on the production of their own tools. It is my hope these open-source art software initiatives[6] will serve as a catalyst for a dramatic shift in the use of software within the arts. ⌂D

Notes

1 BASIC is a programming language invented in 1964 to teach programming to nonspecialists. Variations of BASIC were distributed widely with early personal computers. Logo is a programming language often used to teach children concepts of geometry. The Logo turtle is used to draw lines onscreen in response to simple commands.

2 See http://artport.whitney.org/commissions/softwarestructures/.

3 CEB Reas, 'Who are the progenitors of the contemporary synthesis of software and art?', *The Anthology of Computer Art*, Sonic Acts (Amsterdam), 2006.

4 Jasia Reichardt, *Cybernetic Serendipity*, Frederick A Praeger Publishers (New York), 1969, p 71.

5 Gene Youngblood, *Expanded Cinema*, EP Dutton & Co (New York), 1970, p 193.

6 See http://www.artsoftware.org.

How Do Simple Programs Behave?

Whereas once the world view of the ancient world was shifted by Pythagorean mathematics, scientific knowledge and human perception has been contested in the 21st century by developments in computation. In his ground-breaking book Stephen Wolfram, the British physicist and creator of the Mathematica program, asserted that the complexity of the universe could be clearly understood in terms of simple programs. Here in an exclusive extract, Wolfram describes how one of the most straightforward programs, cellular automata, despite adhering to simple rules, yields some surprisingly complex results.

New directions in science have typically been initiated by certain central observations or experiments. And for the kind of science that I describe in *A New Kind of Science*, these concerned the behaviour of simple programs.

In our everyday experience with computers, the programs that we encounter are normally set up to perform very definite tasks. But the key idea I had nearly 20 years ago – and that eventually led to the whole new kind of science I have since developed – was to ask what happens if instead one just looks at simple arbitrarily chosen programs, created without any specific task in mind. How do such programs typically behave?

The mathematical methods that have in the past dominated theoretical science are not much help with regard to such a question. But with a computer it is straightforward to begin experiments to investigate it. All one need do is set up a sequence of possible simple programs, and run them to see how they behave.

Any program can at some level be thought of as consisting of a set of rules that specify what it should do at each step. There are many possible ways to set up these rules. For now, I will consider a particular class of examples called cellular automata, which were the very first kinds of simple program I investigated in the early 1980s.

An important feature of cellular automata is that their behaviour can readily be presented in a visual way. Thus the picture in Figure 1 shows what one cellular automaton does over the course of six steps.

The cellular automaton consists of a line of cells, each coloured either black or white. At every step there is then a definite rule that determines the colour of a given cell from the colour of that cell and its immediate left and right neighbours in the previous step. For the particular cellular automaton shown here, the rule specifies – as shown in Figure 2 – that a cell should be black in all cases where it, or either of its neighbours, were black in the previous step.

And Figure 3 shows that, starting with a single black cell in the centre, this rule then leads to a simple growing pattern uniformly filled with black. However, by just slightly modifying the rule one can immediately get a different pattern. As a first example, Figure 3 shows what happens with a rule that makes a cell white whenever both of its neighbours were white in the previous step – even if the cell itself was previously black. Rather than producing a pattern that is uniformly filled with black, this rule now gives a pattern that repeatedly alternates between black and white, like a chequerboard.

This pattern is again fairly simple, and we might assume that at least with the type of cellular automata that we are considering, any rule we choose will always give a pattern that is quite simple. But the reality is quite surprising. Figure 4 shows the pattern produced by a cellular automaton of the same type as before, but with a slightly different rule. This time the rule specifies that a cell should be black when either its left neighbour or its right neighbour – but not both – were black in the step before. Again, this rule is undeniably quite simple, but this time the pattern it produces is not so simple.

If one runs the cellular automaton for even more steps, as in Figure 5, a rather intricate pattern emerges – one which has very definite regularity. Even though it is intricate, the pattern actually consists of many nested triangular pieces, all with exactly the same form. As the figure shows, each of these pieces is essentially just a smaller copy of the whole pattern with still smaller copies nested in a very regular way inside it.

All of the three cellular automata examined so far ultimately yield patterns that are highly regular: the first a simple uniform pattern, the second a repetitive pattern, and the third an intricate yet still nested pattern. It might be assumed that at least for cellular automata with rules as simple as those we have been using, these three forms of behaviour would be all that we could ever get. But, remarkably, this is not in fact the case.

Figure 6 shows an example of this. The rule used – rule 30 – is of exactly the same kind as before, and can be described as follows. First, look at each cell and its right-hand neighbour. If both of these were white in the previous step, then take the new colour of the cell to be whatever the previous colour of its left-hand neighbour was.

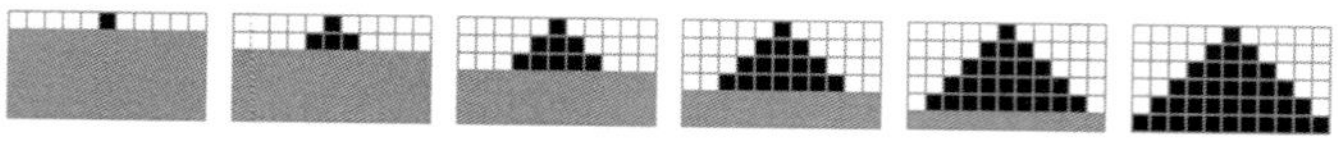

Figure 1. Visual representation of the behaviour of a cellular automaton, with each row of cells corresponding to one step. In the first step the cell in the centre is black and all other cells are white. Then in each successive step, a particular cell is made black whenever it or either of its neighbours were black in the previous step, leading to a simple expanding pattern uniformly filled with black.

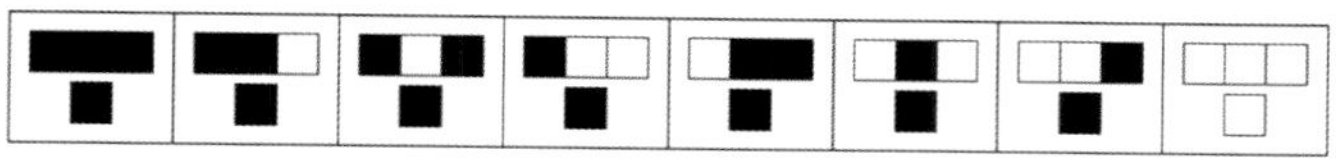

Figure 2. Representation of the rule for the cellular automaton shown in Figure 1. The top row in each box gives one of the possible combinations of colours for a cell and its immediate neighbours. The bottom row then specifies what colour the centre cell should be in the next step in each of these cases. In the commonly accepted numbering scheme developed by Stephen Wolfram, this is cellular automaton rule 254.

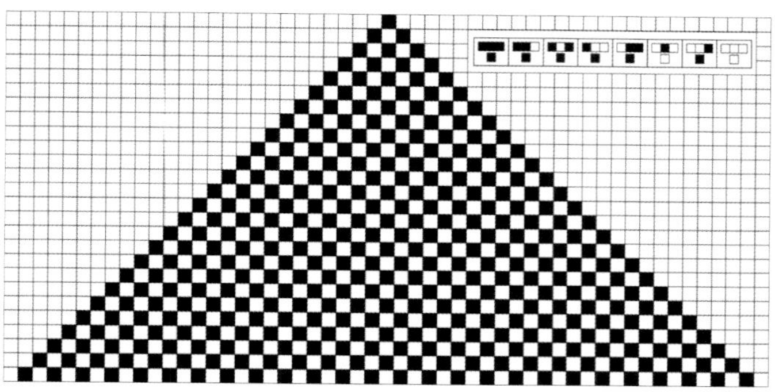

Figure 3. A cellular automaton with a slightly different rule. The rule makes a particular cell black if either of its neighbours was black in the step before, and makes the cell white if both of its neighbours were white. Starting from a single black cell, this rule leads to a chequerboard pattern. This is cellular automaton rule 250.

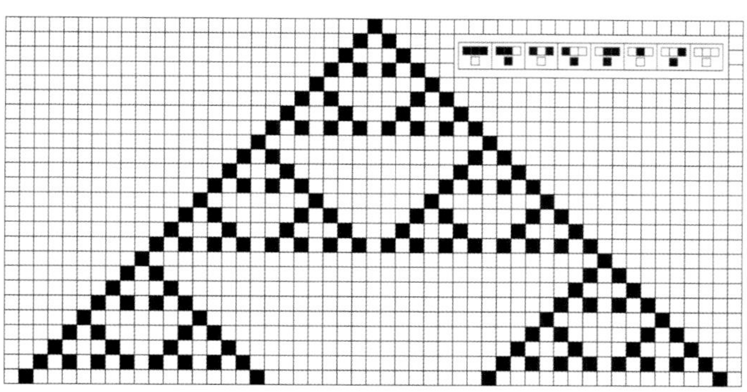

Figure 4. A cellular automaton that produces an intricate nested pattern. The rule in this case is that a cell should be black whenever one or the other, but not both, of its neighbours were black in the previous step. Even though the rule is very simple, the picture shows that the overall pattern obtained over the course of 25 steps starting from a single black cell is not so simple. The particular rule used here can be described by the formula $a_i' = Mod[a_{i-1} + a_{i+1}, 2]$. This is cellular automaton rule 90.

Otherwise, take the new colour to be the opposite of that.

The picture shows what happens when one starts with just one black cell and then applies this rule over and over again. What materialises is something quite startling – and probably the single most surprising scientific discovery I have ever made. Rather than getting a simple regular pattern as might be expected, the cellular automaton instead produces a pattern that seems extremely irregular and complex.

But where does this complexity come from? We certainly did not put it into the system in any direct way when we set it up. For we just used a simple cellular automaton rule, and just started from a simple initial condition containing a single black cell. Yet despite this, Figure 6 shows that there is great complexity in the behaviour that emerges. And indeed what we see here is a first example of an extremely general and fundamental phenomenon that is at the very core of *A New Kind of Science*. Over and over again we see the same kind of thing: that even though the underlying rules for a system are simple, and even though the system is started from simple initial conditions, the behaviour that the system shows can nevertheless be highly complex. I argue that it is this basic phenomenon that is ultimately responsible for most of the complexity we see in nature.

Figure 7 shows progressively more steps in the evolution of the rule 30 cellular automaton. It might be assumed here that the behaviour would eventually resolve into something simple. But again this is not the case.

Though some regularities can be seen – on the left-hand side there are obvious diagonal bands, and dotted throughout are various white triangles and other small structures – given the simplicity of the underlying rule, one would expect vastly more regularities. Perhaps one might imagine that our failure to see any is just a reflection of some kind of inadequacy in the human visual system. But even the most sophisticated mathematical and statistical methods of analysis seem to do no better. For example, one can look at the sequence of colours directly below the initial black cell. And in the first million steps in this sequence, for example, this never repeats, and indeed none of the tests I have ever carried out on it show any meaningful deviation at all from perfect randomness.

Nevertheless, in a sense there is a certain simplicity to such perfect randomness, as even though it may be impossible to predict what colour will occur at any specific step, one still knows, for example, that black and white will on average always occur equally often. However, there are cellular automata whose behaviour is, in effect, still more complex – and in which even such averages become very difficult to predict. Figure 8 gives a rather dramatic example. The basic form of the rule is just the same as before. But now the specific rule used – rule 110 – takes the new colour of a cell to be black in every case, except when the previous colours of the cell and its two neighbours were all the same, or when the left neighbour was black

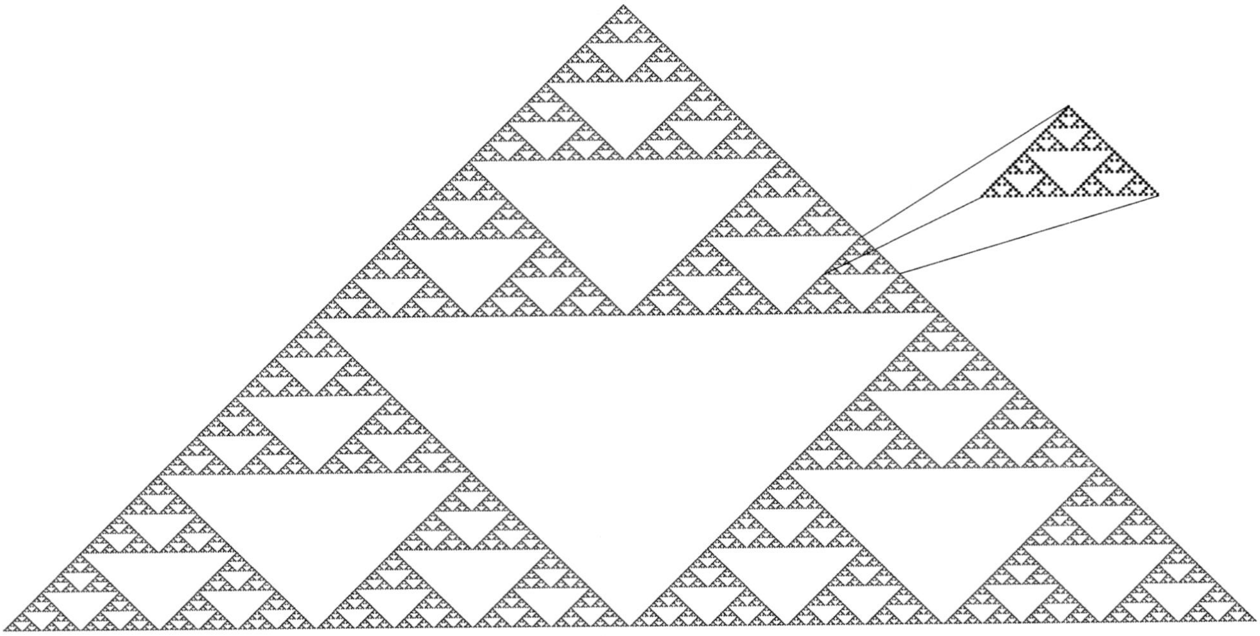

Figure 5. A larger version of the pattern from Figure 4, now shown without a grid explicitly indicating each cell. The picture shows 500 steps of cellular automaton evolution. The pattern obtained is intricate, but has a definite nested structure. Indeed, each triangular section is essentially just a smaller copy of the whole pattern, with still smaller copies nested inside it. Patterns with a nested structure of this kind are often described as 'fractal' or 'self-similar'.

and the cell and its right neighbour were both white.

The pattern obtained with this rule shows a remarkable mixture of regularity and irregularity. More or less throughout, there is a very regular background texture that consists of an array of small white triangles repeating every seven steps. And beginning near the left-hand edge, there are diagonal stripes that occur at intervals of exactly 80 steps. However, on the right-hand side the pattern is much less regular. Indeed, for the first few hundred steps there is a region that seems essentially random. But after several hundred steps, all that remains of this region are three copies of a rather simple repetitive structure.

Soon after, the arrival of a diagonal stripe from the left sets off more complicated behaviour again, and as the system progresses a variety of definite localised structures are produced. Some of these structures remain stationary, while others move steadily to the right or left at various speeds. On their own, each works in a fairly simple way, but their various interactions can have very complicated effects.

As a result it becomes almost impossible to predict – even approximately – what the cellular automaton will do. Will all the structures that are produced eventually annihilate each other, leaving only a very regular pattern? Or will more and more structures appear until the whole pattern becomes quite random?

The only sure way to answer these questions, it seems, is simply to run the cellular automaton for as many steps as are needed, and to watch what happens. In the case of rule 110, the outcome is finally clear after about 2,780 steps: one structure survives, and that structure interacts with the

One might think, for example, that the fact that all the cells in a cellular automaton follow exactly the same rule would mean that they would somehow obviously be doing the same thing. But instead, they seem to be doing quite different things. Some of them, for example, are part of the regular background, while others are part of one or another localised structure.

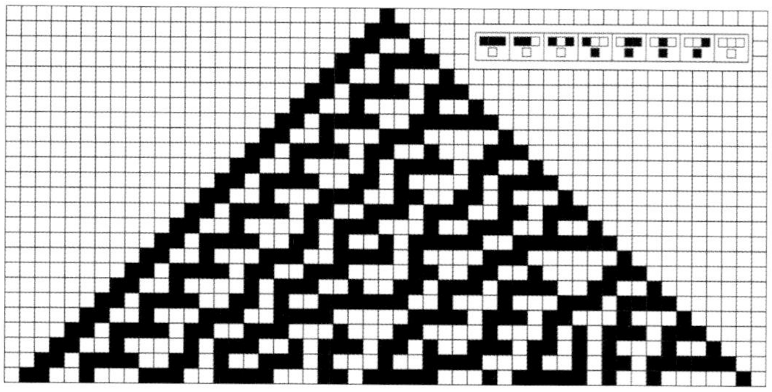

Figure 6. A cellular automaton with a simple rule that generates a pattern which seems in many respects random. The rule used is of the same type as in the previous examples, and the cellular automaton is again started from a single black cell. But now the pattern that is obtained is highly complex, and shows almost no overall regularity. This picture is an example of the fundamental phenomenon that even with simple underlying rules and simple initial conditions it is possible to produce behaviour of great complexity. The cellular automaton shown here is rule 30.

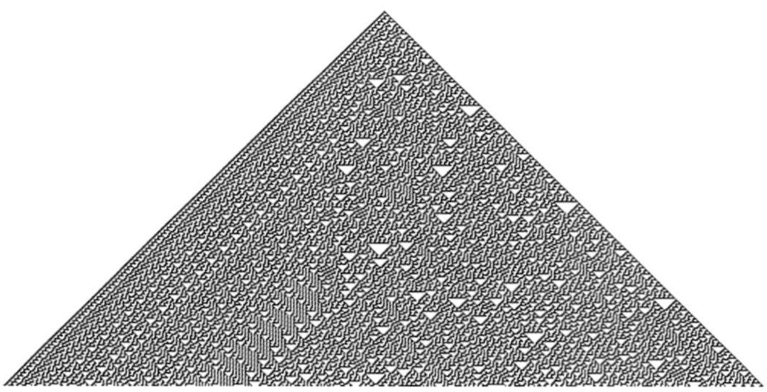

Figure 7. More steps of rule 30 evolution. Some regularities are evident, particularly on the left. However, even after all these steps there are no signs of overall regularity – and indeed even continuing for a million steps many aspects of the pattern obtained seem perfectly random according to standard mathematical and statistical tests.

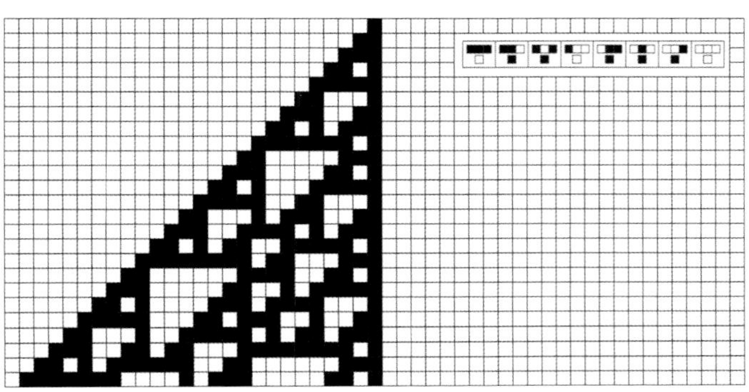

Figure 8. A cellular automaton whose behaviour seems neither highly regular nor completely random. The picture is obtained by applying the simple rule shown starting with a single black cell. Note that the particular rule used here yields a pattern that expands on the left, but not on the right. This is rule 110.

periodic stripes coming from the left to produce behaviour that repeats every 240 steps.

However certain one might be that simple programs could never do more than produce simple behaviour, rule 110 should for ever disabuse one of that notion. And indeed, what is perhaps most bizarre about the picture of rule 110 is just how little trace it ultimately shows of the simplicity of the underlying cellular automaton rule that was used to produce it. One might think, for example, that the fact that all the cells in a cellular automaton follow exactly the same rule would mean that they would somehow obviously be doing the same thing. But instead, they seem to be doing quite different things. Some of them, for example, are part of the regular background, while others are part of one or another localised structure. And what makes this possible is that even though individual cells follow the same rule, different configurations of cells with different sequences of colours can together produce all sorts of different kinds of behaviour.

Looking just at the original cellular automaton rule, one would have no realistic way of foreseeing all of this. But by doing appropriate computer experiments one can easily find out what actually happens – and in effect begin the process of exploring a whole new world of remarkable phenomena associated with simple programs. AD

Figure 9. More steps in the pattern shown in Figure 8. It is a long time before it becomes clear how the right-hand part of the pattern will eventually look.

Metaphysics of Genetic Architecture and Computation

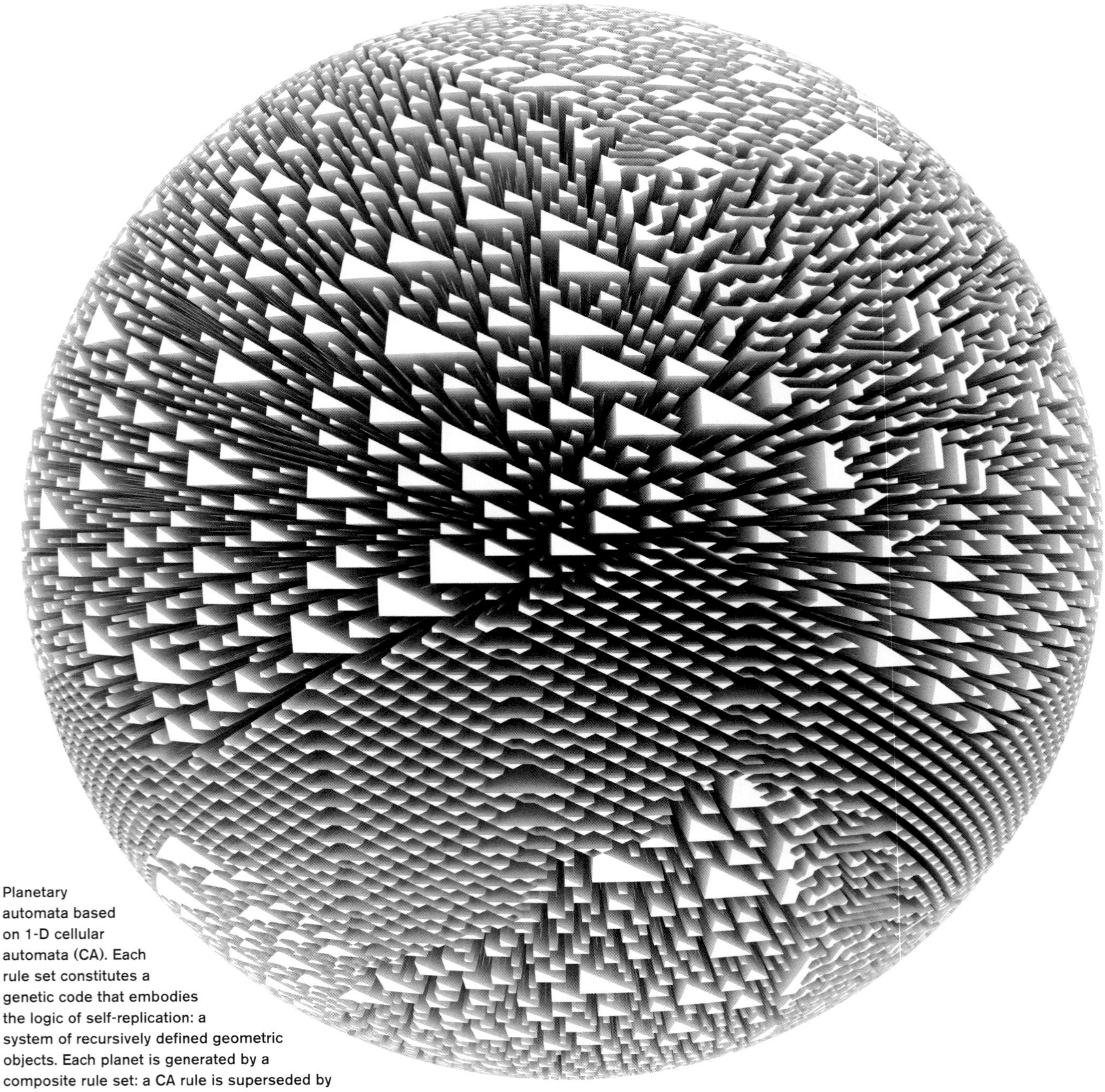

Planetary automata based on 1-D cellular automata (CA). Each rule set constitutes a genetic code that embodies the logic of self-replication: a system of recursively defined geometric objects. Each planet is generated by a composite rule set: a CA rule is superseded by another rule based on either local conditions or random instantiation. The density of each sphere displayed here is the result of a mere 300 generations, which is exceedingly small in relation to the potentially infinite number of generations that each planet can embody. (CA programming and modelling by Kevin Sipes.)

Karl Chu ruminates on the far-reaching impact that the convergence of computation and biogenetics will have on the unfolding history of man and nature. Could the world be 'moving into the so-called Post-Human Era, which will bring forth a new kind of biomachinic mutation of organic and inorganic substances'? How can architects reconfigure the practice of their discipline in order to meet the demands of this computational and biogenetic revolution?

'All is algorithm!'

Gregory Chaitin[1]

With the dissolution of the last utopian project of Man in the name of Communism, the great spectre that once haunted Europe and the rest of the world has all but vanished, leaving in its wake an ideological vacuum that is now being filled by the tentacles of globalisation with its ecumenical ambition. As humanity has become mesmerised by the triumphant spell of capitalism, what remains less apparent in the aftermath of this dissolution is that the world is moving incipiently towards a threshold that is far more radical and fantastic than any utopic vision since the dawn of the Enlightenment. Once again, the world is witnessing the rumblings of a Promethean fire that is destined to irrupt into the universe of humanity, calling into question the nature and function of life–world relations as they so far have existed. These rumblings, stemming in large measure from the convergence of computation and biogenetics in the latter part of the 20th century, have already begun to invoke gravid visions of the unthinkable: the unmasking of the primordial veil of reality.

The evolution of life and intelligence on Earth has finally reached the point where it is now deemed possible to engender something almost out of nothing. In principle, a universe of possible worlds based on generative principles inherent within nature and the physical universe is considered to be within the realm of the computable once quantum computing systems become a reality.[2] For the first time, humankind is finally in possession of the power to change and transform the genetic constitution of biological species, which, without a doubt, has profound implications for the future of life on Earth. By bringing into the foreground the hidden reservoir of life in all its potential manifestations through the manipulation of the genetic code, the unmasking or the transgression of what could be considered the first principle of prohibition – the taking into possession of what was once presumed to be the power of God to create life – may lead to conditions that are so precarious and treacherous as to even threaten the future viability of the species Homo sapiens on Earth. At the same time, depending on how humankind navigates into the universe of possible worlds that are about to be siphoned through computation, it could once again bring forth a poetic re-enchantment of the world, one that resonates with all the attributes of a premodern era derived, in this instance, from the intersection of the seemingly irreconcilable domains of logos and mythos. Organically interconnected to form a new plane of immanence that is digital, computation is the modern equivalent of a global alchemical system destined to transform the world into the sphere of hyper-intelligent beings.

The power of computation is already evident: in the last 70 years since the inception of the Universal Turing Machine,[3] it has ushered in the Information Revolution by giving rise to one of the most significant and now indispensable phenomena in the history of communication: the Internet or what could also be characterised as the universe of the Adjacent Possible. Stuart Kauffman defines the Adjacent Possible as the expansion of networks of reaction graphs within an interactive system into neighbourhood domains of connectivity which until then remain in a state of pure potentiality. He suggests that: 'The Universe has not explored all possible kinds of people, legal systems, economies or other complex systems,' and that 'autonomous Agents tend to arrange work and coordination so that they are expanding into the Adjacent Possible as fast as they can get away with it'.[4]

Like every phase transition, the Internet marks a new world order by reconfiguring the planet with a virtual, albeit an interactive, matrix that is becoming increasingly spatial, intelligent and autonomous: a global self-synthesising organ bustling with neural intelligence feasibly detectable from every corner of the Milky Way and beyond. The implications for architecture are most pronounced at the level of construction of possible worlds. The thesis this paper advances is that architecture is becoming increasingly dependent on genetic computation: the generative construction and the mutual coexistence of possible worlds within the computable domain of modal space.

Yet, what is the nature of computation that is destined to change the world, including architecture? No instrumental concept or logic of implementation since the invention of the wheel has fostered so much enthusiasm and promise as computation. Beyond the normative conception of computing machines as mere instruments for calculation, fabrication and communication, it is important to recognise the nature of the underlying ambitions of computation and its relation to architecture. As controversial and provocative as it may seem, the underlying ambitions of computation are already apparent: the embodiment of artificial life and intelligence systems either through abstract machines or through biomachinic mutation of organic and inorganic substances and, most significantly, the subsequent sublimation of physical and actual worlds into higher forms of organic intelligence by extending into the computable domain of possible worlds. At the most prosaic level, however, computation, like natural languages, deals with information in its most general form. Computation functions as manipulator of integers, graphs, programs and many other kinds of entities. But in reality, computation only manipulates strings of symbols that represent the objects.

It is not surprising that the origin of computation lies in an attempt to embody instrumental reason in an abstract machine with the attendant drive to encode the logic of life and the world around us in all its manifestations.

It should also be pointed out that, according to the late Richard Feynman, computing systems could be constructed at the atomic scale: swarms of nanobots, each functioning in accordance to a simple set of rules, could be made to infiltrate into host organisms or environments including the human body. In its simplest form, computation is a system that processes information through a discrete sequence of steps by taking the results of its preceding stage and transforming it to the next stage in accordance with a recursive function. Such an iterative procedure based on recursion has proved to be astonishingly powerful and is classified as belonging to a class of machines having universal properties.

It is not surprising that the origin of computation lies in an attempt to embody instrumental reason in an abstract machine with the attendant drive to encode the logic of life and the world around us in all its manifestations. The quest for a Universal Language[5] that could encapsulate all the attributes and functions necessary to inscribe the form and structure of all computable worlds is becoming one of the most persistent endeavours in the short history of computation. Since computation is about information-processing at the most fundamental level, John Wheeler, the prominent American scientist influential to a whole generation of physicists in the latter half of the 20th century, initiated an information-theoretic conception of the world by stipulating that every item in the universe has at bottom – at a very deep bottom, in most instances – an immaterial source and explanation that is information-theoretic in origin.[6] The fact that computation is a physical process further stipulates the existence of a self-consistent logical loop: the laws of physics define the allowed mechanical operations and the possible activities of a Universal Turing Machine, which in turn determine which mathematical operations are computable and define the nature of solvable mathematics. In other words, the laws of physics generate the very mathematics that makes those laws computable. The discovery of this inextricable linkage between computation and physics has led to the awareness that physical processes are in fact forms of computation, and nowhere is this understanding made more explicit than in Stephen Wolfram's formulation of the Principle of Computational Equivalence. Wolfram remarks: 'All processes, whether they are produced by human effort or occur spontaneously in nature, can be viewed as computations.'[7]

This proposition reflects a fundamental shift in the way we think about the nature of the physical universe; it is nothing short of a paradigm shift, which would not have been conceivable without an underlying thesis that enables the construction of such a world view: the Church–Turing Thesis, as formulated by Alfonso Church and Alan Turing in the early part of the 20th century. According to Turing: 'Every "function which would naturally be regarded as computable" can be computed by the Universal Turing Machine.'[8]

Although the absolute veracity of the thesis cannot be decided by logical means, all attempts to give an exact analysis of the intuitive notion of an effectively calculable function have turned out to be equivalent. Each analysis offered has proven to pick out the same class of functions, namely those that are computable by the Turing machine.

Parallel to the development of computation is the discovery of the DNA code in the early part of the 20th century, the significance of which has only begun to be realised with the completion of the Human Genome Project. Finally, with the convergence of computation and biogenetics, the world is now moving into the so-called Post-Human Era, which will bring forth a new kind of biomachinic mutation of organic and inorganic substances. Information is the currency that drives all these developments, and nowhere is this more apparent than in the words uttered by Craig Venter, the ex-CEO of Celera Corporation which completed the human genome sequence: 'The goal is to engineer a new species from scratch.'[9]

Notwithstanding theological implications, this statement bluntly announces the unadulterated ambition of the biogenetic revolution. It is only a matter of time before the world will witness biomachinic mutation of species proliferating into every facet of what so far has been the cultural landscape of humanity. Architects take note: this is the beginning of the demise, if not the displacement, of the

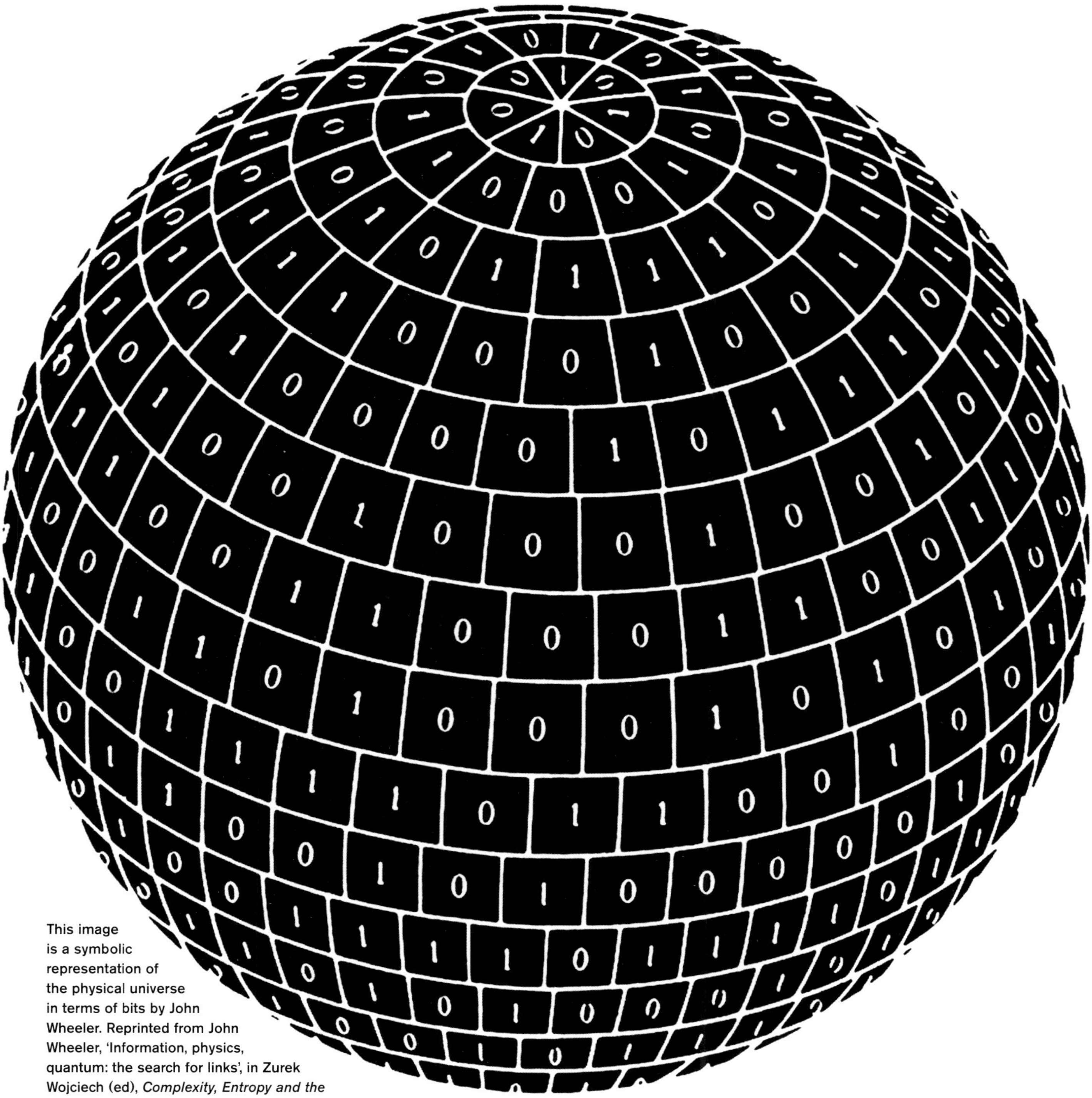

This image is a symbolic representation of the physical universe in terms of bits by John Wheeler. Reprinted from John Wheeler, 'Information, physics, quantum: the search for links', in Zurek Wojciech (ed), *Complexity, Entropy and the Physics of Information (Sante Fe Institute Studies in the Sciences of Complexity Proceedings)*, Addison-Wesley Publishing Company (Reading, MA), 1989.

reign of anthropology, which has always subsumed architecture. Architecture, especially from the standpoint of its mythical inception, has always been a subset of anthropology: the expulsion of Minotaur, the beast, by entrapping it in the labyrinth built by Daedalus, the mythical architect at Knossos. The potential emancipation of architecture from anthropology is already enabling us to think for the first time of a new kind of xenoarchitecture with its own autonomy and will to being. In order to break through the barrier of complacency and self-imposed ignorance on the part of the discipline, what is needed is a radicalisation of the prevailing paradigm of architecture, beyond retroactive manifestos, by developing a new concept of architecture that is adequate to the demands imposed by computation and the biogenetic revolution.

Within the contemporary landscape of architectural discourse there are two divergent trends with theoretical motivations: the morphodynamical and the morphogenetic systems' approaches to the design and construction of buildings.

Even though architects have incorporated computing systems in the design and construction of buildings and environments, the phase of transmodernity that we are now in is perhaps best characterised by the use of computation still operating under the vestiges of the old paradigm. In other words, architecture has still yet to incorporate the architecture of computation into the computation of architecture. Within the contemporary landscape of architectural discourse there are two divergent trends with theoretical motivations: the morphodynamical and the morphogenetic systems' approaches to the design and construction of buildings. These two systems are reminiscent of a strikingly similar problem that exists in modern biology, which is still attempting to synthesise the differences that exist between molecular biology, on the one hand, and developmental biology on the other. What is needed in architecture also is a similar synthesis of the two. After more than half a century of engagement with the avant-garde, the practice of architecture has become increasingly conscious of its embeddedness within the general economy of forces, relationships and the global economy. The morphodynamical approach, which has spurred two different methodological orientations in dealing with programmatic issues, is the more dominant of the two at the moment. The morphogenetic system is still more or less in its embryonic stage, even though it is by far the more fundamental and necessary since it deals with the construction of objects directly.

Having identified some of the salient features that are integral to dominant trends within contemporary architecture, as well as the nuanced relations that each of these trends have with regard to the phenomenon of globalisation, which is increasingly augmented and driven by the gift of Promethean fire that is now saturating the cultural universe of humanity with all forms of transgenic mutation, we are now in a position to articulate a more comprehensive theory of architecture, one that is adequate to the demands imposed by the convergence of computation and biogenetics in the so-called Post-Human Era: a monadology of genetic architecture that deals with the construction of possible worlds. As we now approach what Ray Kurzweil refers to as the Singularity,[10] the myth of matter, which underlies most theoretical and practical discussions of architecture, is about to be displaced by the myth of information. Contrary to Mies van der Rohe's oft-quoted remark that architecture is the art of putting two bricks together, the emerging conception is that architecture is the art of putting two bits together, at least bits that are programmed to self-replicate, self-organise and self-synthesise into evermore new constellations of emergent relations and ensembles.

The use of the term 'monadology' is based on the fact that genetic architecture is an extension and transformation of some of the propositions, especially those that define attributes and properties of relationships among monads, contained in Gottfried W Leibniz's *Monadology* (1714),[11] albeit without its theogony, into an architectural theory of world-making. *Monadology* is one of the earliest attempts in sketching out a system of principles that generalises the nature of the world from an abstract point of view; it shares conceptual properties that are now deemed to be fundamental to the science and philosophy of computation. Even though Leibniz was impeded by the lack of conceptual and technical resources at the time,[12] his ideas nonetheless paved the way for the subsequent development of computation and, according to Gregory Chaitin, Algorithmic Information Theory[13] in the 20th century.

Leibniz's *Monadology* is arguably the earliest endeavour to propose what is now known as an open-source architecture based on the principles of philosophical genetics: the principle of generative condensation, the principle of combinatorial expansion, and the principle of the conservation of information. *Monadology* is a metaphysical treatise; Leibniz

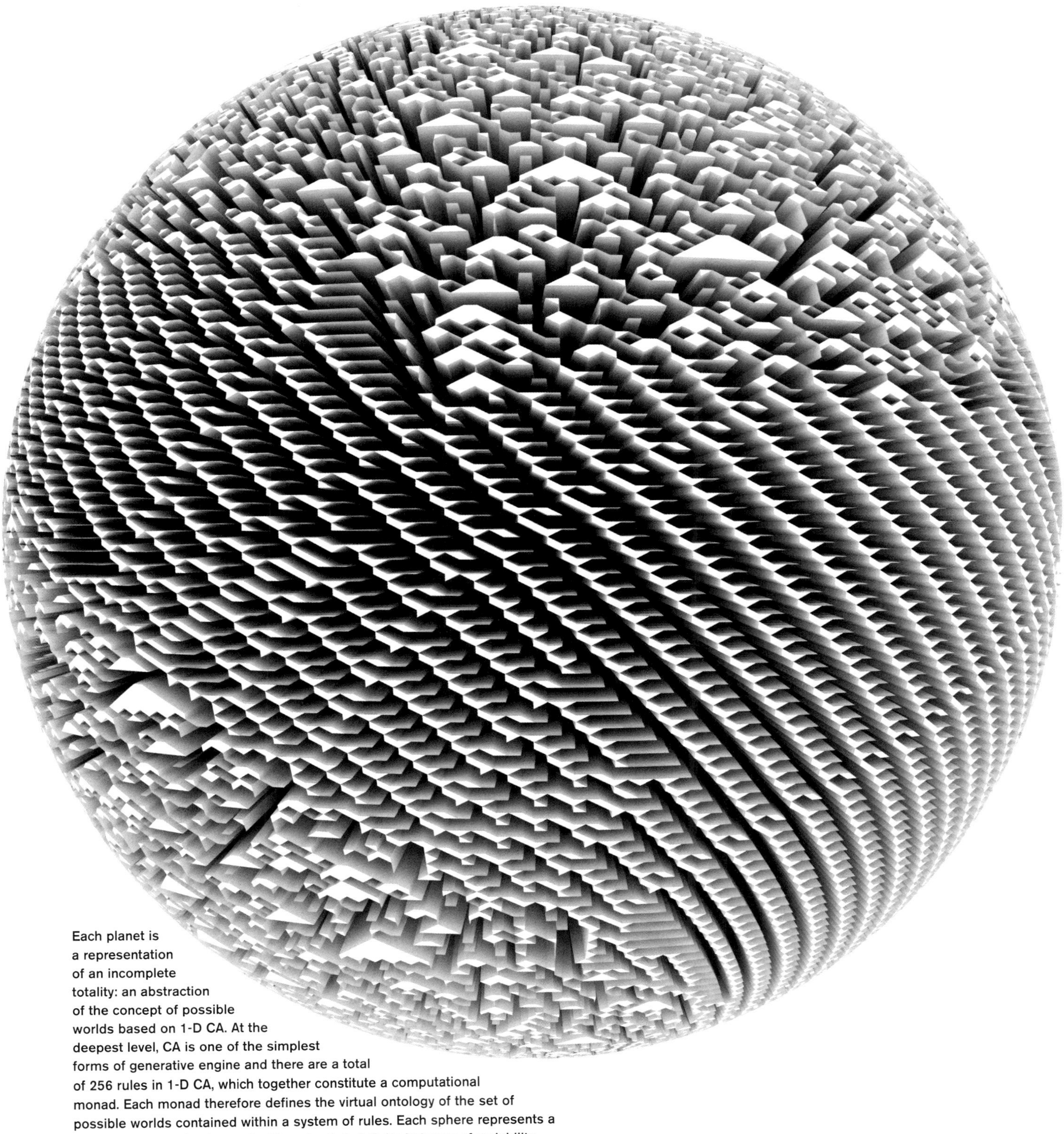

Each planet is a representation of an incomplete totality: an abstraction of the concept of possible worlds based on 1-D CA. At the deepest level, CA is one of the simplest forms of generative engine and there are a total of 256 rules in 1-D CA, which together constitute a computational monad. Each monad therefore defines the virtual ontology of the set of possible worlds contained within a system of rules. Each sphere represents a proto-architectural universe that is potentially infinite in terms of variability and density with regard to its composition. (CA programming and modelling by Kevin Sipes.)

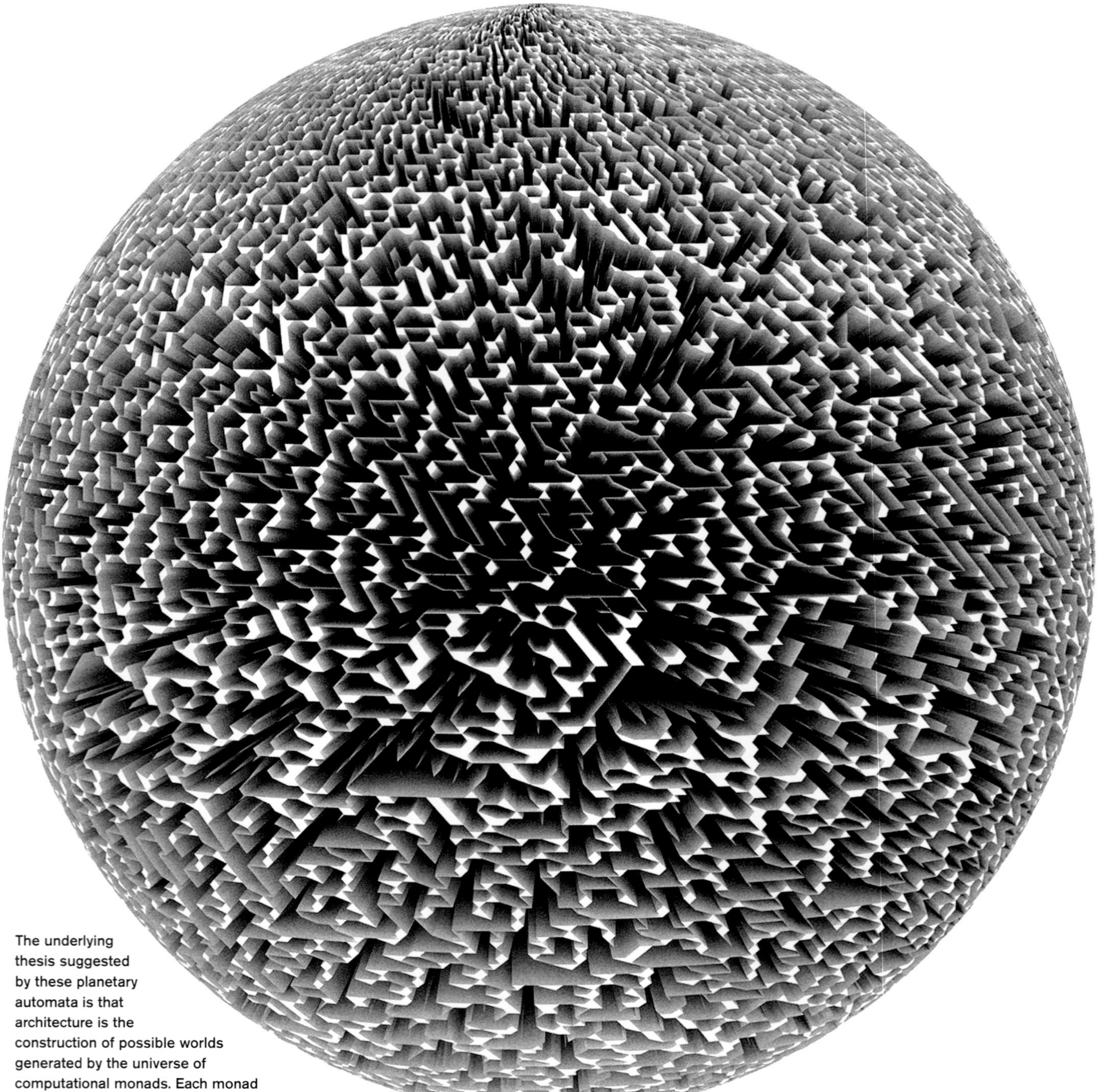

The underlying thesis suggested by these planetary automata is that architecture is the construction of possible worlds generated by the universe of computational monads. Each monad encapsulates an internal principle that is generative, and each generative system transmits and propagates hereditary information. Each monad is at once a self-replicating and self-organising system capable of constituting itself into a cohesive whole or a possible world: in other words, a monadology of genetic architecture. (CA programming by Chris Sandes; modelling by Christian Lange.)

defines each monad as a metaphysical point, an irreducible concept of an atomic entity that is endowed with an immaterial substance. Contrary to Leibniz and without the reference to God as the supreme creator of monads, a computational theory of monadology would instead qualify each monad as one BIT of information at the most irreducible level, and by extension a unit of a self-replicating system. It is based on this conception of a monad as a minimal unit of a self-replicating system that a monadology of genetic architecture is developed here.

Historically, genetic architecture can be seen as an extension and transformation of utopic ideas implicit within the avant-garde to create new worlds by drawing on new sciences and technologies. Genetics is a term coined by William Bateson in 1905 to encompass the study of heredity, and 'gene' was introduced around the same time by the Danish botanist Wilhelm Johannsen, to account for the units within sex cells that determine the hereditary characteristics. The meanings of both terms, 'genetics' and 'gene', are sufficiently abstract and general to be used as concepts that have logical implications for architecture without being anchored too explicitly to biology. Implicit within the concept of genetics is the idea of the replication of heritable units based on some rule inherent within the genetic code, and embedded within the mechanism for replication is a generative function: the self-referential logic of recursion. Recursion is a function or rule that repeatedly calls itself or its preceding stage by applying the same rule successively, thereby generating a self-referential propagation of a sequence or a series of transformations. It is this logic, encoded within an internal principle, that constitutes the autonomy of the generative that lies at the heart of computation.

Even though genetic is a term derived from biology, it is used here as a generic concept based on the interconnected logic of recursion and self-replication whose philosophical underpinnings go far beyond the confines of molecular biology. It should therefore be noted that genetic architecture is neither a representation of biology nor a form of biomimesis; instead, its theoretical origins, insofar as genetic architecture is concerned, can be traced to John von Neumann's invention of the cellular automaton and his 'von Neumann architecture' for self-replicating systems. From the early stages of the development of modern computing systems, von Neumann was proposing the idea of self-replication. Even though he participated in discussions leading to the development of the first electronic computer ever built – the ENIAC – von Neumann eventually came up with what is now known as the von Neumann architecture – the prototype for modern computing systems with its stored memory program. This addressed the idea of a machine that could manufacture itself: a robot that self-replicates and self-constructs copies of itself,[14] a notion that lies at the heart of biology: the essence of self-reproduction is organisation – the ability of a system to contain a complete description of itself and use that information to create new copies.

The von Neumann architecture for a self-replicating system is the ancestral and archetypical proposal, which consisted of two central elements: a Universal Computer and a Universal Constructor. The Universal Computer contains a program that directs the behaviour of the Universal Constructor, which, in turn, is used to manufacture both another Universal Computer and a Universal Constructor. Once finished, the newly manufactured Universal Computer was programmed by copying the program contained in the original Universal Computer, and program execution would then begin again. The von Neumann architecture is, therefore, a precursor to the architecture of a genetic system.

Notes

1 Gregory Chaitin, *Leibniz, Information, Math and Physics*, http://www.cs.auckland.ac.nz/CDMTCS/chaitin/kirchberg.pdf), 2003, p 9.
2 David Deutsch, 'Quantum theory, the Church–Turing principle and the Universal Quantum Computer', in *Proceedings of the Royal Society of London* A 400, 1985, p 3.
3 Alan Turing, 'On Computable Numbers with an Application to the Entscheidungsproblem', *Proceedings of the London Mathematical Society*, Ser 2, Vol 42, 1936. Alan Turing developed the Universal Turing Machine, an abstract machine in the logical sense of the term, in response to David Hilbert's call for the resolution of the decision problem, or Entscheidungsproblem, in mathematics.
4 Stuart Kauffman, *Investigations*, Oxford University Press (New York), 2000, pp 142–4. Kauffman's concept of the Adjacent Possible was applied in the context of his investigations into the origin of life based on autocatalytic systems, which are derived from random interactions of nodes within Boolean networks. See http://www.paulagordon.com/shows/kauffman/.
5 Paolo Rossi, *Logic and the Art of Memory: The Quest for a Universal Language*, University of Chicago Press (Chicago, IL), 2000, pp 145–94.
6 John Wheeler, 'Information, physics, quantum: the search for links', in Zurek Wojciech (ed), *Complexity, Entropy and the Physics of Information (Santa Fe Institute Studies in the Sciences of Complexity Proceedings)*, Vol VIII, Addison-Wesley (Reading, MA), 1989, p 5.
7 Stephen Wolfram, *A New Kind of Science*, Wolfram Research (Champaign, IL), 2002, p 41.
8 Alan Turing, op cit. Note: Apart from the analyses defined in terms of lambda-definability and recursiveness by A Church, there are analyses in terms of register machines by JP Shepherdson and HE Sturgis, EL Post's canonical and normal systems, combinatory definability by M Schönfinkel and HB Curry, Markov algorithms and Gödel's notion of reckonability.
9 Craig Venter, 'Supermicrobe Man', *Wired*, No 10, 12 December 2002, p 191.
10 Ray Kurzweil, 'The Singularity', in John Brockman, *The New Humanists: Science at the Edge*, Barnes & Noble (New York), 2003, pp 215–32.
11 GW Leibniz and Nicholas Rescher, *GW Leibniz's Monadology: An Edition for Students*, University of Pittsburgh Press, 1991.
12 Martin Davis, *The Universal Computer: The Road From Leibniz to Turing*, WW Norton & Company (New York), 2000, pp 180–7.
13 Chaitlin, op cit.
14 William Poundstone, *The Recursive Universe: Cosmic Complexity and the Limits of Scientific Knowledge*, Contemporary Books, Inc (Canada), 1985. See also: http://www.zyvex.com/nanotech/selfRepJBIS.html#vonNeumannArchitecture.

One-dimensional cellular automaton sketch for natural lighting and display walls.

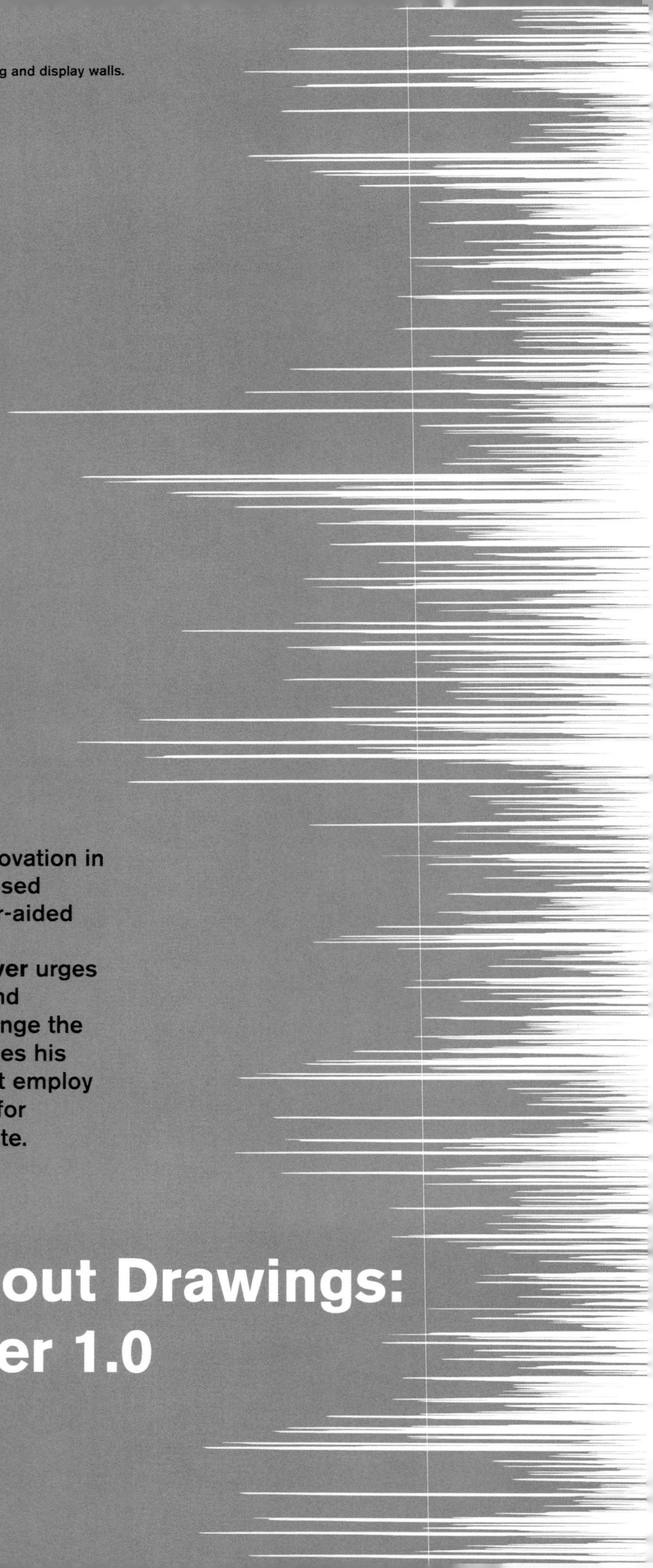

For the most part, technological innovation in architecture has been narrowly focused around the intersection of computer-aided design (CAD) and computer-aided manufacture (CAM). Here, **Mike Silver** urges architects to take up the gauntlet and develop software tools that can change the way buildings are made. He describes his own investigations into projects that employ a cellular automaton (CA) program for conveying design data directly on site.

Building Without Drawings: Automason Ver 1.0

'Technology always lies under the threat of instantaneous ruin, for it inhabits a spot where perfectionism and the litter mentality meet.'

Robert Harbison[1]

While computers have dramatically changed the way architects design, construction in the US and around the world is still very much a diverse mix of processes, often supplemented by hand using both traditional and nontraditional materials. Instead of focusing exclusively on the digital fabrication of building components in the factory, this essay explores the creation of proprietary software designed to effect meaningful changes in the way work is produced in the field. Enhancing the efficiency and formal potential of conventional building techniques in the present requires an expanded definition of computer-aided design and manufacturing (CAD/CAM). For this purpose Automason Ver 1.0 was developed around the analogous operation of cellular automaton programs and masonry construction.

A cellular automaton (CA) program consists of a field of discrete cells divided into small groups, or neighbourhoods. Defined in terms of finite states, on or off, transparent or opaque, white or black, and so on, a CA computation evolves over time. The configuration of each neighbourhood is used to determine the future state of the next generation of cells. Both complex and uniform patterns emerge from the ground up in a network of parts generated by local interactions. The idea of using simple programs to drive the construction of bricks-and-mortar structures comes from the observation that masons work much like cellular automaton programs. By following procedures based on laws of adjacency and iteration, a mason builds by stacking one brick at a time. With a simple set of rules, complex brick patterns can be constructed without reference to an equally complicated index of parts: construction documents, shop drawings, and so on. In fact, cellular automata can facilitate the production of extremely difficult designs without forcing the mason to do more work. An automasonry wall's[2] expressive power is the direct result of its parts and the way they are assembled. This follows one of the guiding principles of Modernism, but with a difference: structures driven by simple programs need not be reduced to a limited inventory of pared-down, predetermined or ideal types (a brick does not only want to be an arch). The only way to know how a given rule will behave is to set it in motion.

With simple programs, building details obtain their complexity for free: no external agency or extraneous system is needed to design them. This kind of complexity is not dependent on the incessant differentiation of parts, but on the application of fixed rules in a discrete system that requires only two components. The overall form of a CA masonry structure must therefore be evaluated in terms of its relationship to specific building requirements interpreted and organised by the architect. Here, Darwin's theory of evolution falls short as a practical model for design. Rather than linking environmental pressures with blind chance to produce morphogenic variation, in an automasonry structure functional constraints are used to wilfully select self-organising patterns that are particular to the rigorous, computational properties of a specific material.

While this link between mathematics and masonry is indeed fortuitous, no approach to bricks-and-mortar construction can be developed without first considering the problem of human error. In a space built with simple programs, anything that interferes with the accurate performance of a given code ends up undermining the intended function of the whole. An automasonry wall must therefore be computed with great accuracy. This can be accomplished through a series of simple training exercises designed for artisans who wish to expand their skills while maintaining a competitive edge. A less artful system of 'error correction' can also be achieved cybernetically with a specially adapted personal data assistant (PDA)cell phone.[3]

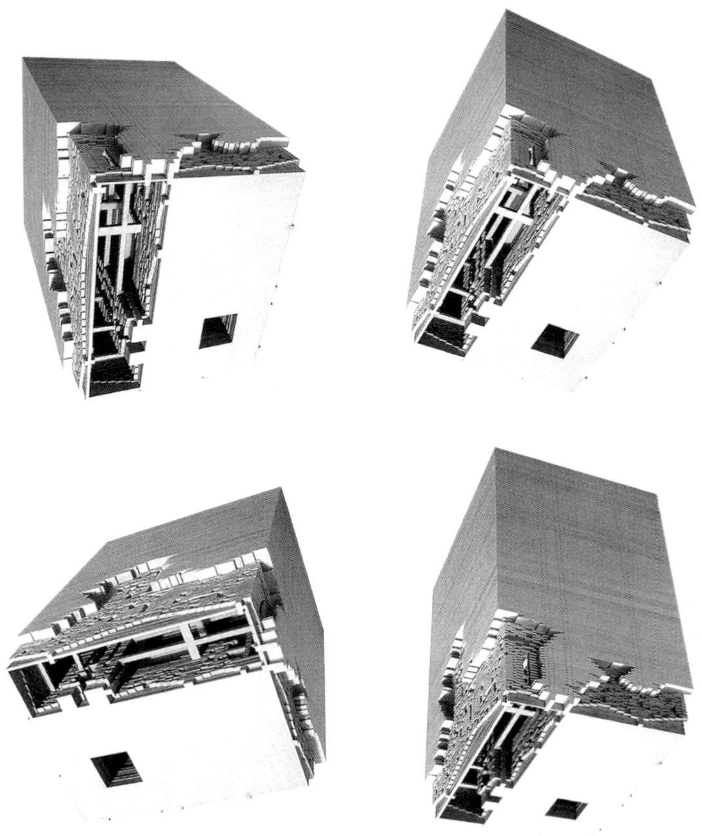

Mike Silver Architects, competition entry, San Jose State University Museum of Art and Design, Silicon Valley, California, 2003
Laser-cut basswood model. Worm's-eye view showing atrium, entry facade and ground-floor fire stair.

A Museum For Silicon Valley

For the San Jose State University Museum of Art and Design competition (2003), we used a 'class two' CA code[4] to produce both complex and simple patterns from straight courses of stone and glass block. Rooms with windows and galleries requiring large, blank display walls were laid out in accordance with the competition brief. Once these parameters were set in place, a search was made through multiple iterations in order to find the most appropriate patterns. For the museum's exterior, internal subdivisions and fire stairs, a five-cell outer totalistic[5] cellular automaton was found that damped out the complexity of the lower floors to create a partly windowless volume with intricate openings at the base (the top of the building is terminated by skylights that draw the sun into a narrow atrium facing east). From the complexity of the lower levels, the project culminates in a quiescent and illuminated void. Vertical supports for the building's interior spaces were determined by the initial conditions of the CA code on the ground floor. A nonregular grid of columns produced different spans with beams of varying depths setting up an exchange between light, gravity and computation.

Rather than being neutral infill, the project's surfaces actively shape an internal concrete armature that rhythmically fluctuates as the CA patterns ascend into space. The parametric relationship between enclosing walls and structure constitutes both the organisational logic of Automason Ver 1.0 (written in C++) and the tectonic interconnections forged by the project during construction. Here in its making, architecture itself is computed (the building's surfaces are not a product of some external image concealing structure, nor are they shaped by a remote database or calculating machine). In the San Jose museum, the nature and position of each masonry unit affects its immediate neighbours and the order of the whole. Because the system is extremely sensitive to small changes, every brick counts in a truly organic architecture created by the rigorous application of simple programs.

The design and organisation of the San Jose project also expresses its code's ability to efficiently produce irregular patterns that are organically linked to blank, homogeneous space. These relationships are produced using local rules that are not based on the recursion of simple motifs, faithfully rendered at different scales (self-similarity). No image of the whole can be found in the details. Neither scale invariance nor the repetition of a standard module can be used to guide the mason's work. While the code for a completed wall can be ascertained through direct observation, the rules on their own give little indication of the kinds of form they can produce. Sameness and variation, periodicity and aperiodicity are therefore binaries that accentuate the morphological potential of simple programs.

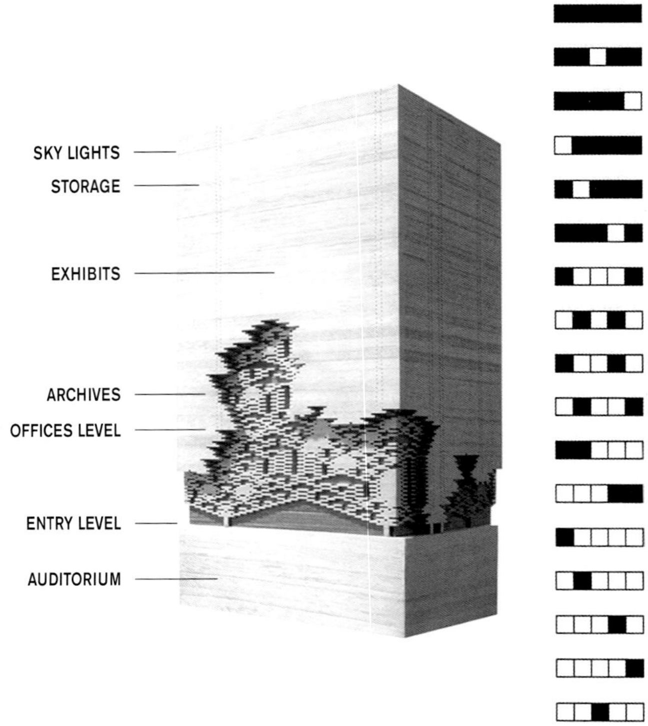

San Jose State University Museum of Art and Design showing brick and glass block patterns generated using simple programs. Right: This Outertotalistic cellular automaton rules set allows masons to generate complex forms without having to look at an equally complicated index of parts. The location and extent of glass and solid walls in the building was determined by internal space requirements. Thousands of calculations were made before the right self-organised configuration was found.

These computational strategies open up architecture to new ways of thinking and are useful as an alternative to one of contemporary design's most pervasive motifs. The ability to integrate different functions and internal space requirements without resorting to antagonistic compositional strategies has been the purpose of 'folding' in architecture. The work of Rene Thom is often used in this context to connect opposing forces on a single, deformed surface. While Thom's catastrophe diagrams are used mostly as a device to exceed the operative limits of collage, an abrupt change in the condition of a system or the integration of contradictory space requirements does not necessarily mandate compositional strategies based on an infinitely divisible logic. Discrete operations can be equally effective in generating networked relationships between distinct elements (and can also be used to produce smooth and continuous behaviour at the macro scale). The fold as a leitmotif for contemporary practice (Eisenman, Gehry, et al) requires 'a continuous variation of matter'.[6] The architectural effects of the fold can be matched by the iteration of programs like cellular automata where simple codes resolve the dynamic and often conflicting demands of function. The following categories, linked to their current formal expression, now give way to a new set of procedures:

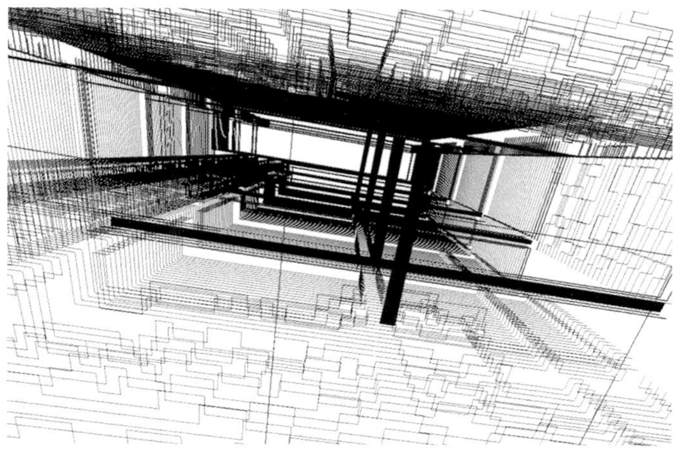

East-facing entry facade with brick and glass block openings on the ground floor. Corner details, views of atrium.

Bifurcation	Folding/Deformation	Simple Programs
Affiliation	Smoothness/Continuity	Discrete Space
Differentiation	Mass Customisation	Complexity for Free
Variation	Self-Similarity	Aperiodicity
Fabrication	Robotics (CAD/CAM)	Augmented Craft

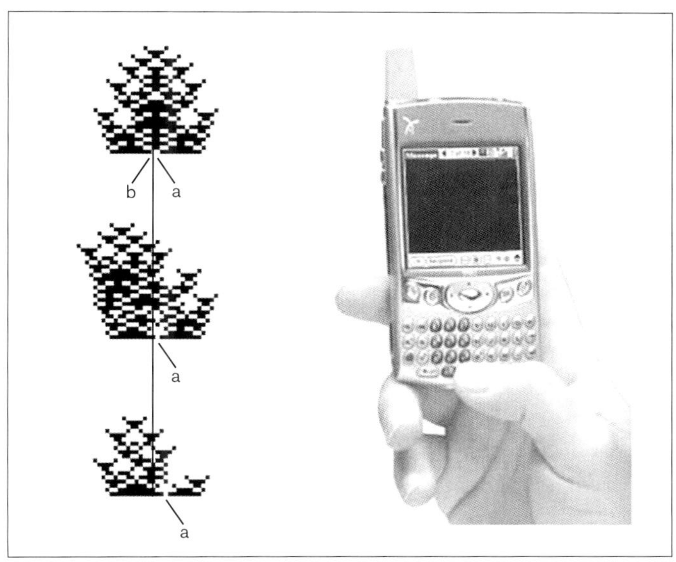

Pattern variations in the above four CA computations are extremely sensitive to small errors. A different arrangement of black and white results if a single cell is shifted. A typical mobile phone could be programmed to alert masons if any mistakes are made in the process of stacking blocks. Mobile communications technologies could also be used in other areas of construction to expand the capabilities of computer-aided fabrication.

Ornament, Entropy and the Picturesque

For the 19th-century architect and theorist Gottfried Semper, ornament was indispensable. As a medium it could exceed function and morphological necessity, transforming utilitarian constructions into great works of art. Semper therefore insisted that a building's structure and material weight should be concealed behind the 'dissimulating fabric' of decoration. This fabric was in turn used to signify the meaning and formal origins of architecture, which he believed had evolved from more primitive techniques such as weaving, pottery and metalwork. (A woven pattern rendered in stone, for example, could actively link the genealogy of a wall to the rich history of textile design.) In many ways Semper's idea of applied decoration presages Robert Venturi's concept of the decorated shed, where signs and symbols are simply attached to raw functional structures. In contrast to Semper and Venturi, Frank Lloyd Wright encouraged the development of integral patterns arising naturally from a building's physical supports.[7] In other words, structure and its articulation equals ornament – a semantically confused formulation that grants the same meaning to completely different patterns (if a given arrangement of columns and beams is considered ornate, then it is either very complex or very inefficient).[8] For Louis Sullivan and John Root, Wright's early mentors, decorative motifs were a means of expression that simply reinforced the primary facts of function and assembly. All of these ideas were, of course, negated by the European Modernists who pushed for the total elimination of ornament.

While the patterned surfaces of San Jose are not themselves a product of organising principles governed by structural necessity, they are also not applied decoration. In the process of unbuilding complexity, class two cellular automata visibly drive the organisation of structure and space. Far from a simplicity achieved through the removal of intricate details, blank homogeneous surfaces emerge out of heterogeneous patterns that negate themselves. Literally, ornament self-organises its own disappearance. This approach escapes the narrow discourse that pits formal excess on the one hand against a strict return to minimal forms on the other. Two distinct systems, masonry veneer and reinforced concrete, are here clearly integrated without having to blur or confuse the boundaries between them.

While the results look as if architecture was being subjected to erosion, this is not a design signifying the unplanned disruption of function and structural integrity: at San Jose form is the result of a code that actively unbuilds the complexity of the project's lower floors to produce a series of useful spaces. The brick walls of SITE's Best department store in Houston, Texas (1974) form a mock ruin by copying an image or picture external to the materials and techniques that produced it. The brick walls of San Jose are self-organised into what looks like a ruin by following a generative process internal to the materials and techniques of building construction. (Progress implies accelerated obsolescence.) The former is a film-still folly, a contrived and unreal snapshot of decay. Its strangeness is predicated on the contradictory tension between movement and stasis, consumerism and death (shoppers menaced by a picturesque simulation of falling bricks), while the latter is a process moving incrementally towards increasing levels of ineffability and emptiness (one critiques function through irony, the other produces an instrumental transition that is both organic and real). Through long rectangular openings located above its blank surfaces, the museum reaches into a vast and unfabricated silence. The vertical progression from intricate fenestration to solid walls is ultimately a move beyond glass and stone, complexity and minimalism, ornament and structure, shadows and light, 0s and 1s. At the roof all dualities come to an end. AD

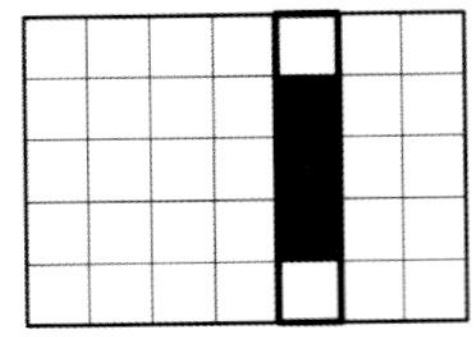

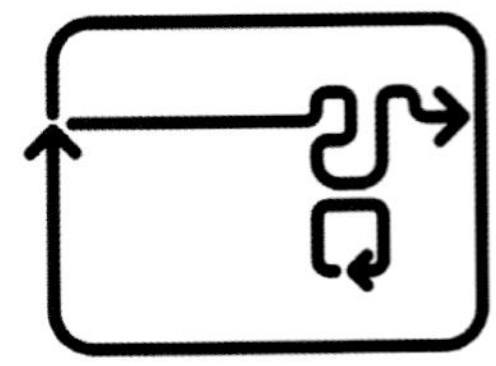

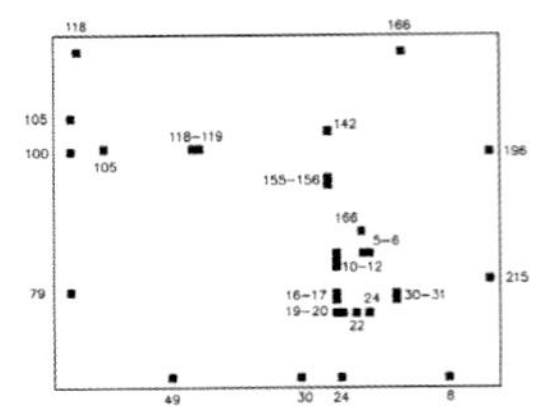

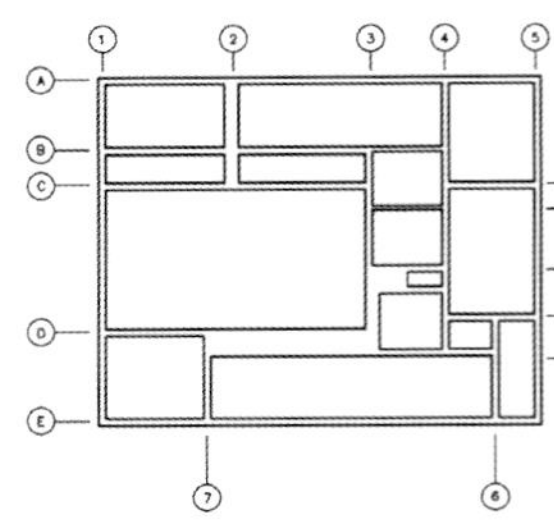

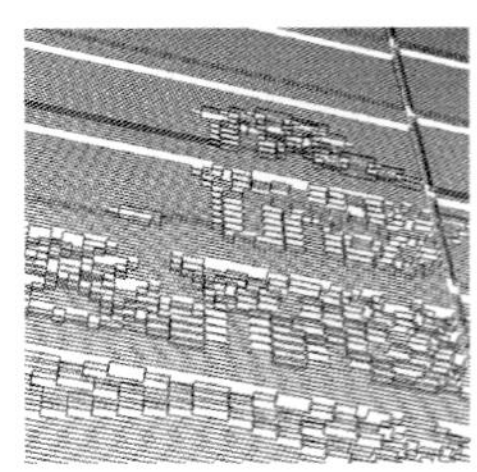

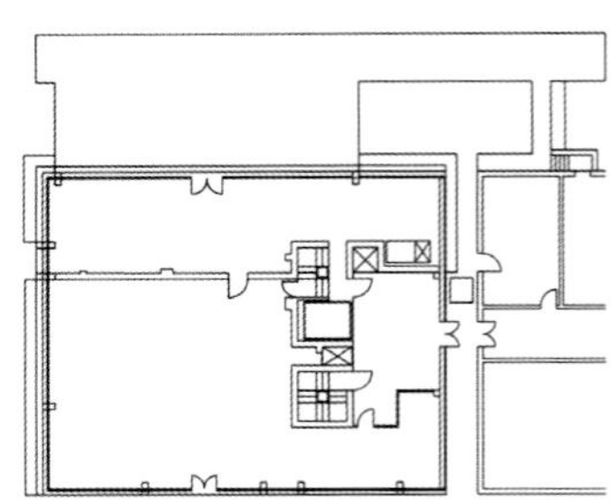

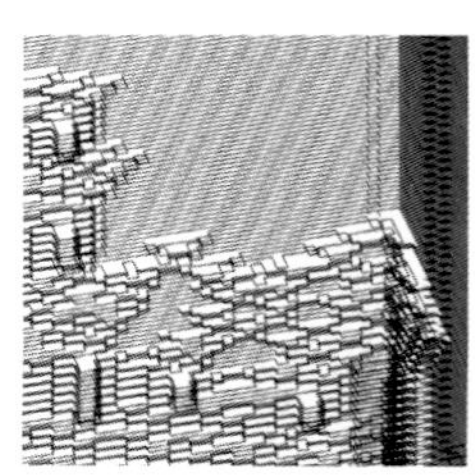

The plan of San Jose is based on a five-cell grid. The building's vertical circulation core is indicated by three consecutive black squares (top). There are three looped walls in the project. The initial conditions for each CA loop also designate column locations for the building's concrete frame.

Notes

1 Robert Harbison, *The Built, the Unbuilt and the Unbuildable*, MIT Press (Cambridge MA), 1994, p 99.
2 An 'automasonry wall' is a wall made with simple programs.
3 With PDA technology, nonstandard brick patterns can be constructed using stored information, digital photographs and pattern-recognition software. The phone's onboard camera can monitor what is happening in real space, while voice commands from its computer help direct block-stacking patterns. By relating pictures taken in close proximity to the user's body with the neighbourhood logic of cellular automata, the system would be able to prevent errors in construction. Using the system, builders could also integrate standard PDA functions into the work flow, making it easy to communicate progress reports to job captains off site using mobile email accounts, organise teams to work simultaneously on different parts of the same wall by forming a wireless network, store and display construction details, read bar codes and track materials, aid in the resolution, redesign and clarification of building information by establishing better communications between architects and builders, and schedule work, access itineraries and organise team members. Of course all of this can be done without paper drawings.
4 For a detailed description of the classification system for cellular automaton programs, see: Stephen Wolfram, 'Universality and Complexity in Cellular Automata', *Cellular Automata and Complexity: Collected Papers*, Westview Press (Philadelphia), 1995, pp 140–57. A class two pattern starts out complex and ends up simple.
5 'Outer totalistic' is a shorthand format for specifying cellular automaton rules.
6 Peter Eisenman, 'Visions unfolding', in Jonathan Cary (ed), *Zone: Incorporations v. 6*, Zone Books (Brooklyn, NY), 1992, p 234.
7 See Frank Lloyd Wright, 'Integral Ornament at Last', from the 'Nature of Materials', excerpt from *Architecture Culture 1943–1963, Columbia Books on Architecture*, Rizzoli (New York), 1993, pp 38–41.
8 If a real column is made thicker than it needs to be it does not become ornament. It is merely an overdesigned column. If a column that does not support any real loads is used in a building to signify structure, then the column is only ornamental. If structure is concealed by ornament the results are the same: ornament is not structure.

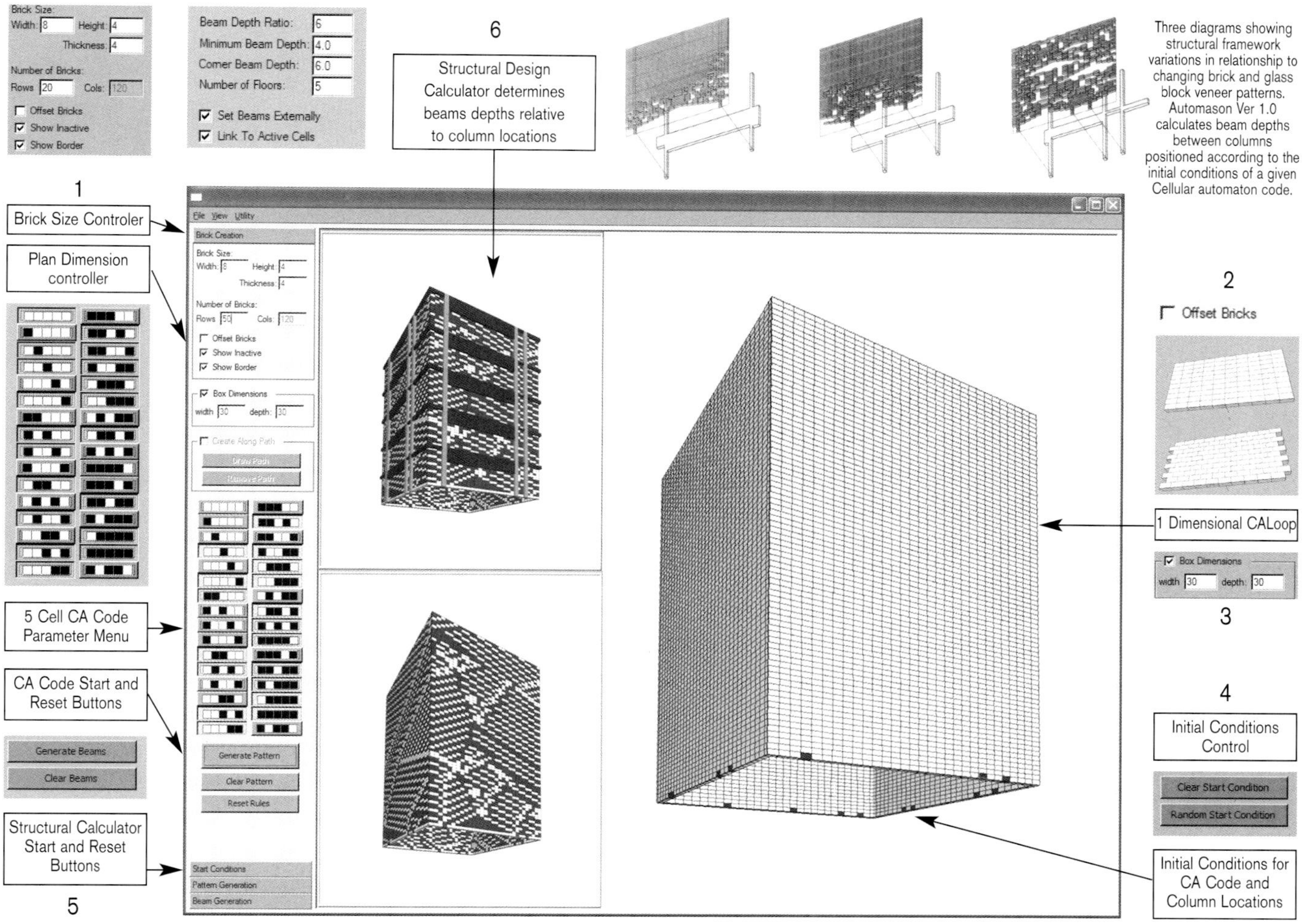

Automason Ver 1.0 software controls
Automason brick pattern and concrete frame calculator determines beam depths relative to the initial conditions of the wall's cellular automaton code. The software was written in C++ by Yee Peng Chia and Eric Maslowski. Automason software controls: Steps 1–6. (1) Set block size and layout dimensions using the number of bricks and brick-size selection boxes. (2) Activate grid or ashlar pattern control. (3) Set building height using the brick course button. (4) Set the initial conditions on the ground floor by moving the selection box with the keyboard arrows then press 'ALT' to set conditions ON or OFF. (5) Design CA rule set by pressing any combination of 32 buttons. (6) Calculate structural framing dimensions by setting the 'Beam Depth Ratio' controller.

The Milgo Experiment: An Interview with Haresh Lalvani

For just less than a decade, Haresh Lalvani has been working on a series of projects with Milgo/Bufkin, a leading architectural metal-fabrication company, seeking to economically integrate the shaping and making of metal surfaces into elements that create a seamless whole. Here, **John Lobell** interviews Lalvani about his pioneering work with computer-aided design and manufacturing and how it has been informed by his development of the Morphological Genome, a universal code for mapping and manipulating form, whether natural or man-made.

Soft AlgoRhythms, surfaces with softer, rounded bends as morphological extensions of bent-surface AlgoRhythms.

Milgo's laser-cutter, one of the several digital-fabrication devices used for different Milgo experiments.

'The dilemma posed to all scientific explanation is this: magic or geometry.'

Rene Thom, 1972[1]

'A more important set of instruction books will never be found by human beings.'

James D Watson (on the human genome), 2003[2]

In recent decades there has been an increase in the use of curved surfaces in architecture, although to date more often in computer simulations than in realised projects. The most common use of curved surfaces is cylindrical column covers that are created from sheet metal on press brakes, with skilled workers continually moving the sheet of metal under the machine's blade by hand. This process curves the metal without warping or deforming it.

Compound curves, along which one cannot place a straight edge in any direction (for example, a bowl), are far more difficult to fabricate for architecture. They are commonly used in the automobile industry, where they are created by pressing the metal between curved male and female dies, which stretches and deforms the metal. However, such dies are expensive – a cost that can be justified only by making large quantities of identical pieces. Compound curves in sheet metal can also be created by hand, for example with an English wheel, though this technique is also expensive and it would thus be impractical to make an entire building using this method.

In 1997, Haresh Lalvani began working with Milgo/Bufkin, a leading metal-fabrication company, to find a way of creating developable curved sheet-metal surfaces using an economical process that recognises both the characteristics of sheet metal and the digital capabilities of metal fabrication, such as laser cutting, water-jet cutting, press braking, digital punching. The fabrication of sheet metal at a scale economical for architecture inhibits compound curves and requires developable surfaces – curved surfaces that can be folded or bent from a flat sheet without deforming the material. This work launched the AlgoRhythms project that Lalvani terms the 'Milgo experiment'. According to Lalvani:

'There is more than one Milgo experiment in progress, AlgoRhythms being the first. All relate to genomic architecture.[3] The objective of these experiments is to integrate shaping (morphology) and making (fabrication) into a seamless whole. In nature, the two aren't separate. In these projects, I am interested in architecture as surface, not mass. Mass focuses on material performance (strength of material), while surface depends on its geometry (strength of form). This approach has several motivations. First, it is deeply connected with sustainability, as limited resources require us to maximise performance. Second, the bulk of the morphological universe (morphoverse) is inhabited by curved forms that need to be discovered, mapped and accessed. Straight lines and flat planes are in a minority within this universe. Third, new building technologies closer to those found in and beyond nature need to be invented to deal with these new vocabularies.

'We focused on metal because Milgo is a metal-fabrication company, though our experiments extend to other materials and forms. The question was as follows: Using sheet metal as it is used in architectural metal fabrication, could we form surfaces to define architectural space using techniques available at Milgo? We wanted to modulate the stiff metal surface to make rigid curved surfaces without deforming the metal. This way the sheet metal would preserve its integrity and become what "it wants to be", to borrow Kahn's words. It would also become stronger. Strength "emerges" from curvature when 2-D becomes 3-D during the forming process. We have called this new kind of forming "nondeformational bending". By comparison, standard methods of forming sheet metal, for example stamping, deep drawing and so on, yield stronger 3-D surfaces by deforming the metal sheet as, for example, in the making of automobile bodies.

'As we proceeded with these projects, three things happened. First, on a more practical level, we found that we could bend sheet material in a new way. We produced AlgoRhythms, a line of architectural products, column covers, wall panels and ceilings, and proposed other products.

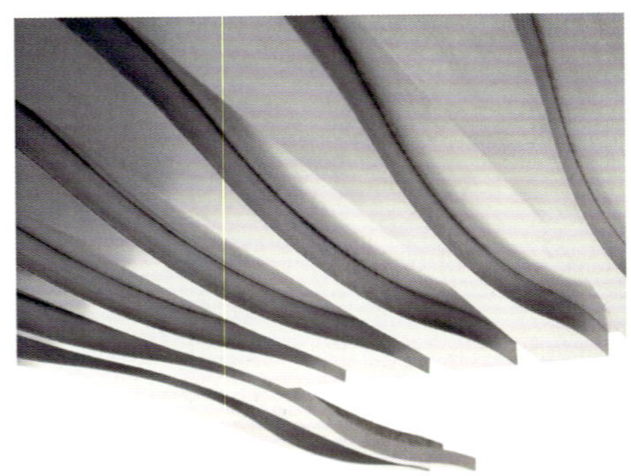

The first line of AlgoRhythm products – columns, walls and ceilings – using nondeformational bending of sheet metal.

Second, it was satisfying to demonstrate that theoretical ideas could be translated into practice. The Milgo experiment is an application of the "Structures on Hyper-Structures" work I did in 1981[4] and establishes that metastructural thinking can lead to real products. My work at NASA-Langley from 1989 to 1990 had touched on this in the context of structures for outer space. Third, this experiment has opened a window in the morphoverse where process is added to form. This is the universe of form I have been mapping. Thus the project-within-project became mapping the family of AlgoRhythmic forms as an example of forms generated by a physical process and not a computational one. The Milgo experiments attempt to marry software (morph genome) with hardware (fabrication genome!) in the making of physical objects.

'It is important that the products we produce have an intellectual integrity throughout the process, from the mathematics of surfaces to fabrication techniques, to the detailing we use in installation. Working with Neil Katz, we derived AlgoRhythms through a computational algorithm based on my generalised morphological model that defined new families of surfaces from "solid" forms. The result allowed infinite variations of form, as one iteration could continually morph into another.'

There is currently much 'computer architecture' around – exotic curved forms on the screen that may not be buildable. Lalvani's work with AlgoRhythms, although based on higher mathematics, is more rooted in the realities of construction than many other approaches:

'The interesting question is whether there is a fundamental link between form and form-making. I assume there is. The form of a seashell or a bone, though based on different growth principles, is intimately connected with its process of growth. Form *is* process.[5] In AlgoRhythms we linked the approaches to form and fabrication from the very beginning. Our approach leads to a new kind of mass-customisation that should eventually make it possible for us to make many units, each one different, as efficiently as we can make them all identical.

'We have installed AlgoRhythms in various buildings and showrooms. Most prominently, we have an iteration of AlgoRhythm columns in folded titanium in the permanent design collection of the Museum of Modern Art (MoMA). And in March and April 2004, at an exhibition at the Municipal Art Society in New York, we showed the Hyperwall system, an AlgoRhythms beam and an AlgoRhythms structural truss to extend the concept into forming structural shapes.

'As we scale up AlgoRhythms and apply our theories to more building components – for example, to curtain-wall systems and glass envelopes, to beams and trusses and, eventually, to entire buildings – we encounter real structural problems. We have designed the entire exterior and lobby of a 12-storey apartment building in Chelsea, New York. The

HyperWall system, an irregular modular wall system using AlgoRhythmic principles (exhibited at the Municipal Art Society, New York, 23 March to 30 April 2004).

important next step is to go beyond surfaces and begin investigating entire building systems, especially structures. We are now working on a residential building we are calling Project X that is AlgoRhythmic from the structural system out to the facade.[6] Since the late 1990s I had been thinking of AlgoRhythmic skins (such as in glass) for tall buildings,[7] so when Stanley Perelman asked me to design a 25-storey apartment building in Manhattan, here was an opportunity to mine the universe of columnar forms we had been developing at Milgo for a completely different application.

'We are interested in developing Soft AlgoRhythms, where the hard edges of the folded surfaces disappear, but here the fabrication technologies are in the way. We are looking into Kinetic AlgoRhythms as well, but here we need some bright ideas, as we don't know how to proceed without making the continuous into discrete.'

The approach behind AlgoRhythms began with Lalvani's work on the Morphological Genome, a universal code for mapping and manipulating all form: natural, man-made and artificial. By conceiving the morphological universe as a hyper-universe, and by using higher dimensional geometry, we gain the power to understand and manipulate it. Lalvani says:

'The morphological universe is infinite and open-ended, with a fractal hierarchy composed of recursive levels within levels through which one can access and navigate in a number of ways from any level. This is a universe where each structure (and each type of architecture) can transform from one to another in a continuum of space and time, within and between levels. This hyper-universe map provides the basis for the Morphological Genome.

Project X, an apartment building in Manhattan, designed for Stanley Perelman. The morphology of the building skin and structure are derived from AlgoRhythm columns.

An AlgoRhythm truss, a NYSTAR project, inspired by the flow of milk and derived from AlgoRhythm columns. Photo taken at Milgo in the factory setting.

Soft AlgoRhythms, surfaces with softer, rounded bends as morphological extensions of bent-surface AlgoRhythms. Their forming technology is yet to be determined.

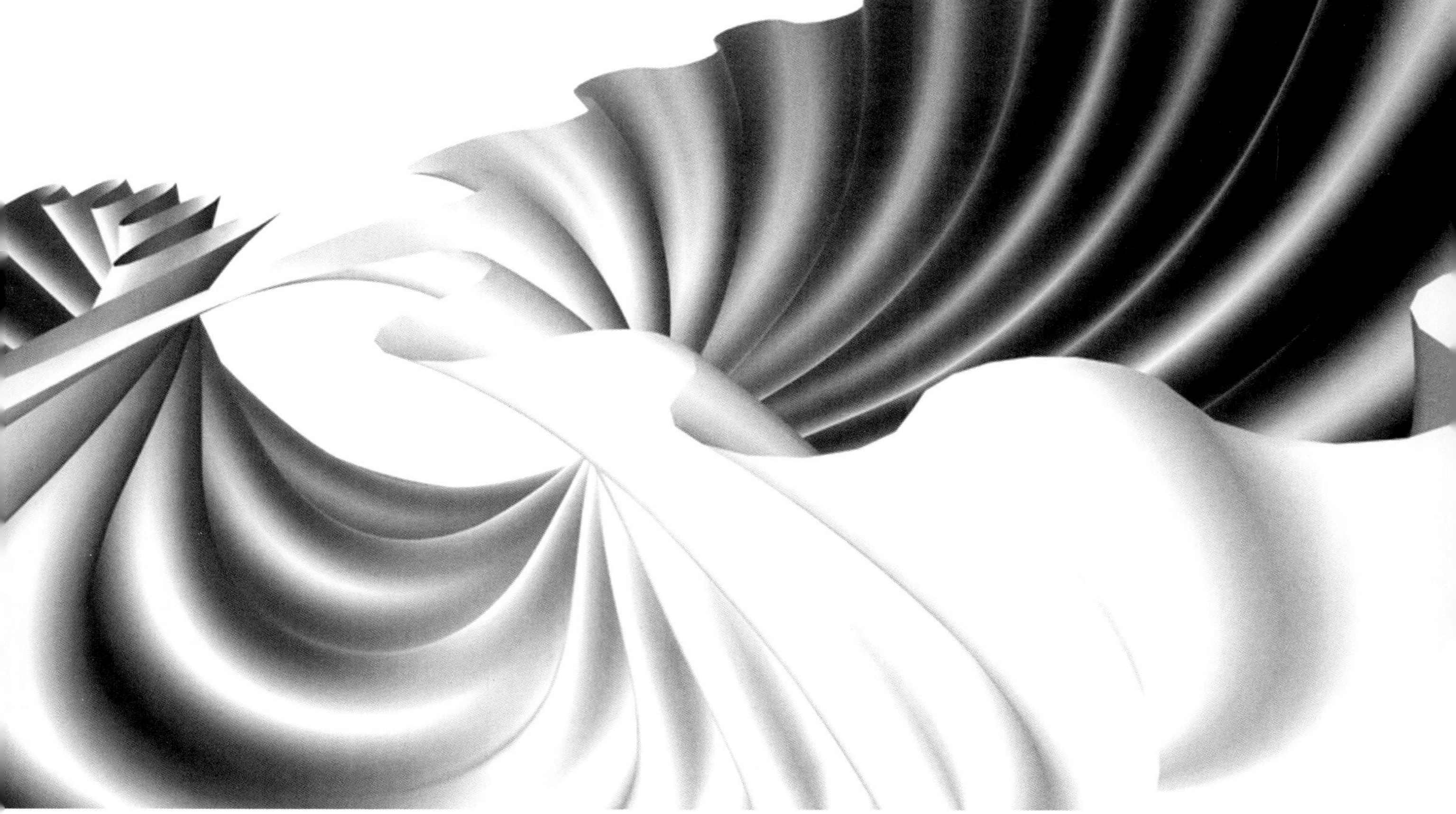

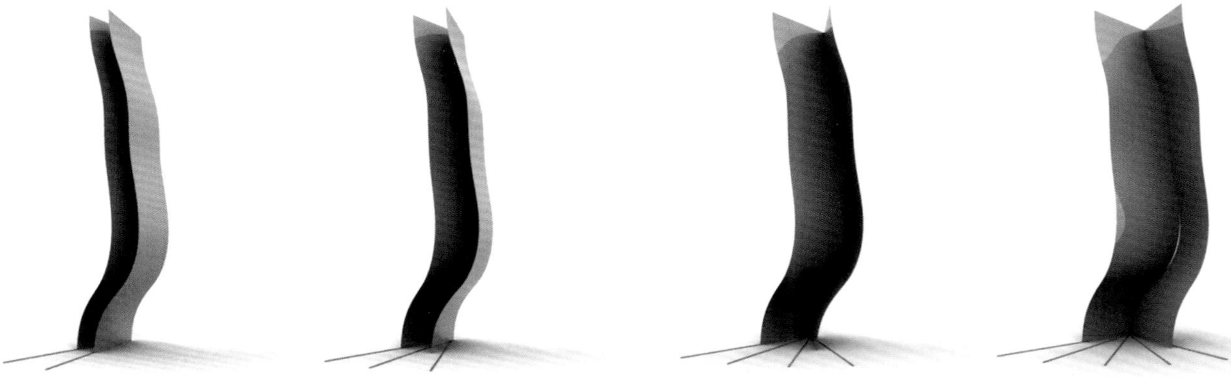

The computer sequence shows an example of Kinetic AlgoRhythms, a kinetic version of the HyperWall system folding dynamically. This is another example where the forming technology is yet to be invented.

'The Morphological Genome is a direct inspiration from biology, something I began wondering about in the mid-1970s. In biological terms, it is an epigenetic code[8] that lies outside the biological genome. I have always wondered if there is a "shape gene" in nature and, as far as I understand, the answer today is still "no". If the answer were to become "yes", it would be easy to reverse-engineer biology and construct every shape in nature through genetic engineering. The absence of a shape code in nature provides the need to invent a shape genome. This is the agenda of the Morphological Genome[9] project.

'The Morphological Genome is a model experiment for mapping other genomes. It is composed of morphological genes (morph genes), where each gene specifies a family of related parameters, and each parameter is controlled by a single variable of form equivalent to a "base" in DNA. We are working on this universal structure of form, similar to Crick and Watson's structure of DNA, and mapping and manipulating it at this genetic level.'

In deriving AlgoRhythms from the Morphological Genome, Lalvani and his associates took a series of algorithmic steps:

'At the first level is the genomic concept, a meta-algorithm, which defines a family of interrelated, intertransforming shapes tied to a fabrication process. At the second level is a computational algorithm of developable surfaces, surfaces that can be formed from flat sheets by bending without deforming.

'I want to point out that the issue of mapping all form is like counting to infinity, many times over, since there are infinite infinities within the morphological universe. So as a practical matter, the morphoverse is not mappable. However, what is possible is to provide a framework and show the workings within it with some examples. The expedient way is to identify the morph genes. The key idea here is that the infinity of possible forms can be specified by a finite number of morph genes. I am expecting this to be a small number.[10] Besides the difficulty of identifying these as universal morph genes, you run into unsolved mathematical problems. Only a few years ago I discovered that there exist topological surfaces that violate Euler's famous equation that relates the number of topological elements.[11] The fact that new morphologies (which lead to new mathematics, and new architecture) are possible, is a feature of the morphoverse. This makes mapping the morphoverse more challenging to accomplish.'

Interestingly, several architects now refer to their work as 'genetic'. Lalvani speculates:

'All these genetic and algorithmic approaches to architecture, including our genome project, mark an evolving path in our relationship with the computer – from a labour-saving device to an intelligent problem-solving machine, to an autonomous entity capable of independent creativity. We hold the latter as sacredly human, but this may change.[12] The point I want to make is that as we pass on our skills, knowledge and intelligence to the computer, we must be prepared to pass on creativity as well. This trajectory inevitably leads to architecture without architects, in a different sense from Rudofsky,[13] of course. In "Meta Architecture",[14] I had referred to this as the end of architecture (as we define it presently), an architecture liberated from the architect.'

Lalvani's morphogenomic model seems to imply continuity, but at the moment there appears to be a bias towards seeing the universe in terms of binary discreteness. On whether reality is continuous or discrete, Lalvani comments:

'The binary view of the universe, exemplified by discrete computational sequences of 0s and 1s, does not appear to capture the continuum we see in life. In my morphological model, there is a continuum, infinite states between 0 and 1. Yet I am unable to carry this through to all aspects of form. I would like to believe that all topology, the bottom-most level of form, is a continuum and it is also emergent. But the quantum nature of integers that describe many topological features makes it discrete. For example, the number of sides of a polygon is, say, either three or four, both discrete states. Yet a few years ago I discovered that the space between three and four is filled with fractional regular polygons with sides in between these two numbers. So what appears discrete may be hiding a continuum.

'However, there are clear instances, like cellular automata, that resist the continuum.[15] Additionally, when you apply the bottom-up cellular automata rules, a one-gene phenomenon in the morph genome, to smooth topological surfaces we need to impose a top-down topology from a completely different gene.[16] The emergence of top-down from bottom-up is an intriguing idea. Nonetheless, the coexistence of discrete and continuous systems leads me to think that the universe may have a variable dial that can be set to binary or continuous states, or any state in between. After all, movies, which have 24 discrete frames per second, appear continuous when we run them. Physical reality may have a discrete basis at the root level, though at the experiential level it appears perfectly continuous.'[17]

Lalvani's work seems to have broader implications for architecture:

'At the very least it would be satisfying to show that the "alphabet" of form is not restricted to simple shapes like the cube, cylinder, cone and sphere, but that it is an extensive family of intertransforming alphabets embedded in an integrated framework. This framework, an open-ended, expansive, continually extendable higher-dimensional periodic table of all forms, is an interesting idea. You are no longer limited to existing architectural vocabularies, you can generate your own vocabularies, morph any vocabulary to any other, or existing vocabularies (architectural contexts) to new ones. Any language becomes an instance of the other. Here is a universe where the particular and the universal coexist, as do complexity and diversity in a dual relationship to one another. This understanding can be liberating, and empowering.

'The known issues of architecture, programmatic, structural, poetic, visual and spiritual, will not go away. The challenge is to

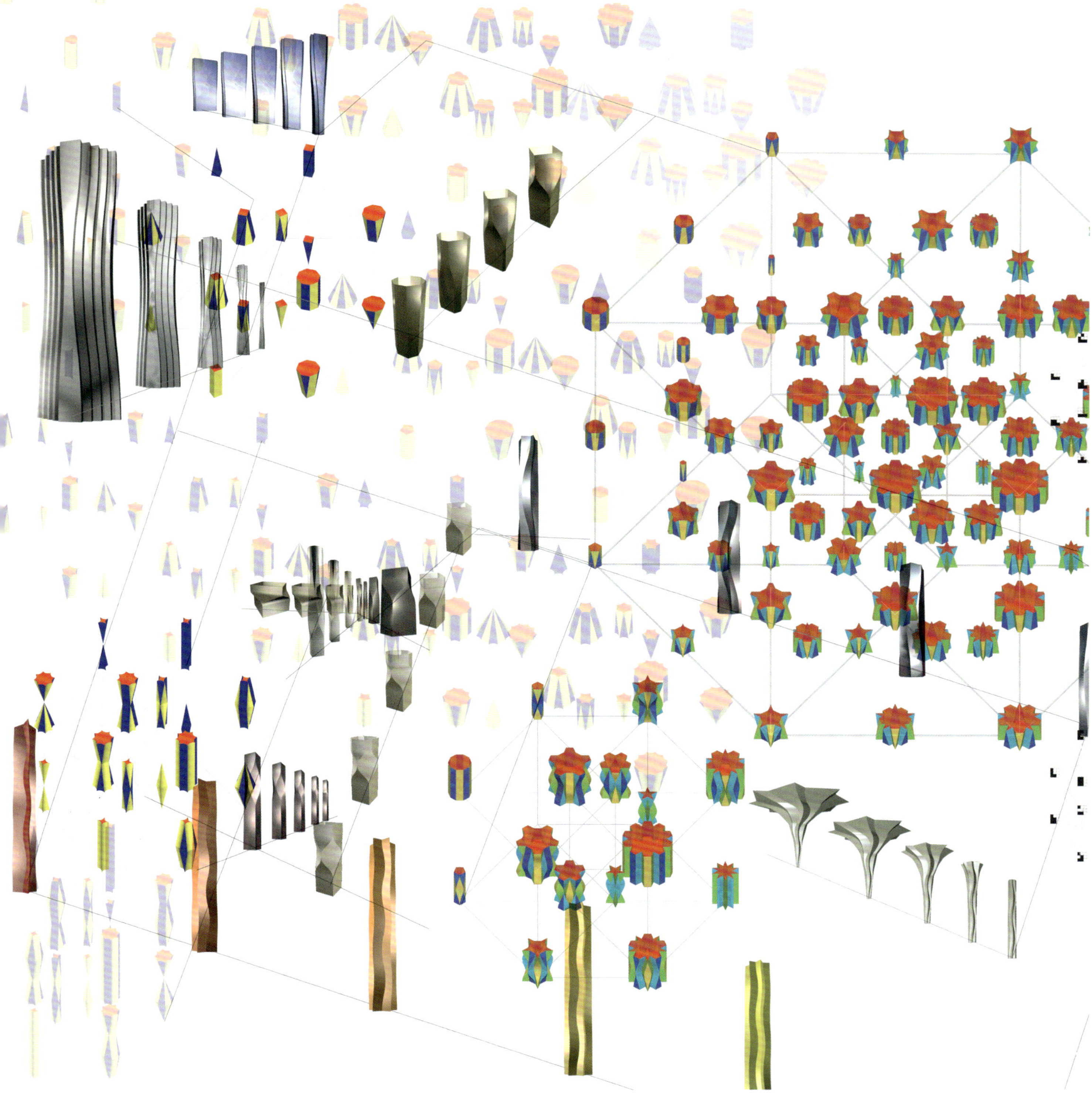

A portion of the morphoverse suggesting a continuum of AlgoRhythm columns. These columns, fabricated from single metal sheets, are genetically coded and are based on one algorithm, one material and one method of forming. Adding process to form opens a new window in the morphoverse and requires the expression of 'fabrication genes' in addition to selected 'form genes'.

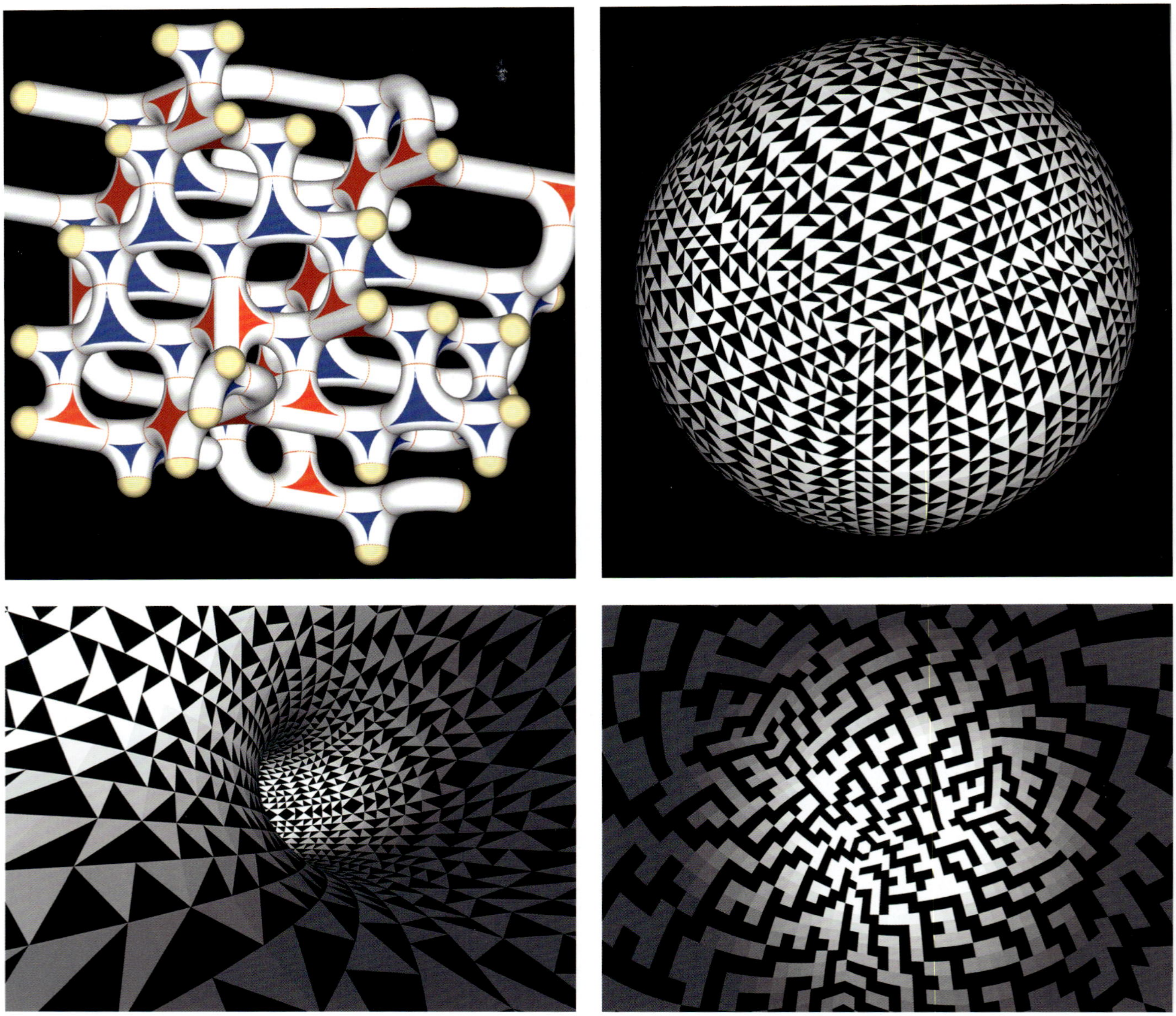

Wolfram's cellular automata rule 30 applied to a sponge-like surface (top left), a sphere (top and bottom right) and torus (bottom left). Such surfaces require the activation of at least two morphological genes.

infuse new formal vocabularies with meaning. The morphology of meaning (and hence of language and thought) is one of the most interesting unsolved problems. A coherent mapping of form and meaning is our challenge and architecture is the best experimental medium for that.'

And his Morphological Genome appears to have implications that go far beyond architecture. He has been applying this approach to dance, chemistry, metrics in physics, and so on:

'The Morphological Genome could impact how we approach different areas of knowledge. At this time we are pressing forward in several areas outside architecture. The challenges are enormous. Each new area has its own knowledge base and to overlay an extrinsic model would be naive. The challenge is to find the intrinsic structure of native knowledge.

'However, the Morphological Genome does have significant ramifications in all areas of shaping and making. It can be embedded in a morph chip and linked with new fabrication techniques including nanotechnology (for example, in Drexler's "assembler" at the nano level),[18] or in some universal forming machines (that do not exist) at the architectural level. This forming ability must include the integration of bottom-up and top-down mentioned earlier. Think of this in terms of the stem cell, a universal cell that differentiates into different specialised cells that perform completely different functions in a co-coordinated manner. At the purely formal level, the Morphological Genome has the same intent, a universal code that can produce the infinite variety of forms we find in nature, technology and beyond. At this point we are far from realising this. The genome is in progress, and Milgo's experiment is just one case study. The goal is auto-morphogenesis, human products (including architecture) that design themselves physically, not just virtually[19] out of encoded forms, processes, materials – something the biologists are likely to achieve first as a neat counterpoint to artificial life'.[20] AD

Acknowledgements
School of Architecture, Pratt Institute, for its support of the Center for Experimental Structures; Bruce Gitlin, Alex Kveton and Robert Wrazen of Milgo/Bufkin; Neil Katz, Ajmal Aqtash, Che-wei Wang and John Gulliford for computer-modelling/rendering as members of Lalvani's studio team; NYSTAR grant (2002–04) to experiment with AlgoRhythms Structures involving Pratt students at Milgo.[21] Some ideas in this paper were first published in notes 3 and 7 below.

Notes

1 From Rene Thom, *Morphogenesis and Structural Stability*, WA Benjamin (New York), 1972.
2 From James D Watson, *DNA: The Secret of Life*, Alfred Knopf (New York), 2003.
3 Haresh Lalvani, 'Genomic Architecture', in Deborah Gans and Zehra Kuz (eds), *The Organic Approach to Architecture*, Wiley-Academy (Chichester), 2003, pp 115–26.
4 Haresh Lalvani, *Structures on Hyper-Structures*, Haresh Lalvani (New York), 1982; based on author's doctoral dissertation entitled 'Multi-Dimensional Periodic Arrangements of Transforming Space Structures', University of Pennsylvania, 1981.
5 In nature, process results from force. D'Arcy Thompson's dictum 'Form is a diagram of forces' is another way of saying the same thing.
6 This project began in September 2004. Vince DeSimone has analysed the structure and proposed a method of construction, and Israel Berger has been advising Milgo/Bufkin on the exterior skin construction. Che-wei Wang, working in Lalvani's studio, has been assisting with the modelling and visualisations shown here.
7 The first example, called 'Fractal High-Rise', was published in Haresh Lalvani, 'Meta Architecture', in Giuseppa di Christina (ed), *Architecture and Science*, Wiley-Academy (Chichester), 2001; article reprinted from AD *HyperSurface Architecture*, Sept/Oct 2000.
8 D'Arcy Thompson, in his classic *On Growth and Form*, has already pointed out physical forces and mathematics as the guiding principles of form lying outside genetics. See D'Arcy Wentworth Thompson, *On Growth and Form*, Cambridge University Press (Cambridge, UK), 1942. Dr Loren Day, a structural biophysicist in New York working on the structure of viruses, who reviewed this text, sent Lalvani the following remark on this speculation of his: 'I think "mathematics and physical forces" do, in fact, guide genetics. It's more than a possibility.'
9 The Morphological Genome defines just one chromosome of architecture and other chromosomes of architecture could be added through genomes of materials, processes and so on, and the most complex of all, the genome of meaning to complete the entire architectural genome.
10 At present, Lalvani is focusing on a dozen or so genes. Several of these genes are infinite-dimensional, yet rounding that off to a small manageable number gives an exact count of the number of dimensions active in the morph genome.
11 The simplest of these surfaces is one with a singularity (ie, with a single vertix at the centre) where all edges and faces meet. This is an infinite class of surfaces obtained by taking all Eulerian structures (like a cube, tetrahedron, dihedron, and so on that satisfy the Euler relation Vertices – Edges + Faces = 2) and collapsing the vertex to its neighbours or to a common centre. The resulting structures violate Euler's equation. Adding holes to these generates an additional infinite class of new topologies not defined by the more general Euler relation where the 2 on the right-hand side of the equation is replaced by 2 – 2g, where g is the number of holes.
12 For the exponential change in the power of the machine and its ramifications for society see, for example, Ray Kurtzweil, *The Singularity is Near*, Viking (New York), 2005. Kurtzweil argues that 'We won't experience the 100 years of progress in the 21st century – it will be more like 20,000 years of progress [at today's rate] ... Within a few decades, machine intelligence will surpass human intelligence, leading to The Singularity ... [that will include] the merger of biological and non-biological intelligence.'
13 Rudofsky used this term for indigenous architecture: Bernard Rudofsky, *Architecture without Architects*, University of New Mexico Press (Albuquerque, New Mexico), 1987 (reprint).
14 Haresh Lalvani, 'Meta Architecture', op cit.
15 Lalvani asked Neil Katz (who modelled the CA surfaces for him) to take Wolfram's one-dimensional cellular automata (see Stephen Wolfram, *A New Kind of Science*, Wolfram Media (Champaign, IL), 2002), index his 256 rules in an 8-dimensional cube as part of the morphoverse so that each vertex is one rule, and check for a continuum between any two adjacent rules. Surprisingly, the result showed no such continuum.
16 This top-down component comes from the topology of the surface, for example the surface of the cube has six squares with three squares meeting at every corner, a rule that is independent of cellular automata rules and is specified by a different morph gene. This gene is the same gene that establishes the square grid of the cellular automata, an a priori grid that has to be 'imported' to demonstrate the bottom-up nature of a cellular automaton. A fully bottom-up phenomenon requires the emergence of (primary) topologies as well. This means a minimum of two genes is required for a cellular automaton.
17 Loop Quantum Gravity theory suggests something similar for physics. See, for example, Lee Smolin's article 'Atoms of space and time', *A Matter of Time*, special edition of *Scientific American*, Vol 16, No 1, 2006.
18 Eric Drexler, *Engines of Creation*, Anchor Books (New York), 1986.
19 This is related to the idea of growing architecture. For the origins of this idea see William Katavolos, *Organics*, Steendrukkirj de Jong & Co (Hilversum), 1961; Vittorio Giorgini, 'Early experiments in architecture using nature's building technology', in H Lalvani (guest-editor), *The International Journal of Space Structures*, 11:1 & 2, Multi-Science, 1997. Lalvani's own ideas were proposed in an unpublished article 'Towards Automorphogenesis: Building with Bacteria', 1974. For more recent work, see John Johansen's *Nanoarchitecture: A New Species of Architecture*, Princeton Architectural Press (Princeton, NJ), 2002.
20 The genomics pioneer Craig Venter foresees creating life in the laboratory from gene sequences in 10 years. On a related note, earlier, in the 1990s, the idea of originating 'from nothing' had led the physicist Alan Guth to suggest the possibility of creating a 'universe' in the laboratory.
21 NYSTAR, New York State Office of Science, Technology and Academic Research, gave Milgo/Bufkin a two-year grant to experiment with two different AlgoRhythm structures: AlgoRhythm glass-panel systems and the AlgoRhythm truss system. The following participated in the various prototyping experiments at Milgo: Henry Harrison and Jenny Lee (production managers), Neil Katz (consultant) and Pratt students Ori Adiri, Ezra Ardolino, Ajmal Aqtash, Daniel Barone, Christopher Devine, Thorsten Foerster, Brandon Gill, Gershon Gottlieb, Seo Kiwon, Jeff Mitcheltree, Matthew Peterson, Sabrina Schollmeyer, Reza Shricker, Jarrett Shamlain, Che-wei Wang, Hiroshi Yamamoto and Albert Zuger.

Oblique view looking down at Auto Braids membrane from the corridor roof-scape. Rendered image intended to highlight the range of variation intrinsic within the parametric surface due to computational modifications as well as perspectival distortion.

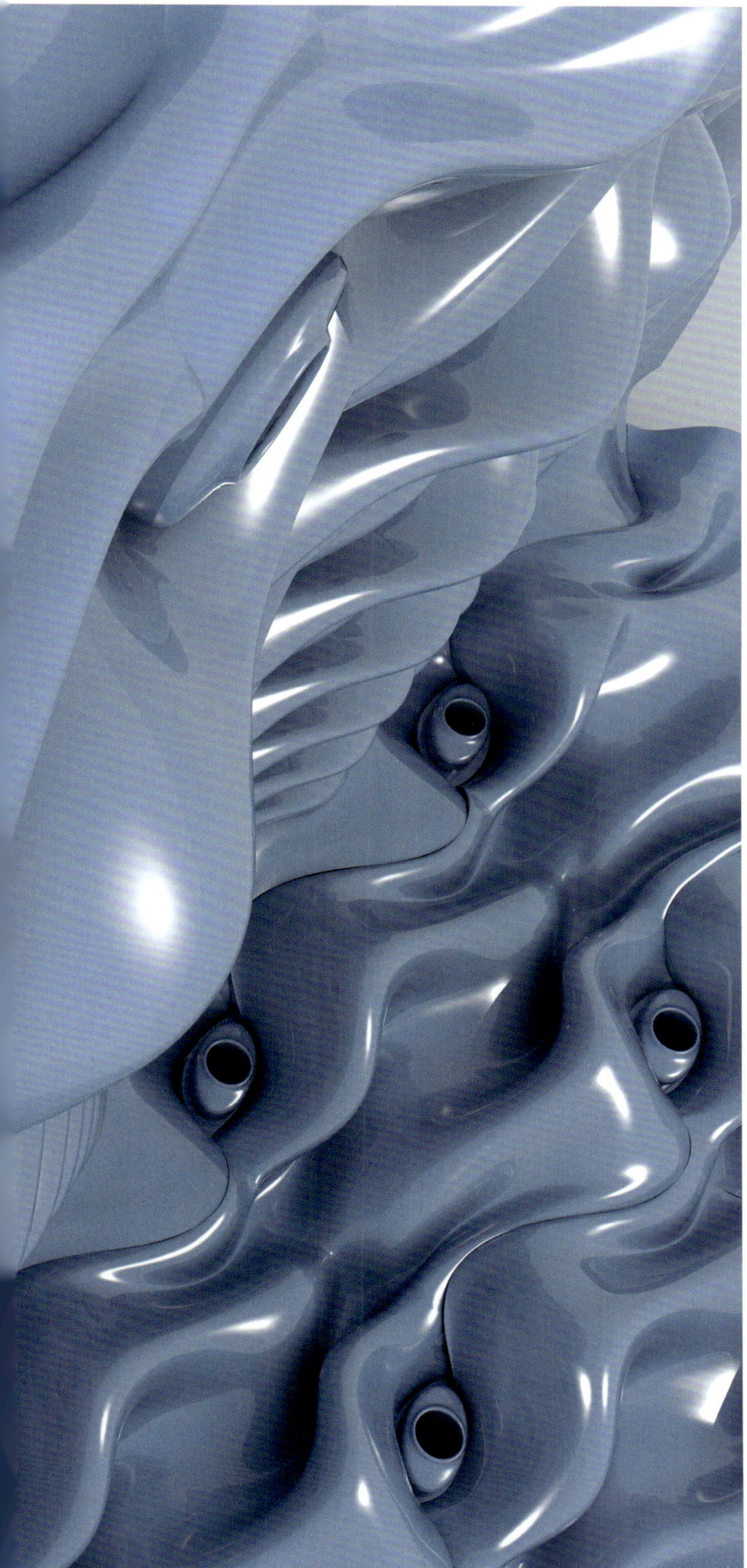

From a studio in Brooklyn, New York, Evan Douglis has carved out an international reputation for innovative research into self-generative systems, membrane technology and contemporary fabrication. In the last decade, this work has largely been expressed through interactive installations, a medium that is compatible with Douglis's curatorial interests (he was the director of the architecture galleries at Columbia University for eight years). However, with the opening last year of the *RE*ptile, Haku Japanese Restaurant in New York, and the ongoing development of the *RE*ptile tile product line, Douglis is currently working at new building and manufacturing scales. As Chair of the Department of Undergraduate Architecture at the Pratt Institute since 2003, his influence on a generation of younger designers has been palpable. Here, guest-editor Mike Silver discusses with Douglis the significance for him of the interface between the algorithmic and the material.

One of the founding myths of the digital age holds that information, treated as a statistical phenomenon, can exist apart from the context and material conditions in which it has become instantiated. The ability to transmit error-free data through a communication channel filled with noise is one of the great achievements of modern communication technology. It is also one of the most powerful means yet devised for separating matter and information. In other words, if one can transmit signals through a communication channel, without interference (without resistance), then the material properties of the system become neutralised. The medium is not the message. The material facts of the system and the context of their operation become inactive properties. This engineering miracle has had an enormous impact on our conception of architectural practice; it has driven the way we make space by affecting the way we perform computations.

Bridging the gap between matter and code has been one of the main tasks for Evan Douglis as an architect. In much of his work we see a deliberate relationship forged between different software tools, materials and new computer-numerically controlled (CNC) fabrication machines. Translating algorithms into real objects and spaces tests both the specificity of data and the limits of matter. The importance of this move cannot be overestimated since it brings the computer into a direct relationship with the act of making.

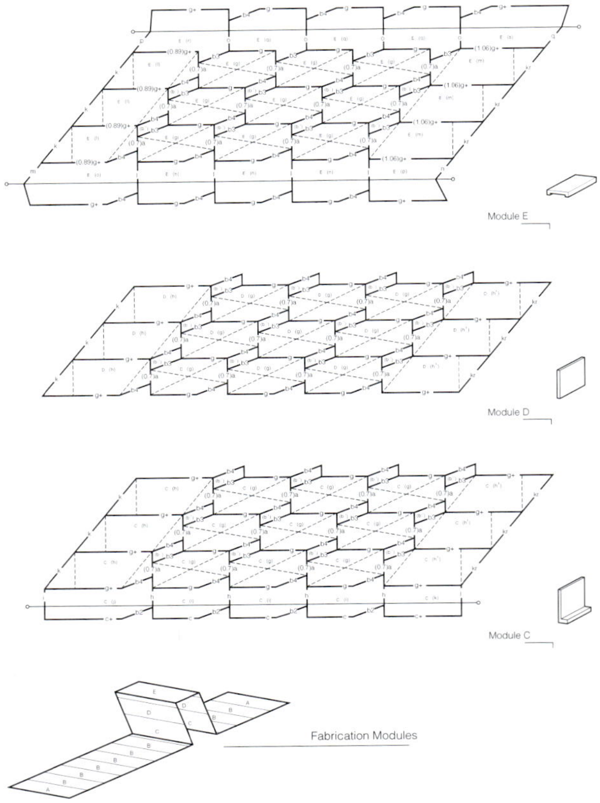

Auto Braids/Auto Breeding tiling program. The codification system designates the zoning pattern for all topological expressions.

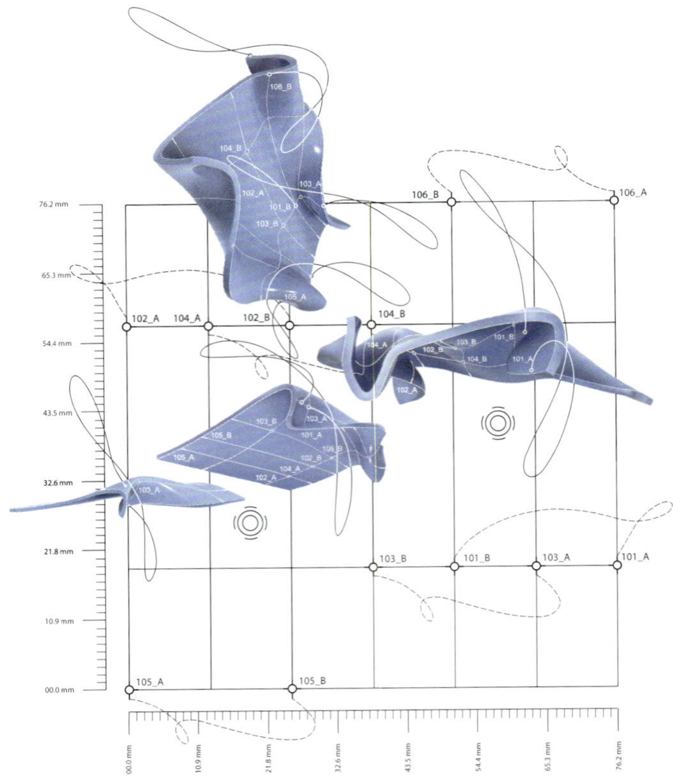

Early modelling phase of Auto Braids unit module. Views showing evolutionary stages of sheet foam undergoing morphological transformations due to tactical pinching procedures.

View of high-density Auto Braids foam block cut to size on a five-axis CNC milling machine. Once the designated tool pass is deemed operational, a single block can be milled to its desired figuration within a 24-hour period.

Auto Braids/Auto Breeding display-scape, Columbia University, 2003
Entry view of 16-module membrane with Jean Prouvé artefacts suspended above the surface.

In Douglis's work this relationship is both excessive and precise. Computer code does not lead to a dry and desiccated reality. Instead, the unfolding of code into architecture is suffused with a libidinal energy. Like the infinite desiring machines of Marcel Duchamp or Francis Picabia, technology and Eros combine to produce abundant and overflowing life. Whether it is the blue, liquid-crystal light that shines on Prouvé's furniture or in the Quicktime movies of love hotels cross-pollinated by curious spectators, these effects are both metaphorical and programmatic.

Morphologies

In his own practice and through his pedagogy at Pratt, Douglis focuses particular attention on the design of units, parts or modules that are repeated to form a larger whole from the ground up. Both the rules for designing the part and the procedures for aggregating the whole seem to be based on a series of very specific laws, and yet the whole is not given in advance as some kind of fixed or predetermined image. I was curious to know from Douglis what is the significance for him of this method of working. He explained:

'I have always been committed to the proposition that the production of architecture is one of emergence. It is not about a preordained image, icon or aesthetic that is imposed on the world, but rather an opportunity to devise and experiment with a conceptually rigorous methodological system offering a broad range of adaptations in relation to an ever-increasing body of interests. This approach is obviously tainted with risk and unpredictability for those who aspire to instant gratification, but most importantly its unique contribution for our current generation of architects is one of utilising controlled chance as a means to managing complexity and taming the unfamiliar.'

In counterpoint, Douglis elucidated how this strategy might differ from the Modernist approach to repetition: 'In our particular case, the rule sets that govern our topological surfaces are both directive and pliable in order to sustain a continuously evolving archive of expressions. Through the deployment of a recursive gaming strategy sympathetic to heterogeneous effects, one resists the natural tendency towards monotony or sameness that often emerges within any replication process.'

Douglis expanded further on the rules for these procedures and how they affect the production of architecture: 'The paradoxical correspondence within our work between the unit modules and their respective fields calls attention to the significant priority we also place on managing complexity across a range of scales. It is imperative for us to assess the performance of any area of these surfaces as a segment of a larger evolutionary string. And as a result of these efforts we encounter a more supple and excitable topological surface well equipped to handle the ever-increasing demands of a contemporary modular system.'

Auto Braids/Auto Breeding, Columbia University, 2003

To bring this into specific focus, I asked Douglis how complexity was managed across a range of scales in one of his best-known projects, Auto Braids/Auto Breeding. Fabricated out of aerospace foam with a high-gloss automobile finish encapsulating every exposed surface, this 16-piece modular system provided a contemporary display-scape for a collection of Jean Prouvé's artefacts. The exhibition, entitled 'Three Nomadic Structures', and curated by Douglis and Robert Rubin, was originally presented in 2003 at Columbia Architecture Galleries in New York. Originally conceived as a travelling exhibition celebrating three of Prouvé's lost buildings (the Glassmaking School of Croismare, the Tropical House at Niamey in Africa and the Aluminum Centenary Pavilion at Villepinte), the installation is now attracting an international audience and in autumn 2005 made its debut at the Los Angeles Museum of Contemporary Art's Pacific Design Center.

'The relational correspondence between the smallest surface folds and the larger serial wave patterns generated in our Auto Braids/Auto Breeding project is testimony to the latent intelligence manifest at the smallest incremental measure. Here we intentionally installed fluctuations within the base unit that showed a clear predisposition to initiate a variety of effects as they reassembled at increasing scales across an ever-expanding field. Through a combination of operative techniques comprising reflective mirroring, tactical slippages and purposeful oscillation, we experienced an increase of the overall emergent properties, as the membrane evolved forwards into a programmable skin.

'It is important to note that we are attempting to develop these surfaces along the logic of our theory of "dazzle topology". The instrumentality of the surface achieved through specific computational commands is aimed at producing a taxonomy of illusory effects at the moment when occupation is finally introduced. In turn, these sentient apparitions are intentionally derived in anticipation of the spectator as the prime recipient of this broad range of phenomenological behaviour.'

Programming and Ornament

One of the most striking aspects of Douglis's work is its rich sense of patterning. In terms of a formal genealogy, Douglis appears to be reviving a line of historical thought that was cauterised by the Modernists. In the 19th century, architect and theorist Gottfried Semper espoused that ornament was a primary condition for architecture: he wanted to conceal structure behind decoration. By the time of Louis Sullivan and John Root, ornament was already becoming secondary to a building's primary spatial and structural organisation. The European Modernists, however, believed they could eliminate ornament altogether. I was eager to find out from Douglis how his programmed units and the patterns they generate fit into a

Helioscopes travelling media-scape, 2004
Reflected ceiling plan showing a series of Helioscope travelling media-scape units aggregated across an ever-expanding field. The packing strategy utilises blending techniques to increase the variety and complexity of all surface effects.

broader cultural picture. He responded by explaining his interests in complex patterning in the context of emergent technologies and contemporary biological mimesis:

'It's a question of mining this vast archive of topological complexity, available to us with this technology, for a very specific set of architectural intentions. In our case, all of the projects showcased here explicitly favour a topological and perceptual exuberance that subscribes to the potential of developing a new species of architectural components that offer ornament and structure as a unified yet complex organisational system. This would consist of producing membranes that reassessed the classical split between these two distinct modes of production in favour of acquiring a more intelligent and enigmatically charged skin capable of satisfying structural, programmatic and chimerical considerations.

Oblique view of ever-expanding Helioscope field. Vision slots located on the interior of each helical tail contain LCD screens for the curious consumer.

'In the context of a more radical body, consider for the moment the array of contemporary artefacts within our mainstream culture that are currently simulacrums of nature and advocate for a more complex organisational structure within their material programming in order to accomplish these remarkable feats. Voice-activated software, artificial organ implants, memory retention alloys and self-sustaining robots all share a common reliance on biological mimesis as a new paradigm at the turn of the century. As we leap forward exponentially from one year to the next in our understanding of how nature works and the opportunities afforded with a new generation of smart materials, it is only appropriate that we ask architecture to put forth a more ambitious agenda on the merits of new membrane technology and the new possibilities of bringing architecture to life.'

Helioscopes Travelling Media-Scape, 2004

The Helioscopes multimedia exhibition, which is part of the FRAC Centre's permanent collection in Orléans, France, is also earmarked to travel to Los Angeles, Chicago and New York in the months ahead. Produced as a lightweight fibreglass resin shell suspended like baroque tongues across an aerial terrain, this surrealist diorama offers a unique glance into the future of a more excitable architecture. Sharing many common threads with Auto Braids/Auto Breeding in terms of what Douglis refers to as 'dazzle topology', Helioscopes takes 'the idea of exuberance and implicit animate behaviour to the next level'.

Douglis elaborates: 'If, in principle, we are capable at this moment in time of replicating certain biological expressions within the surfaces of our artificial counterparts, then the promise of Helioscopes lies in our intent to elevate the status of a delirious realism in the form of a new breed of perpetual desiring machines. Posited as a "hyper-excitable cloud-scape comprised of swirling helical tails magically suspended above a frenzied crowd of thrill-seeking consumers", this new topological flesh represents an alternative strategy for the production of eroticism in architecture.

'In the context of situating the project culturally for a moment, it is important to note that while we were in the early stages of developing Helioscopes we came upon the most curiously perverse example of a current service industry dedicated exclusively to commodifiable desire and the management of fantasy. There is a thriving industry of love hotels dispersed throughout the major cities in Japan where consumers can select for rent a fantasy room of their choice from an extensive menu of options. The rooms vary from historic re-creations to *Pulp Fiction* interiors and in all cases are fabricated with the utmost attention to detail in order to sustain the illusion that the fiction may actually be real.

'Independent of the unsettling portrayal of architecture as a collection of caricatures, the more fascinating aspect of this cultural phenomenon is its extreme adeptness as a conceptual

View of single Helioscope under construction. The fabricator applies metal foil as a seal to the foam surface in anticipation of a 15-piece urethane mould. The final cast of the helical tail will produce a super-lightweight fibreglass shell.

desiring machine within the marketplace. As an ideal example of the substantial psychological dimension underlying all forms and products of mass consumption, the precedent of the love hotel offers deep insight into the plethora of subliminal impulses that surround any architectural surface as it comes into contact with an audience of consumers.

'In recognition of this remarkably agile "system of attraction", as a compilation of techniques that systematically increase desirability, the morphology of Helioscopes was explicitly created to re-enact these effects within the performative logic of a single continuous surface. We decided from the beginning that in order to imbue these phenomenal qualities within the syntactical expressions of the surface, we first needed to select a radical position in space from which the surface of Helioscopes would emerge. By orienting this seemingly animate jungle of helical tails downwards, we consciously made reference to a long-standing legacy of science-fiction narratives that depict the sky as a polemically charged terrain ominously poised to address a potential threat from afar.'

I asked Douglis to explain in greater detail the rationale behind the particular morphology that was applied and how, in itself, it could be regarded as a programming strategy. He

The most recently completed project by Evan Douglis Studio, a Japanese restaurant in New York which Douglis conceptually entitles *RE*ptile for reasons that are apparent when you see the scaly tiles in the interior, has enabled Douglis to import cutting-edge techniques into a commercial environment.

responded first by outlining the development of the topology: 'In the context of developing the actual surface for the project, we set in motion two independent script commands in the software responsible for generating helical surfaces at two different scales and rates of growth. The first one regulated the overall exponential growth of the tail as it seamlessly reduced in mass and circumference from top to bottom. The programmatic aim here was to utilise the dynamically excitable geometry of the spiral to guide the spectators along its surface en route to a middle space large enough for a single occupant. Upon arrival, the curious spectator would discover a small LCD projection screen recessed at eye height into the tail's surface displaying a continuous loop of photographic images of the interiors of the Japanese love hotels. Ironically, the place in the field one would assume was the most psychologically vulnerable, due to the spectator's unexpected role as a public voyeur, is curiously the safest due to the fact that the tail visually obscures their faces once they look into the viewing window.

'The second script we applied regulated the deep surface ridges that coiled around the tail downwards at varying speeds from top to bottom. The surface inscription here was crucial to sustain the illusion that the tail was continuously undergoing metamorphosis and flight like the swirls in soft ice-cream. The juxtaposition between these two distinct but correlated surface algorithms created the emergent tension necessary to sustain the extreme exuberance critical to the actualisation of our theory of dazzle topology.'

_RE_ptile, Haku Japanese Restaurant, New York, 2005

The most recently completed project by Evan Douglis Studio, a Japanese restaurant in New York which Douglis conceptually

Oblique view of custom-modular *RE*ptiles showing animate features installed across the entire length of the surface modelling. Periodic rotation of pyramids contributes to an increase of light reflectivity dispersed throughout the room interior.

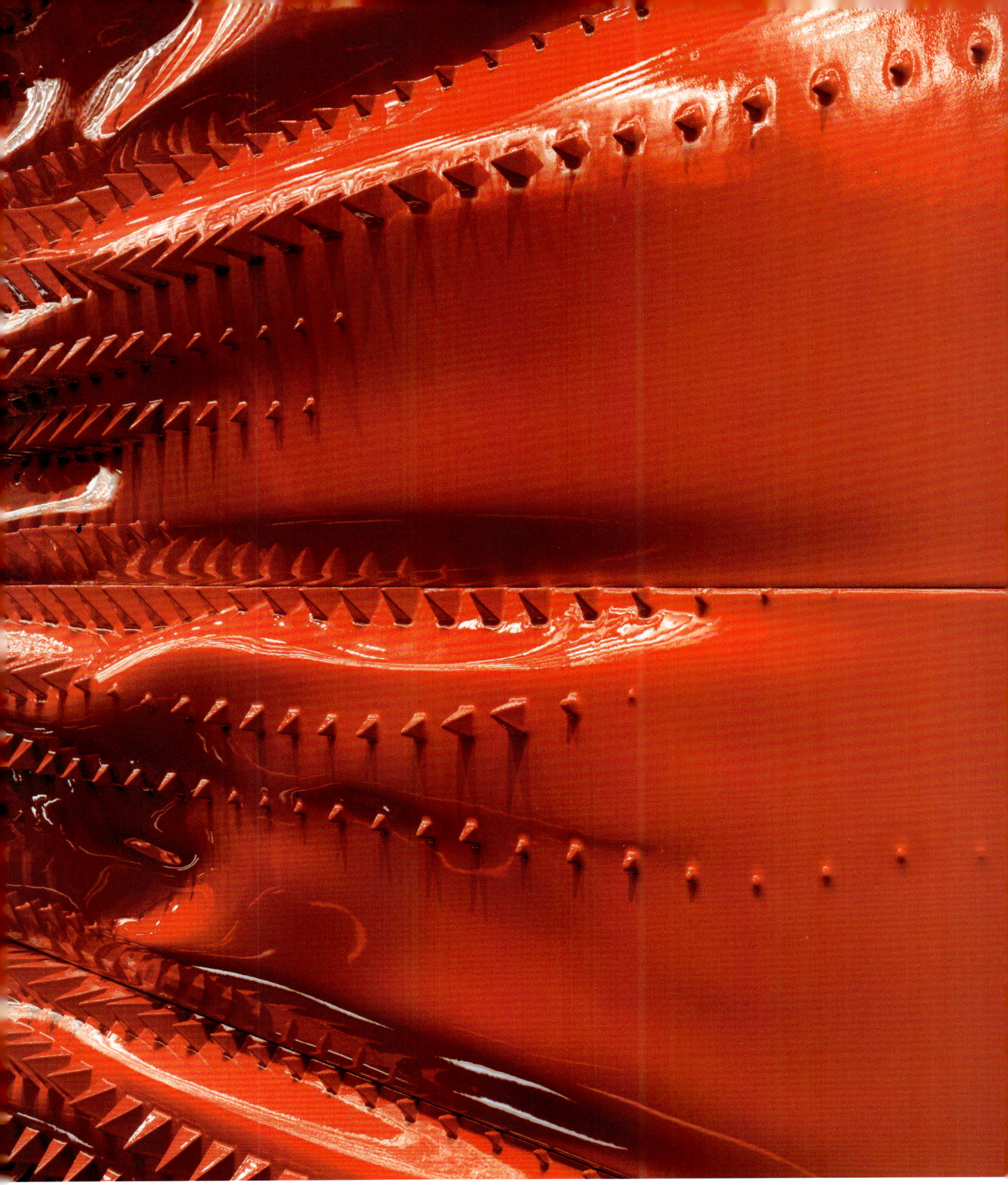

***RE*ptile, Haku Japanese Restaurant, New York, 2005**
View of the entire restaurant interior from the perspective of the sushi bar. Custom wall-mounted modular *RE*ptiles blend in to the sushi bar fixture to create an integrated approach.

entitles *RE*ptile for reasons that are apparent when you see the scaly tiles in the interior, has enabled Douglis to import cutting-edge techniques into a commercial environment. In the design development of the restaurant, he continued to work with 3-D modelling software, but his experimentation using animation software was particularly vital to the development of these surfaces. Our discussion continued, as he explained how an enlightened client allowed him to adapt 'dazzle topology' in this scheme:

'Our client for this project approached us to design a Japanese restaurant that would aim our new research with animate membranes in a direction that celebrated a specific cultural or mythological theme related to Japanese cuisine. He was familiar with our development of complex surfaces and our current use of high-end fabrication technology for our mass-produced architectural components. As a sign of support, he enthusiastically challenged us to make a new building block that continued our theoretical interests and at the same time satisfied his specific design concerns.

'Given the high demand to maximise the floor area for seating, we were obligated from the outset to abandon a more ambitious morphological strategy for the project in favour of a more normative spatial layout. Although subtle in its minimalist sensibility, in retrospect it offered us an ideal foil to develop once again an exuberant set of surface expressions for our new custom wall tiles installed throughout the interior perimeter of the restaurant.

'In terms of the initial design development of the *RE*ptile module, we began by searching for a range of associative material in response to our desire to imbue the surface with specific signifying qualities. After examining a wide range of source material, we decided to use certain topological expressions specific to reptile skins. Curiously, we found an illustrious history connected to the great symbolic significance of the reptile in Japanese mythology. We discovered that, assigned a dual status given its role historically as both a benevolent and threatening character, it resides in a rather ambivalent yet mysterious domain. Given its compelling literary dichotomy as well as our appreciation of its intriguing set of anatomical attributes available for architectural experimentation, we selected the reptile as our conceptual and topological guide for the project.

'The extreme variation one finds in the tiles are due to a "mixing operation" that was devised specifically to utilise productive chance during the initial generative phases on the computer. Beginning with a pyramidal matrix and a smooth plane as our prime surface expressions, we set out to write specific scripted programs within the animation software that enabled these field characters to oscillate in continuous juxtaposition in relation to each other. Choreographed in favour of establishing a wide range of scalar and animate effects, the final tile surfaces selected for the project offered the flux and indeterminacy essential to sustaining a fiction of an architecture in motion.'

Computation and Artistic Intention

In Douglis's work, the computer is linked to a whole universe of techniques both conventional and high-tech. In fact, he is one of the few architects working today who has been able to strike a productive balance between total automation and handcraftsmanship without the results looking ad hoc. This is something that Douglis puts down to being able 'to manage complexity to the extent that the local and global scale is equally regulated with respect to a performative rigour. The same ethic applies to the relational correspondence that needs to be met between the virtual bodies born in a computational arena in juxtaposition to their equivalent twin within the material world. There are so many translative thresholds that we as architects confront throughout the generative phases of our work en route to the full-scale manifestation that it is absolutely imperative that we be obsessively attuned to the priority effects that need to be sustained from one moment to the next. One of the most difficult challenges we face as architects committed to emergent systems is our ability to move any form of radical abstraction conceived digitally into a realisable domain without compromising the integrity of its original aim.'

This, however, brings under the spotlight the balance between the idea of automatic rule-based computation and artistic intention dependent on desire and subjectivity. Douglis explains this in his own terms: 'Rather than seek to categorise the creative process, I would prefer to propose that any critical project needs to move continuously between a bottom-up and top-down approach in order to integrate a full range of interests. Certainly in appreciation of the profound opportunities afforded in particular with rule-based computation today, an infinite array of potential still remains unclaimed for our discipline. Yet, it is equally important to be reminded that the crystalline purity of the number will always be tainted in its fall by ideology and the real-time pressures of human existence. I don't see this as a problem, rather an affirmation that the affiliation between an algorithmic command and its material outcome comprises both risk and fortuity.' AD

Exterior store-front elevation of Haku restaurant showing powder-coated red, custom-extruded aluminium profiles surrounding a large showcase window. Theatrical interior surface effects are exposed as an urban spectacle for all to see.

All-Over, Over-All: biothing and Emergent Composition

In the last decade, the impact of the digital on form-finding in architecture has been conspicuous. Could working with computational algorithms as the primary generative material, however, have deeper, more far-reaching effects on the creative field? Here, **Pia Ednie-Brown** asserts that a new paradigm in composition is being articulated, as exemplified by the Invisibles installation, created by the New York-based practice biothing.

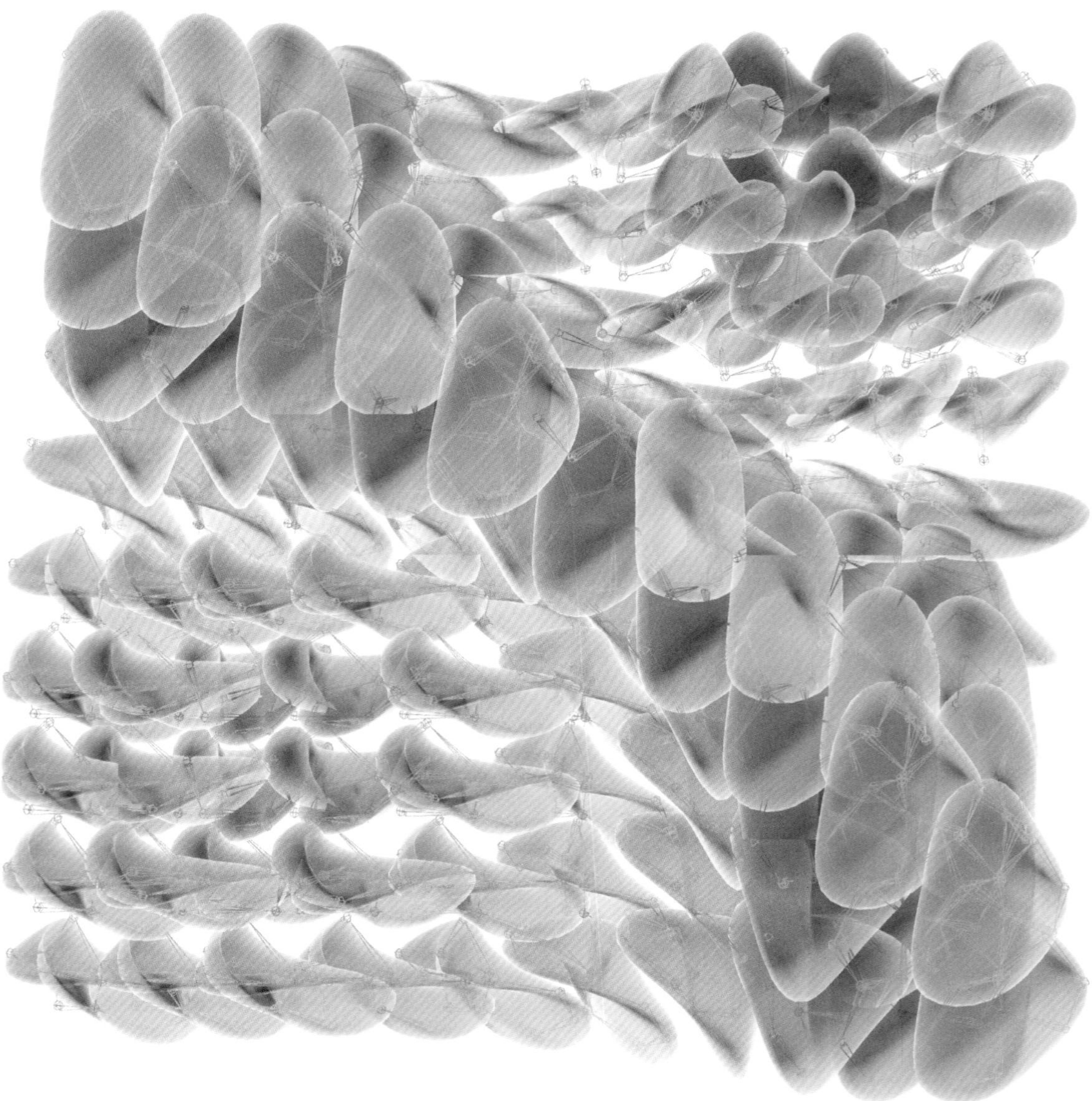

Alisa Andrasek/biothing, The Invisibles interactive installation, Prague Biennale, 2003
Sample morphological stance from the Invisibles animation. The skin inflection emerges through the active relationship of a digital skin and a correspondent field of skeletal 'cells'.

'A nonsensuous perception is an over-all perception, or an all-over perception, irreducible to its constituent parts.'
Brian Massumi[1]

'Composition is less a critical thought project than an integrally experienced emergence. It is a creative event.'
Brian Massumi[2]

Diagramming is often associated with a dry, skeletal tone: the work of de-fleshed data spared of anything extraneous to a set of crucial relations. Bubble diagrams, massing studies, organisational charts and their functionalist leanings have helped foster such a reputation. Programming involves diagrammatic thinking, operating through notating and mapping out the interplays of relations. Both diagramming and programming seem rather abstract or, at least, reductively systematic in a technical and functional orientation. In this sense, they are often felt to be at odds with the more creatively inflected, generative approaches to design – as if the more embodied, intuitive designer-sensibilities are distinct from abstract modes of working. The analytical, reductionist tendencies of the sciences and the creative, critical practices related to aesthetics are often seen to be adjacent and in conflict. Contrary to these kinds of general, commonly held assumptions, the philosophical efforts of radical empiricism[3] assert and sketch out how embodied feeling is inseparable from abstract relations.

This suggests that aesthetics and abstract compositional techniques could revive and refresh some old relationships. But this does not imply a nostalgic return to past compositional principles. Working with computational algorithms as primary generative material offers a different bent to, for example, the mathematical ratios of the Renaissance or the flow diagrams of Modernism. I am suggesting here that a new paradigm in composition is being articulated through the opportunities offered by digital technology, exemplified here in the work of biothing. A now more-or-less familiar word indicative of the nature of this paradigm is 'emergence'.

Given the preoccupation with emergence within the sciences, it might seem desirable here to offer a scientific explanation of the term – a good bit of foundational bedding to grip on to as we heave our way through the complex vagaries of composition. But as desirable as this might be, science has no such explanation to offer, and this is precisely its poignancy. However, there does exist a well-understood description. John Holland's influential book on the subject describes the hallmark of emergence as 'much coming from little'.[4] And Steven Johnson's popular book, *Emergence*, summarises it as the 'movement from low-level rules to higher-level sophistication'.[5] These are provisional definitions to strap around an elusive problem because science is unable to explain how it could be possible for so much to come from so little. As Mark Bedau writes: 'All the evidence today

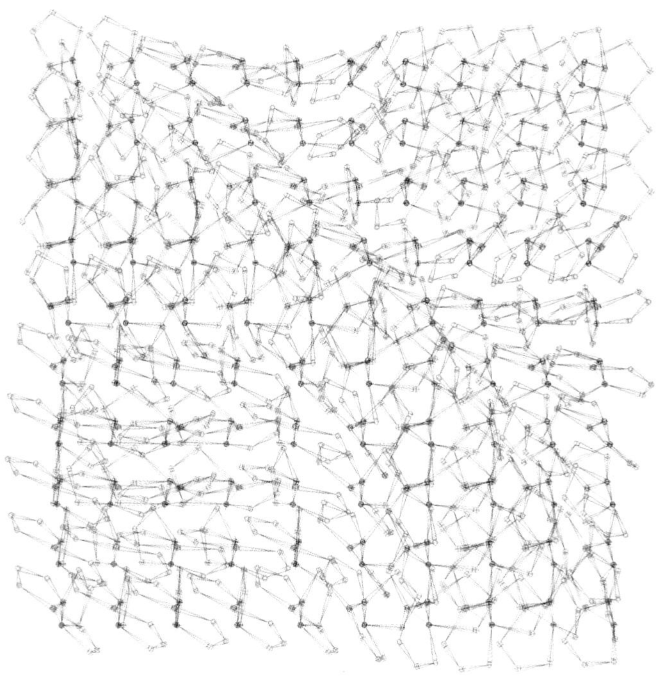

A series of morphologies captured from the Invisibles animation.

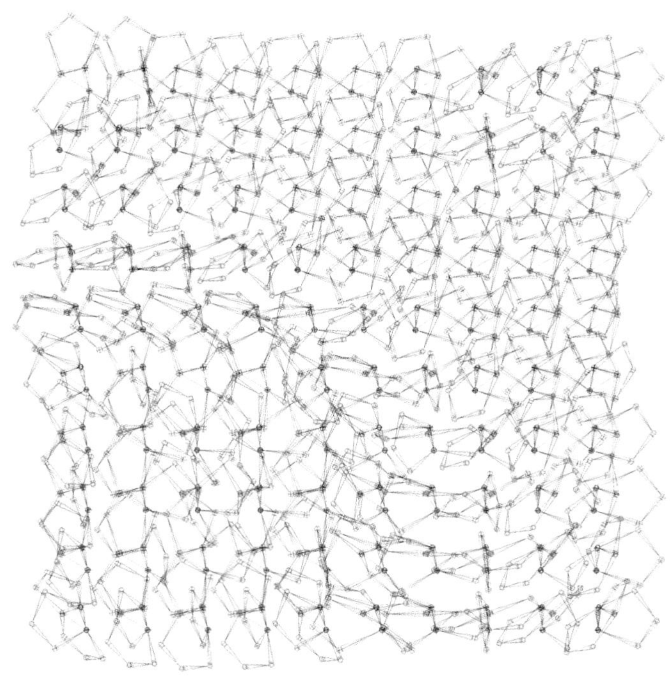

Sample morphological stance of the skeletal field in the Invisibles animation. The field is constituted by an interconnected network of simple 'cells' programmed through inverse-kinematics-based skeletons in MEL script.

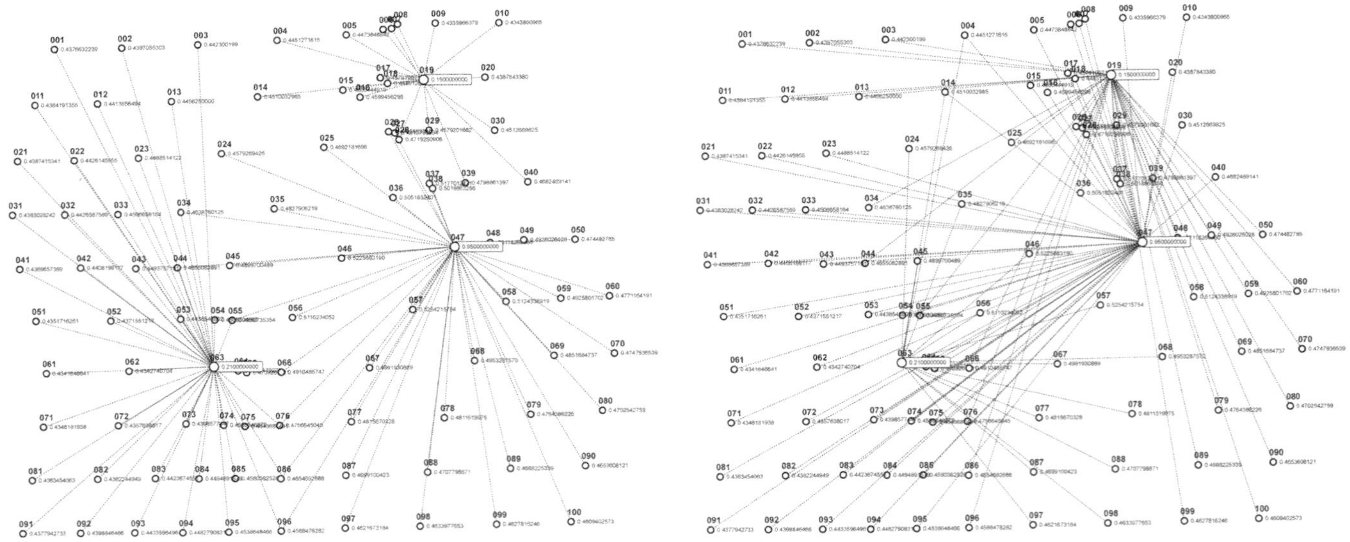

Diagram of algorithmic speed-distribution and cellular relationships. The field of speed distribution affects the rotations of the joints in the skeletal field. Speed of rotation is derived from a weighted average based on the speed of each of the three transitional activators. Three dominant cells act as input points for data from the changing sound frequencies bred through a process of granular synthesis (as part of the overall installation). All other cells adapt their speed of rotation to these master cells.

suggests that strong emergence is scientifically irrelevant ... Strong emergence starts where scientific explanation ends.'[6] This is where aesthetics comes in.

Interest in the issue of emergence and design has recently intensified in architectural discourse. This arena of design research tends to focus on emergent form-finding, where the emergent outcome is the form of a building. Significant precursors of this field can be identified in the work of Karl Chu, John Fraser, Marcos Novac and Greg Lynn, for example. NOX, the office of Lars Spuybroek, is among the more creatively thoughtful of those currently contributing to the discourse. And a recent issue of AD, *Techniques and Technologies in Morphogenetic Design*, guest-edited by the Emergence and Design Group, offered a very useful probing into the potential of emergence for design practice. Both Spuybroek and this group draw significantly on the work of Frei Otto, who exemplifies a focus on embedding structural behaviour in guiding emergent form-finding. Such issues are enormously interesting and, I believe, hold great as-yet-unrealised potential.

This article, however, approaches the subject with a different question in mind: What does emergence imply for the aesthetic nature of thinking-doing in architectural practice? Or, more specifically, how might the practice of architectural composition be considered in relation to models of emergence? The implication that emergence-oriented design research might freshly inflect aesthetic forms of architectural knowledge has not been explored to any significant degree. Emergent phenomena are always aesthetic phenomena.[7] This closely knit relationship can be seen as the core of the problem that confronts the sciences in their speculations on the unanswered conundrums of emergence. And yet, when architects pick up the tantalising threads that scientific formulations of emergence throw to the winds of wonder, they tend to avoid aesthetically oriented questions as well, largely preferring to rest their enquiries on the authorisations of scientific understandings.

In general, enquiries into the nature of emergence are inseparable from computation. Cellular automata, for example, have been a key tool for research. These enquiries are also inseparable from the question: 'What is life?' Life itself is the most mysterious of emergent phenomena. Where emergence has been used within architectural discourse, it is almost always closely affiliated with digital tools. It is frequently employed for its life-mimicking powers, or as forms that seem, in some more-or-less defined way, lifelike. The problem with most biomorphic approaches is that form is generated in *terms of form*, with the morphologies of living or organic things as the compositional measuring stick. The self-contraction implicit to this approach lies in the fact that, as Brian Massumi writes: 'Any potential the process may have had of leading to a significantly different product is lost in the overlay of what it already is.'[8] Emergence, in other words, gets left out of the equation.

Practices that generate work with microscale algorithmic procedures to generate emergent morphological outcomes at another scale and ontology are not especially common. However, the work of biothing is one such rare moment.

Based in New York, the practice is directed by Croatian-born architect Alisa Andrasek, who also teaches at Columbia and the Pratt Institute. biothing is a research-design laboratory whose various projects emerge through the use of computational systems that underscore multiple-scaled expressions. My aim here is to explore some of the intricacies of biothing's manner of working – sketching out or depicting an event of generative composition before turning to consider the aesthetic implications therein. In doing so I concentrate on one very specific biothing artefact: the animation that was part of the larger the Invisibles installation project[9] produced for the 2003 Prague Biennale. In order to maintain a deep focus of attention, I do not discuss here the role of the animation in the larger framework of the installation. The animation is explored as indicative of a mode of composition active throughout all of biothing's work. Other projects featured here, such as bifid and reticulars, give a sense of the consistency of the practice as a whole. And genware, a broad-reaching biothing research project, represents a core aspect of the firm's approach to generative design practice. This project explores how computational patterns can actively link projects, traverse scales and function through a network of practitioners collectively developing material in an open-source manner.

I will start by leaping into the deep with a particular kind of analysis, one that I call an 'affective diagram', a configuration wherein affective and abstract relationality explicitly coalesce. This particular affective diagram is drawn through words, in a little density of text I wrote in response to watching the Invisibles animation:

Watch biothing's the Invisibles animation.[10] It washes through you. Caressing the senses nonsensically, sensuous waves unfurl and curl, nonsensuously foaming perception.[11] It strokes in plush gushing rushes. This velvety vigour is both qualitative enumeration and relational enunciation: in each case both crystal clear and ungraspable. It is effective in that it causes a strong impression and affective in that this cause is indiscrete. Effects are fielded and we fly affected with the flock. Simple trajectories and links are swamped in a more expansive sense and sensibility. Stunning.

This passage aims to diagram the indelibly intertwined relations between abstraction and affect, its impetus to analyse the aesthetic nature of the animation. Such issues are difficult to articulate. Any event of heightened aesthetic power tends to leave us, momentarily at least, speechless. We pause or falter, groan or gasp. We just don't know what to say.

(pause)

As feeling blows in the face of speechless wonder, let's slip back to the beginning and feel our way through the process of coming into being.

Diagram of 'genware' network.

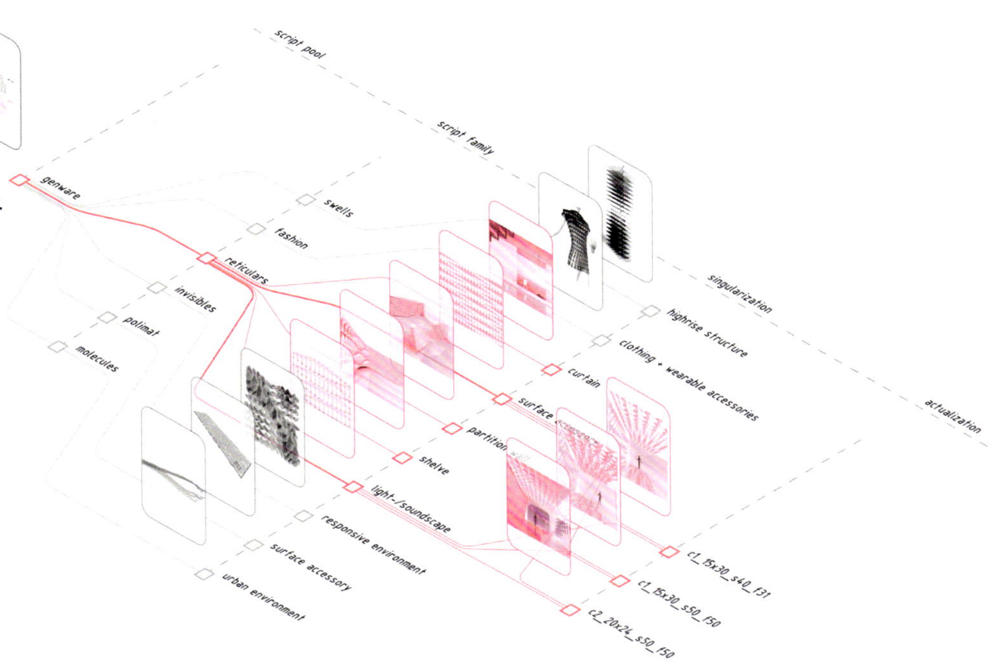

Alisa Andrasek/biothing, genware algorithmic library, 2001–06
The genware project was conceived as a sharing collaborative platform. Incorporating both aspects of *gen*etic engineering and soft*ware* design, it allows a designer to work at the scale of information. Not unlike a genetic engineer, the designer writes and manipulates computer scripts and code sequences in the generation of abstract forms of digital intelligence. This intelligence is then channelled into any number of potential material sites and scales. Like a virus it circulates through a number of disciplinary contexts such as architecture, product design and fashion. In each case, abstract geometric transformations are linked to specific material and fabrication constraints as well as scales of production, allowing for a synthesis of design intuition, algorithmic programming and parametric limits as the very foundation of the design process.

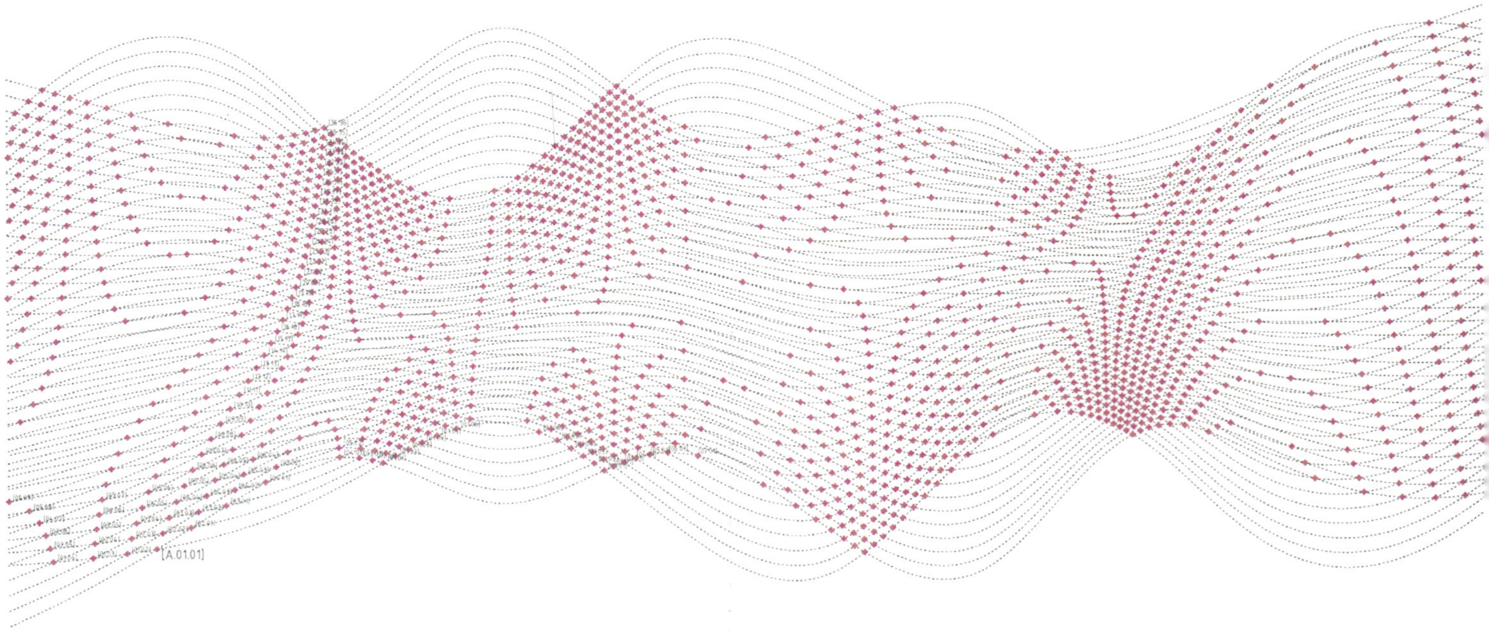

Alisa Andrasek/biothing, bifid ceiling prototype, 2005
The bifid project explores the mode of composition discussed through the Invisibles while involving material computation. The differential behaviour of the material system is a composite of: (1) algorithmically derived intersections between components; (2) constraints of the laser-cut fabrication method; (3) material properties of the polycarbonate material. Initial small-scale tests were scaled proportionally to a large-scale field fabricated using CNC milling.

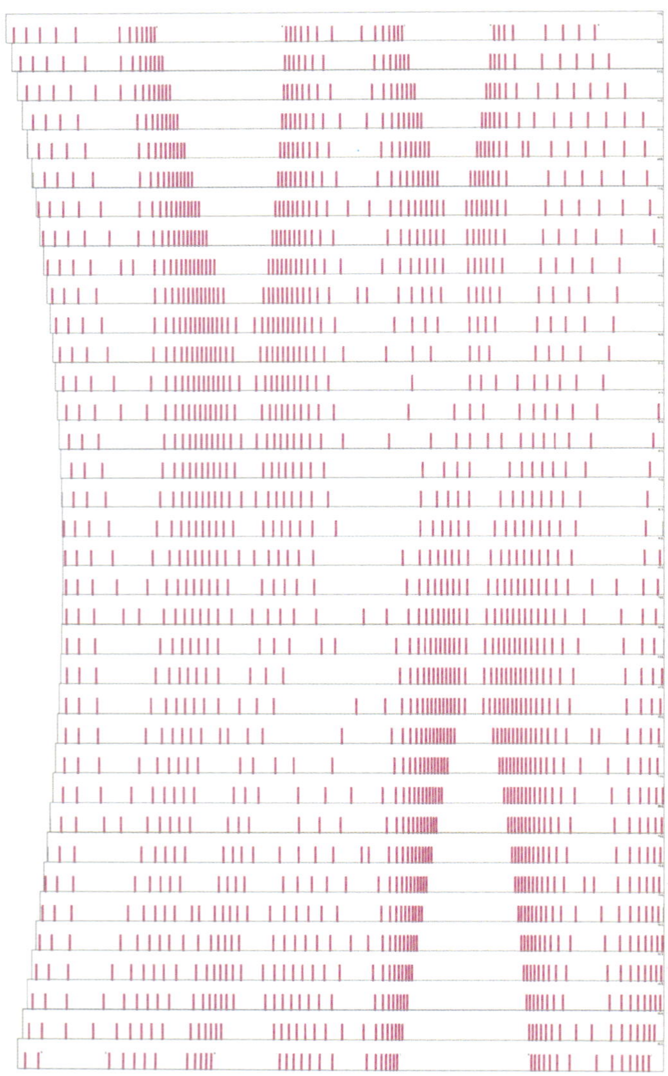

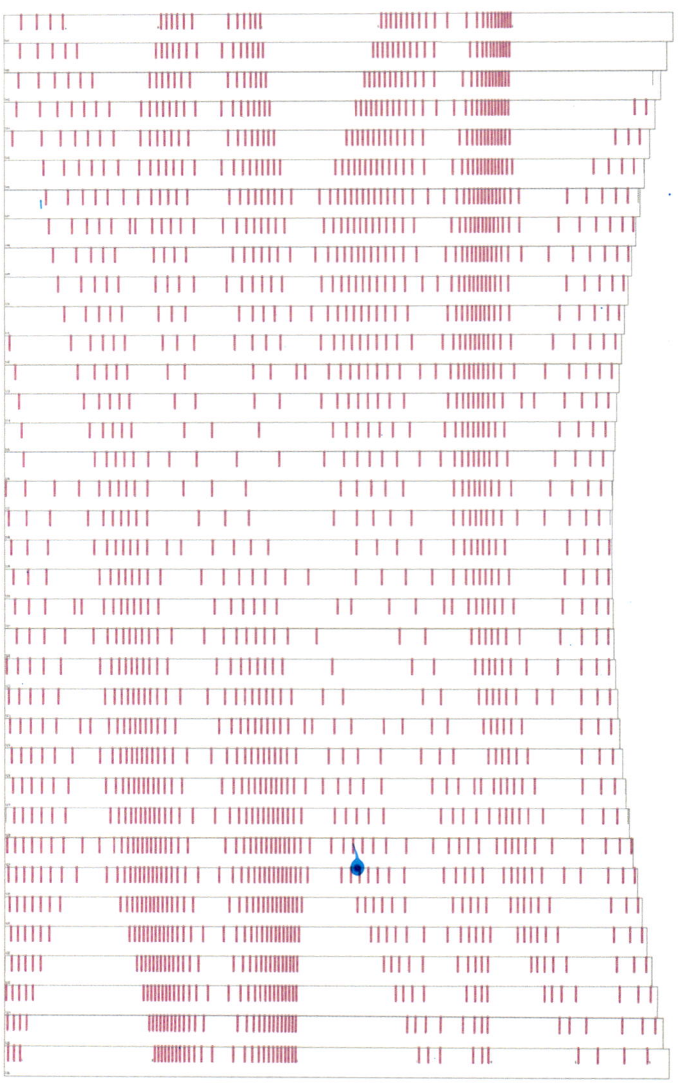

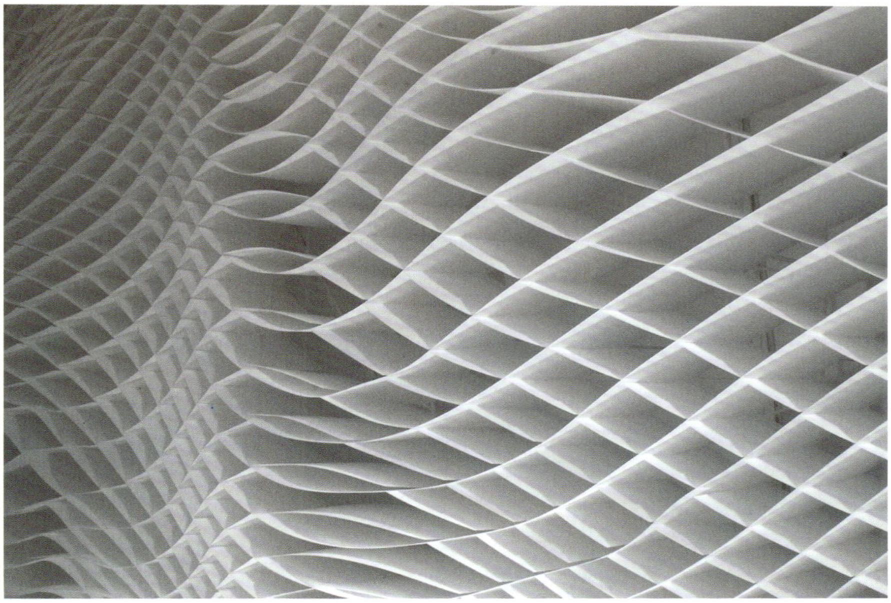

The intersection and fabrication pattern was generated algorithmically. The algorithm was based on wave interference logic. Parametric differentiation imbedded into the script derived multiple offspring conditions.

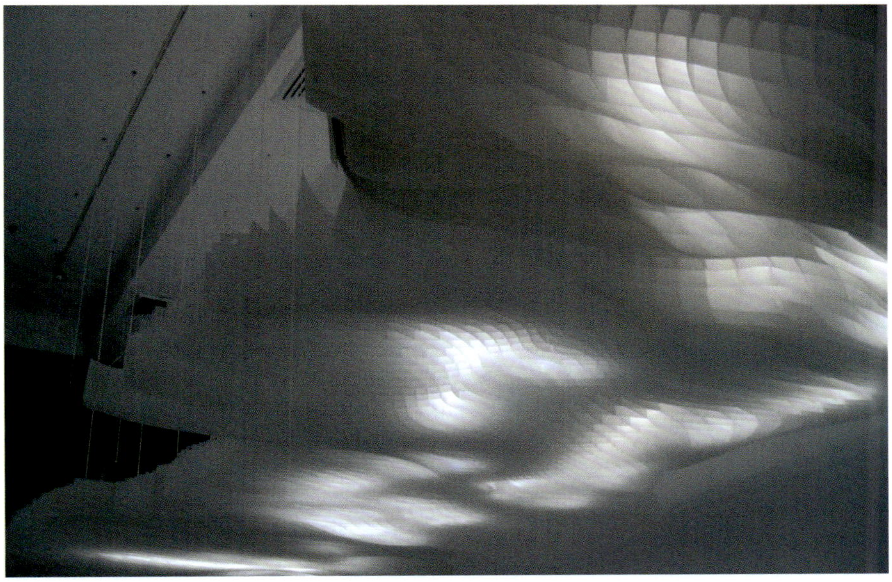

Ceiling detail. A field of LED lights which were programmed through the same logics of interference as the intersection patterns.

bifid v1.5. Alisa Andrasek and her algorithmic fabric 'creature' during installation at the KSA Gallery, Austion E Knowlton School of Architecture, Ohio State University. In often referring to her systems as 'creatures', Andrasek evokes their inherent dynamically behavioural coherence. This becomes powerfully manifest in her material computation techniques that intrinsically involve 'playing' with physical models, as can be seen in the bifid project.

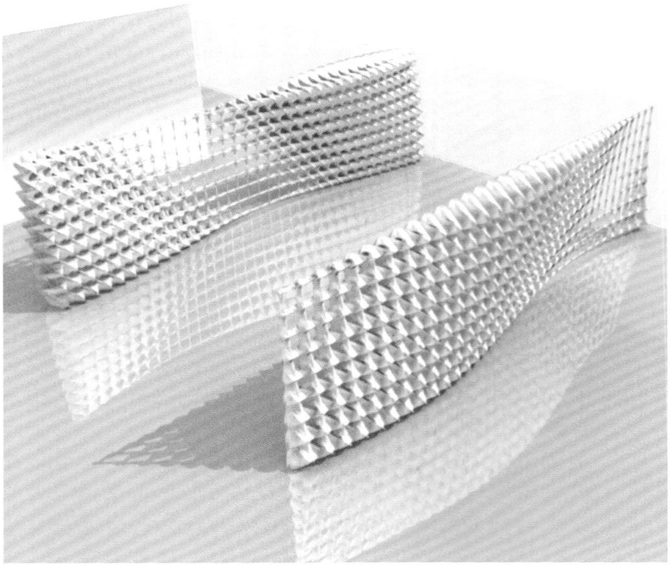

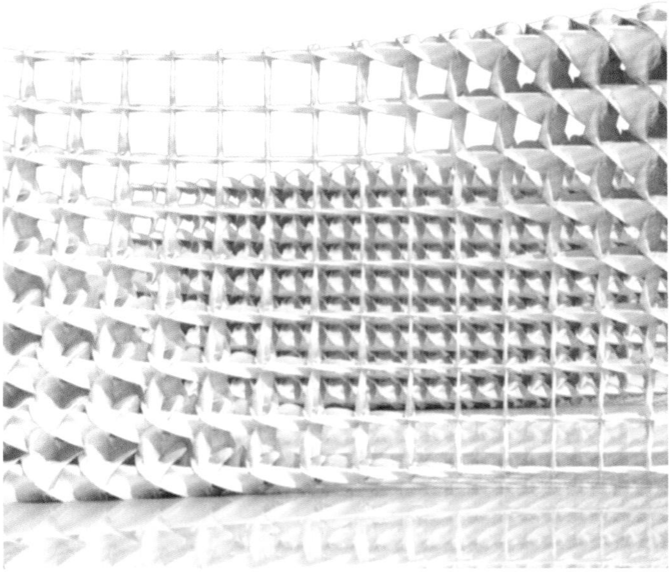

Alisa Andrasek/biothing, reticulars (smart) surface accessory, 2005
The reticulars project investigates the production of architectural systems using algorithmically differentiated geometry. Such systems are designed to distribute various 'soft' infrastructures such as lighting, sound or light storage systems. Cellular units can be parametrically varied into a range of scales, orientations and densities that can provide variant storage capacities, different paths of lighting or sound distribution and different transparency levels. Lighting and sound can be programmed to emit distinct and, over time, variable behaviours.

But first, I will sketch out an outline of the dynamic system that constitutes the Invisibles morphology. The system is made up of three interrelated layers: a skeletal field, a speed-distribution field and a skin or surface field. The skeletal field starts with a simple geometrical unit sketched out in 'bones' connected by rotating joints. This unit, or 'cell', is programmed through inverse-kinematics-based skeletons in MEL script. Each is built with algorithmically defined constraints or limits to movement, so that it is programmed to operate within a range of potential postures. This simple unit is multiplied into a network of connected units, setting up a field of internally held tendencies of movement or behavioural properties, and becoming a tightly packed 'colony' of units.

This resulting colony-field needs to be provoked into action; it needs stimulus for its microbehaviours to leap into a collective swarming. And this is where the speed-distribution field comes in. This layer is a loosely gridded mass of data nodes that propel the rotations of the skeletal unit joints. Within the mass of nodes, three 'sense nodes' (or data-input points) are designated to provide the anchor points to which all other nodes are related. Streams of variational data (related to sound frequencies in the larger installation) enter through the sense nodes, the effects rippling out into all of the other nodes. As the ripples spread, their effects are registered through skeletal joint rotations, inducing a complex set of relations in a skeletal swarming.

Over these two interrelated fields lies the third, skin-surface layer. Components of the surface-skin are behaviourally linked to corresponding units in the skeletal field. The skin leaps into patterned gestures that emerge out of this field of behavioural interrelations.

The description above roughly, or broadly, sketches out the technical, relational make-up of the morphologically dynamic system that constitutes the animation. But there is something missing in this account of its construction: the process through which it all 'came together', which enfolds more than one can simply mention. The enfolded complexity occurs through one dominant processual entity that tends to get left out of the accounts of generative systems: the designer. Behavioural properties or patterned gestures may emerge in the animation's different fields, but they do not emerge on their own. The emergent design process is not as simple as a purely bottom-up unfolding (as emergence theory would often have us believe). It is part of a larger event.

The animation's field system is emphatically, even if invisibly, part of a broader ecology through which parameters that do not enter into the digital data are enfolded. This involves a complexity of project criteria of many different kinds, along with the tendencies of the designer, knitted together by her habits, attentions, memories, affections and so on – a cluster of potential that can be folded into what we call 'personality', described by Brian Massumi as a 'pattern of preferential headings'.[12]

Personality enters into a dance with the potentials of the medium of design manipulation, accompanied by a range of other pragmatic and intangible influences. In the event of negotiating an undulating ground of criteria-meeting-potential, the designer becomes part of a depth of complex relationality so that the totality of the compositional event becomes one evolving 'thing'. Within this larger thing, the developing digital system described earlier is a material in the making. As a collective composite it develops resistances and potentials that interact with other material resistances and potentials in the midst of this complex occasion. A series of textured materialities meet one another in a co-determining process of being made.

In the cacophony of this event there is a striving that tempers development: to create or compose the morphologically dynamic system that constitutes the animation. Creating such a systemic entity involves discerning a coherence that we might recognise as a kind of life-of-its-own. The designer leads, but not bluntly or brutally. Likening the process to the training of a pet, she talks about 'teaching it, guiding it, stirring in certain directions, but at the same time learning from IT'.[13] The compositional process reaches a breakthrough point and enters another phase when IT's 'life' first flickers forward and the compositional event bifurcates into a clarity of differentiation between her and IT. It is at this moment that it also develops a 'pattern of preferential headings', or an abstract 'personality', and starts to lead as well as being led, to affect as well as being affected. Such a personality or character emerges through resonant intersections between the many materialities and potentialities.

This phase shift is a paradoxical moment: everything comes together at the same time that a clarity of differentiation emerges. The compositional event-thing bifurcates: IT and 'her' pop out into a distinction. Following this phase shift the designer's role within the compositional event changes. She is no longer the only source of 'push' amidst a scattering of material because she now has an IT (a system) to play with. She, as designer, can now manipulate or play something that has developed a consistency of its own. It is a system of behavioural tendency, albeit one that requires further development.

The system *is* something. It becomes a system defined by *tendencies of behaviour* that give it a *consistency*. By consistency I mean the sort of thing we refer to when discussing the consistency of a cake mix. Rather than some idea of sameness or uniformity, consistency is the texture arising from *the way in which something dynamically holds together*. Its consistency means, by definition, that it is not limitless, but full of limits, tendencies and resistances. The strength of this consistency means that it develops enough behavioural tendency (or 'patterns of preferential headings') to have character, becoming something of a creature. Alisa Andrasek often refers to such systems as 'creatures', evoking their inherent dynamically behavioural coherence. This is powerfully manifest in her material computation techniques that intrinsically involve physical models, as can be seen in the bifid project, a ceiling prototype exhibited at the New Museum of Contemporary Art in New York in 2005.

The first physical model for bifid was laser-cut at the Spatial Information Architecture Laboratory at the Royal Melbourne Institute of Technology (RMIT). In this context I was able to literally play with the model, feeling out the behavioural tendencies of Andrasek's creature. This occurred while the designer was in residence, running her Material

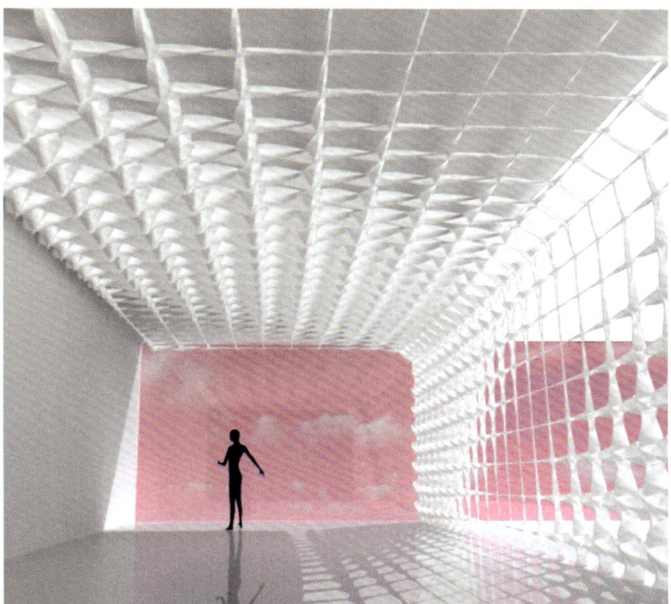

Cellular partition system.

Potency seminar as part of a design studio,[14] in which she would often evocatively orient the design investigations of the RMIT architecture students towards the production of a 'creature'. This is quite different to biomorphism as an approach because it is not about looking like or formally resembling a living thing. Rather, a pattern of relations is built into a physical model so that the behaviours of both the manufactured pattern (a colony of variationally repeated units constructed from strips of material) and properties of the physical material actively co-determine the nature of the creature's swarming morphology, which comes into being at a different scale and ontology to the ecology of relations through which it emerged.

The behavioural material-pattern system of bifid is another example of the mode of composition that tempers the algorithmic one of the Invisibles. In both, the cohabitation of a series of behavioural influences, each of which is constituted by multitudes of dynamic micro-interrelations, intricately and precisely collaborates in the emergence of an over-all, all-over consistency. Importantly, such cohabitation produces interference patterns through negotiations between interacting fields, influences and parameters. No component of the design event, including the author,[15] remains unaffected by the cohabitation.

The aesthetic power of biothing's projects is integral to this mutual affectivity. Aesthetics is a form of knowledge that studies the experience of relation or relatedness. Aesthetic experience is the experience of interrelatedness. The relations that constitute biothing's compositional entities cannot be singled out: they are never experienced in isolation, not even as some part of a whole. As a multitude engaged in an emergent process of composition, they generate patterns or textures of multiple, mostly invisible, relations: a consistency. So, what we (aesthetically) experience is an all-over, over-all consistency. This is the aesthetics of emergence.

While I am suggesting that we are witnessing the development of a new compositional paradigm, the configurations I have sketched out and detailed here are not in any way exclusive to the domain of working with digital media. The history of art and architecture has long been privy to these issues. Work such as that by biothing foregrounds

Partition screen system.

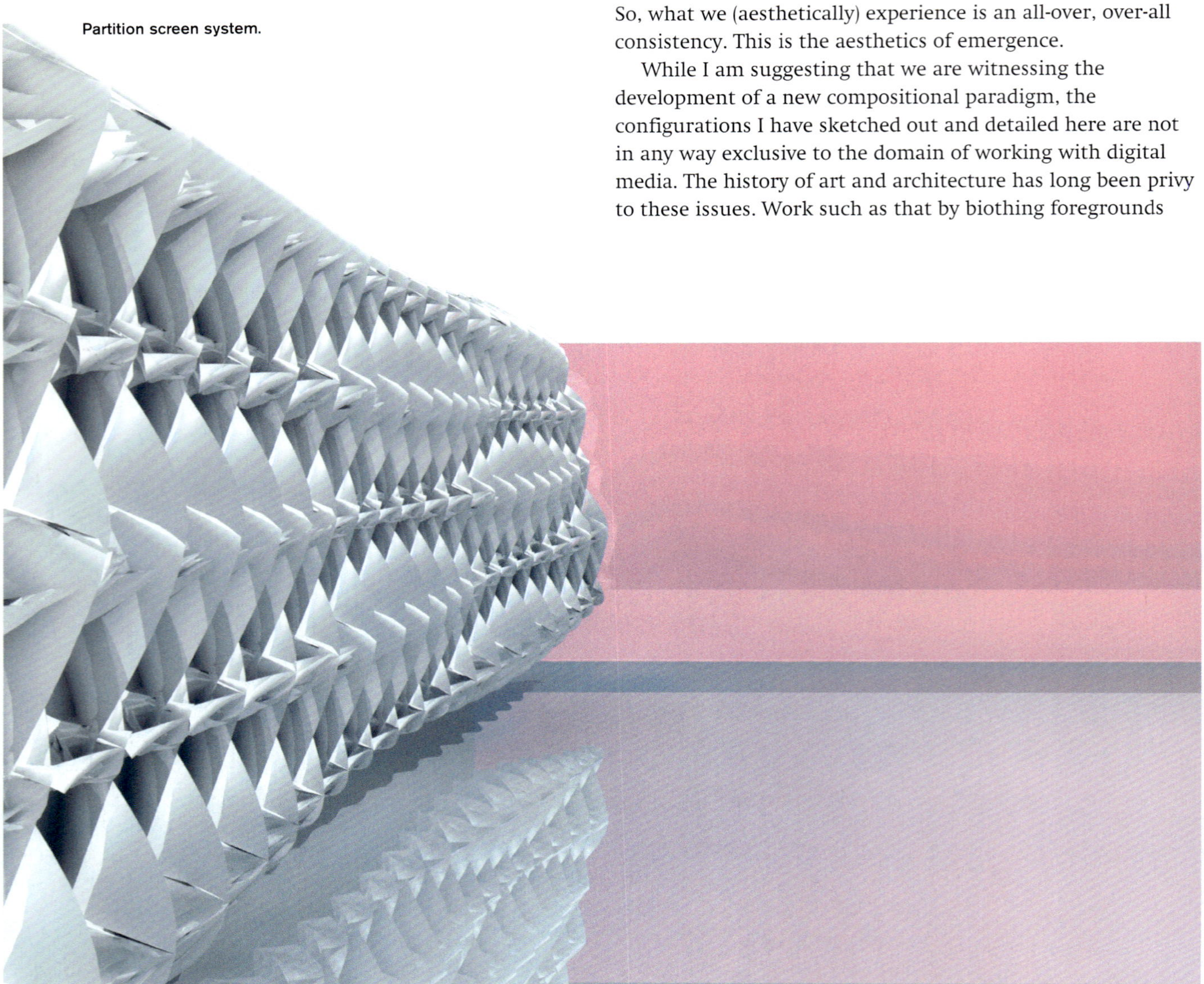

largely unspoken, implicit operations that more or less quietly, I would argue, massage all acts of creative composition. The newness lies in the degree to which the implicit is becoming *explicitly* articulated, or where the invisible becomes undeniable. ◬D

Notes

1 Brian Massumi, unpublished statement from early draft of 'Building Experience' in Lars Spuybroek, *NOX Machining Architecture*, Thames and Hudson (London), 2004.

2 Brian Massumi, *Parables for the Virtual: Movement, Affect, Sensation*, Duke University Press (Durham and London), 2002.

3 I am referring here to the field spawned by William James in the late 19th/early 20th century, as notably developed in the work of Brian Massumi.

4 John H Holland, *Emergence: From Chaos to Order*, Basic Books (New York), 1999, p 3.

5 Steven Johnson, *Emergence: The Connected Lives of Ants, Brains, Cities and Software*, Scribner (New York), 2001, p 18.

6 Mark Bedau, 'Downward causation and the autonomy of weak emergence', *Principia* 6, 2002, p 5.

7 I argue this in my current doctoral research at RMIT: 'The Aesthetics of Emergence' (to be submitted in 2006).

8 Brian Massumi, *A Shock to Thought: Expression After Deleuze and Guattari*, Routledge (London and New York), 2002, p xviii.

9 This installation is documented on the biothing website: www.biothing.org.

10 The animation can also be viewed on the biothing website: www.biothing.org.

11 This refers to that which Alfred North Whitehead, among others, referred to as 'nonsensuous perception'.

12 Massumi, *Parables for the Virtual*, op cit, p 205.

13 Email correspondence with Alisa Andrasek, 22 December 2004.

14 This was run in 2005, with the assistance of Chris Perry (servo), myself and Jonathon Podborsek (kokkugia).

15 This whole scenario can be usefully illustrated with the following: Research in *Neuroscience* tells us that if a rabbit smells a carrot, this smell induces a particular pattern of neuron firings in the brain. When the rabbit smells rabbit poo, a different pattern is provoked. These patterns are patterns of recognition. But should a rabbit encounter a smell that it can't recognise because it's never smelt it before, like coffee perhaps, not only is a new pattern of neuron firings established, but every previously established pattern becomes altered. This rabbit encountered an atmospheric character (a smell) that was utterly new to its experience of the world. The rabbit could not have perceived that smell without a 'smell intelligence': a capacity to sense it and place it in relation to every other smell it knows, so that from that moment onward nothing would ever smell quite the same again. That rabbit and its sense of the world had palpably, even if minutely, been reconfigured. The effect is all-over and over-all in a moment of nonsensuous reshuffling and a shift in the rabbit's whole texture or consistency. This was provoked in the encounter with a new pattern through smell, but every pattern is part of a broader nonsensuous, synaesthetic texture or consistency.

Tectonics, Economics and the Reconfiguration of Practice: The Case for Process Change by Digital Means

The current programming culture in architecture could all too easily be written off as a youthful, geeky obsession with the algorithmic and the parametric among nascent practitioners, who have had little if any opportunity to build. The activities of Gehry Technologies run counter to this stereotype. Building on 15 years of experience at Gehry and Partners, Gehry Technologies was founded in 2002 as an independent organisation dedicated to the business of technological innovation and the development of architectural software tools. Dennis R Shelden, chief technology officer, discusses the wider implications of a concentrated focus on technological tools and organisational processes for designers and the business of building.

Gehry Technologies is a relatively new organisation, representing a new organisational model in the spectrum of building practice. The organisation pursues an enquiry into the processes of building and the emerging practices and roles suggested by technological advances. The impact of this focus on process translates into architectural form through the tectonic aspects of design, and a view of building from the process of making back towards architectural design, rather than the prevailing view of making as design's outcome. There are several reasons for this focus on tectonics and process, not the least of which is that consideration of these aspects has been downplayed in the development of tools and methods in favour of the more obvious architectural drivers of schematic and planning-level thinking about building. At Gehry Technologies we perceive there to be a gap in the available tools sets and methodologies for these aspects of design, and great opportunity for the profession as it moves into these areas of interest.

The opportunities and potential value of retooling contemporary building practice are well documented, as are the potential pitfalls. There is great potential for design in expanding the set of forms available to architecture, along with a corresponding sense that the rules of engagement have to be different to realise this potential in built form. Capabilities for the geometric expression of form – enabled by advances in digital media – have moved beyond the capacities of 'conventional' project descriptions to effectively capture, and processes project intentions into building. Meanwhile, the contractually structured conventions of project team organisation and roles have inherent, deliberate limitations on communication, whose utility has now been exceeded.

Reconfigurations of Practice

Building has a history of a hierarchically structured organisational model and supply chain that stems from the 'limited bandwidth', or limited capabilities for the transmission and processing of information, of the predigital age, and suggests a preference for 'command and control' over collaboration.

Other businesses have advanced their organisations in light of recent technology. While the heavy manufacturing industries have optimised around such hierarchical command-and-control structures, others have developed around more decentralised, webbed business organisations, including light manufacturing, retail and the entertainment industry.

The business of building has yet to do either. It has been noted that building teams are constructed as networked organisations, but are contractually restricted from functioning in this manner. The process of building has remained – officially – hierarchically structured in control, and linearly structured in time. Contract, finance, information and control flow-gates control the process and communications between players. These structures are legislatively defined, and there is considerable inertia in the current model, and risk in pursuing new models. There are many issues with the existing organisation, perhaps most notably that it has isolated architectural practice from the centre of value of construction. This has occurred nominally in the interests of protecting architects, the argument being that architects cannot be experts at everything, and construction processes – which have high risk (but also high value) – are too detailed or too complicated for generalists.

Digital practices offer the potential for expanding the reach of design deeper into the process of building, and the potential emergence of a new, digitally enabled, master-builder role for architecture is the topic of much discussion. Digital tools offer a catalyst for pursuing alternatives to traditional project controls, by reducing the risk of innovation below the level of current practice. We are now seeing new ways in which designers and builders provide new value by forming new project organisations that branch across the tree. This has the appearance of the direct violation of the formal ways that information flows through projects. So the risks of making change are high, but firms are moving in these directions because of the inherent opportunities in doing so. Whether the architectural profession will take the lead in this industry reconfiguration remains to be seen, but, under any circumstances, the opportunity of control through improved access to information does not seem to be a zero-sum game.

A key aspect of this catalytic force is the potential for directly repurposing information through various stages of project definition and execution, between specification and execution, and between form and economics. This is radically new, in that previously human intervention, and presumed quality control, was required to transfer intent across usages. Each division or reprocessing required an authority to be taken and documents to be stamped. The notion that project definition might flow freely and automatically between players without specific human action threatens to make the traditional ways of controlling responsibility obsolete. Yet it is in this streamlined connection of process that new opportunities are available.

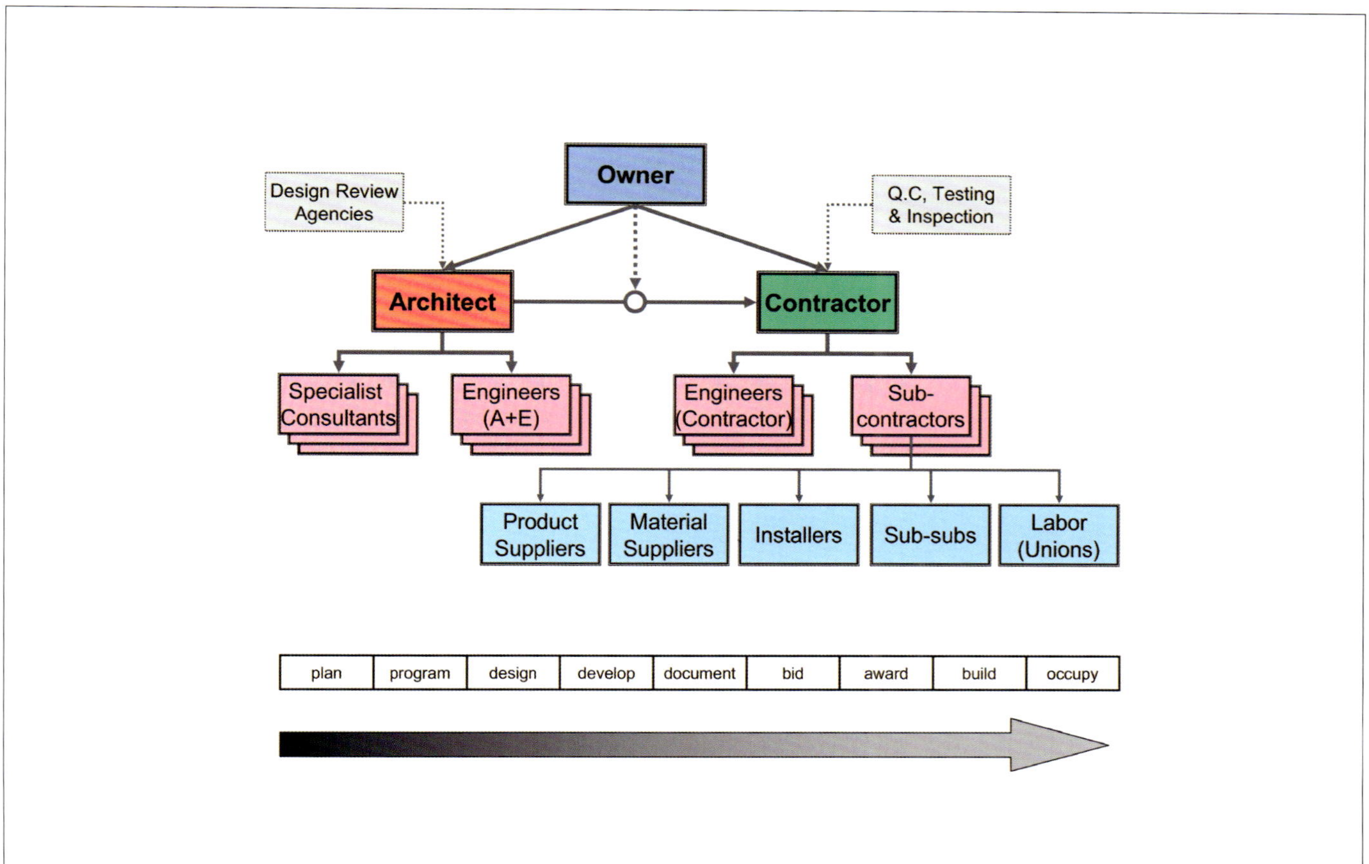

Conventional building delivery is structured hierarchically in terms of control and linear in time. Digital tools are providing a catalyst for rethinking the structures of project delivery, presenting opportunities for firms to expand their roles, offer new services and change the sequencing of how and when design information is developed and consumed.

The third dimension has so far been the locus of this new communication. One of the drivers of information integration is the understanding that miscoordination occurs at connections and interfaces, precisely where the inherent gaps of contemporary process are defined.

One of the hallmarks of emerging design tools is the ability to expose cost–benefit analysis as an aspect of iterative design. This requires exposing information developed late in the game and hidden internally in specific delivery roles, upstream and into the mix of high-level project decision-making.

The 'single building model' has been an attempt to coordinate project knowledge around a framework for the integration of spatial occupancy. This view of the net result of specification as geometric location is an obvious one, and substantial efficiencies are being realised by digitally simulating the spatial configuration of building elements prior to construction.

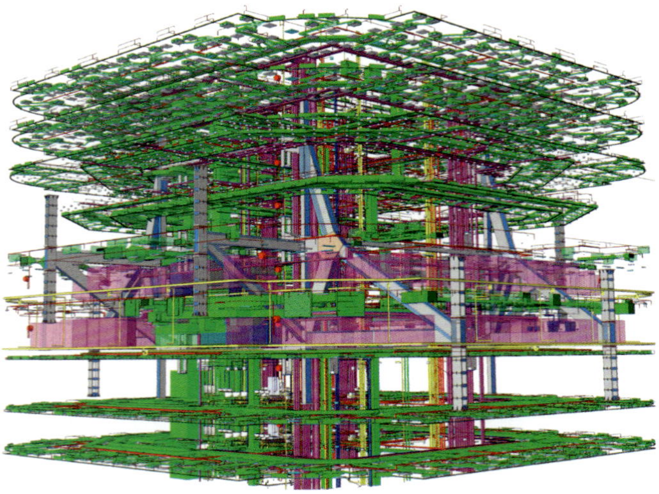

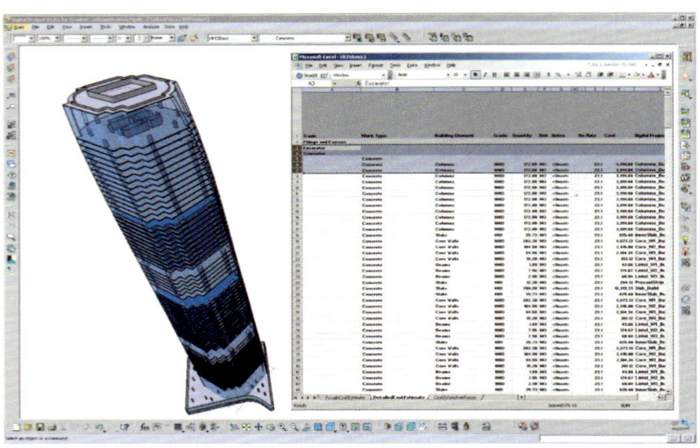

Swire Properties supported the development of a digitally integrated building delivery team for the One Island East project (Hong Kong, 2004–). The project database was used to produce detailed quantity extractions and cost estimates, which were provided to bidders as part of tendering phase documents. The 'single building model' is, in fact, an integrated view of numerous trade- and discipline-specific design documents.

Yet even as this view of the spatially integrated building model begins to take hold in practice, there is the sense that technology – and opportunity – have already moved beyond. The reason is simple: much more is known internally about the nature of products than can be exposed to the process simply as occupancy of space. The notion is that design or engineering intent *generates* occupancy of space in a given building configuration, and that this intent can be coordinated in a much more direct manner. Parametric modelling is the technological basis for this expression of intent. The opportunity of parametric modelling is that we can express design, engineering and fabrication intentions independent of geometry, so that these intentions persist over geometric variation. It is this capability that allows the conventional notions of the linearity of process to be reversed, that late-stage decisions can be potentially back-propagated upstream into design iteration without the inherent cost of the conventional generate–test–discard model.

Digital Tectonics

One net affect of algorithmic design on practice has been a new emphasis on tectonics as a key driver of architectural expression. The trajectory of tectonic intentions towards a central role in design has occurred independently of digital processes, but expansions of formal possibility through digital media have necessitated increased attention to these practical aspects of building.

There was a sense in 20th-century practice that what was critical was to get the more 'architectural' aspects right – aesthetic intentions and the relationship between form and programme – and that these intentions could be abstracted from project execution. Modernist forms allowed for the abstraction of form from materials, and for a primacy of geometry over materials. Tectonic specifics were at best second-order drivers of form, and were 'hot swappable': one material could be substituted for another late in the process as part of 'value engineering' without requiring substantial revisitation of higher-level project intentions. The move away from tectonics and process is expressed in the contractual distinction between the roles of architects and builders, and corresponding distinctions between specification and execution.

Of all the unanticipated trends that the digital has produced, none is more surprising than its role in the re-emergence of craft and increased intentions towards materiality as important design themes. We might question whether these arose as first-order drivers in themselves, or emerged as necessary topics with design's move beyond the forms of Euclidean geometry, a development in which digital media certainly have played a profound role.

The expanded potential of architectural forms has mandated a consideration of material and tectonics as first-order drivers, key enablers or constraints that impact the potential realisation of form as building. The limits of our

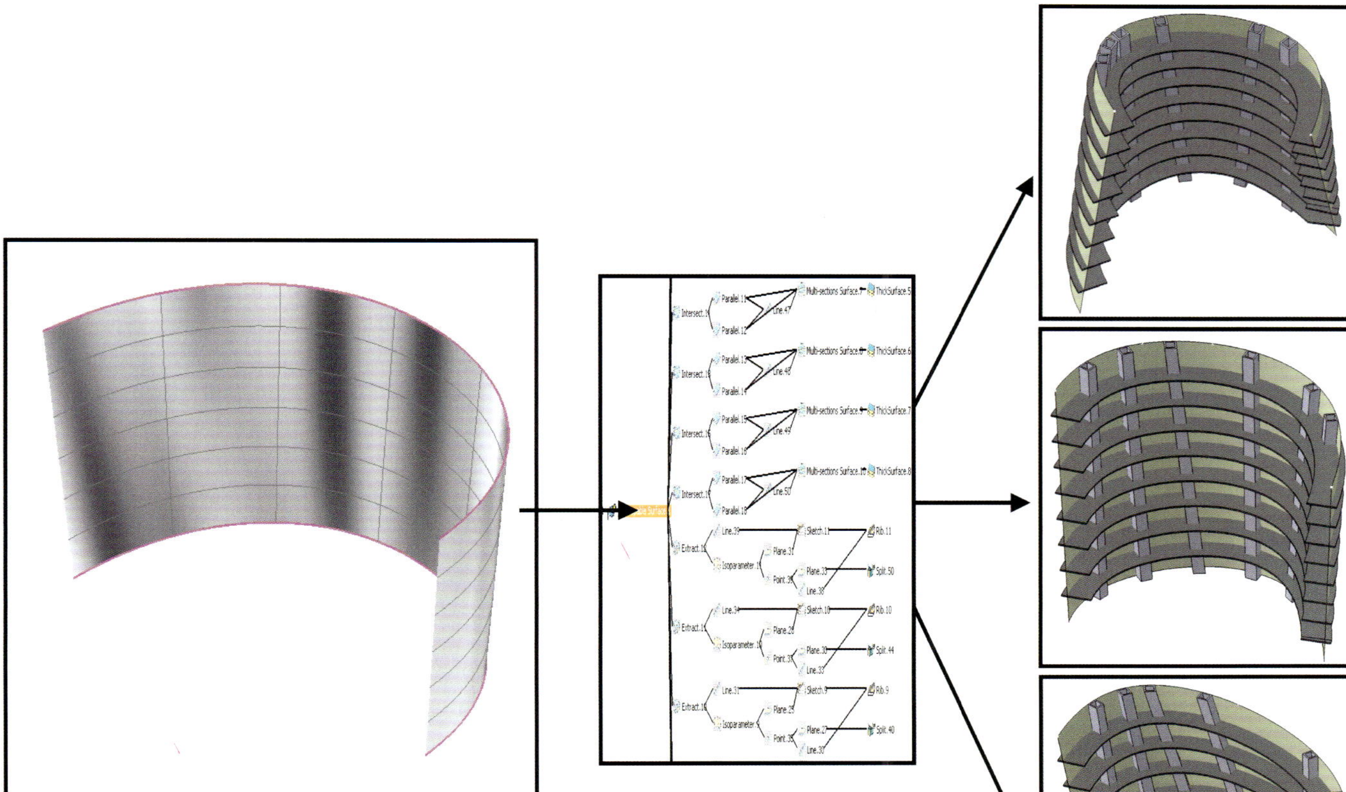

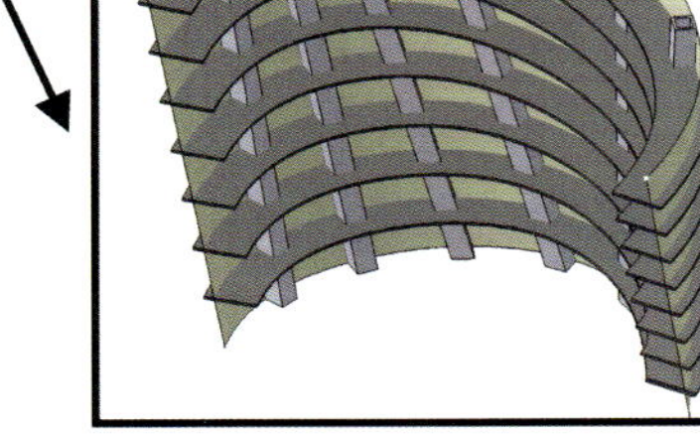

Parametric models are developed as networks of geometric relationships, which can be replayed in different spatial contexts. These techniques have radically changed the costs of detailed system engineering, providing opportunities for 'mass customisation' of building systems.

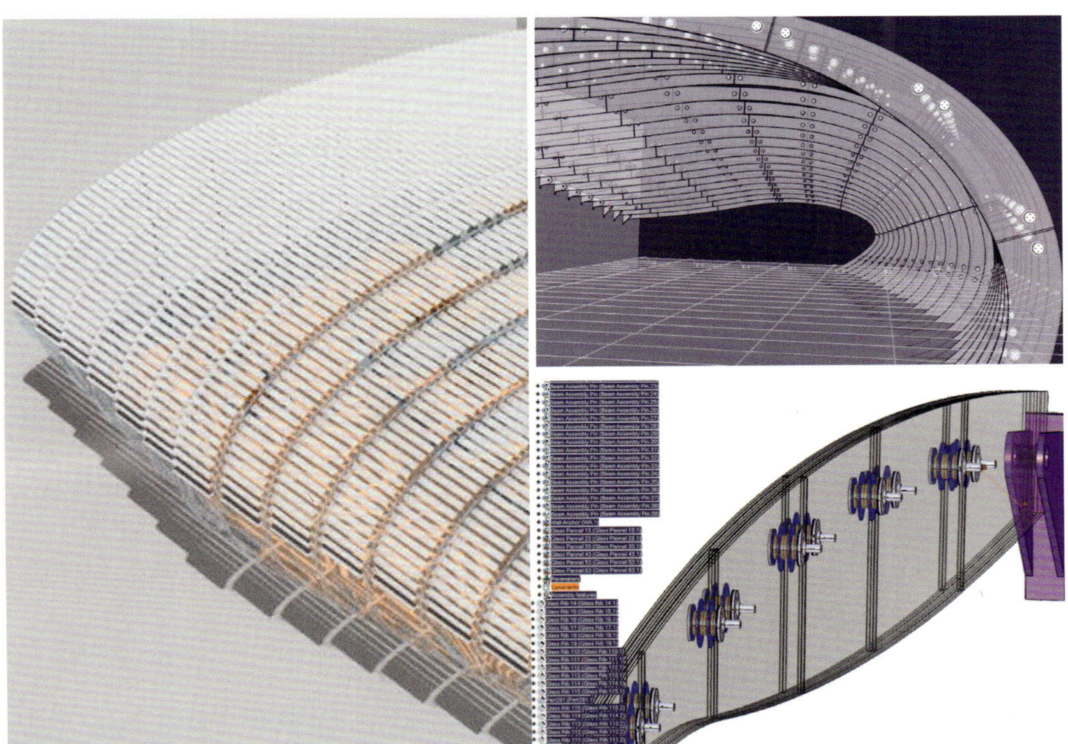

Front Inc adopted a parametric approach to the design of the Yatala Glass Showroom (Brisbane, Australia, 2004–). The firm provides design, engineering and detailing services, and is expanding into self-performing the delivery of building envelope systems. Front's practice demonstrates the potential of new technologies to support innovative business models and opportunities for practice.

capacities to express or control the *descriptions* of form are no longer the main barriers to exploration: digital media have taken care of that. Rather, the limits are economic, and are resolved by bringing the efficiencies of fabrication processes into the sphere of formal design considerations.

Part of this trend may be transitory, due to the current limitations of the economics of spatial control. For while digital media have afforded an almost unlimited availability of information at continued reductions in cost, the same is not (yet) true of our ability to project this information into the spatial environment. This limitation has been breached in schematic-phase design activities, where prototyping capabilities provide low-cost, high-fidelity translations from digital to physical. However, such technologies are not yet scalable to building-size objects of singular configuration, at unit costs competitive with those of traditional construction. It might be argued that digital design media have produced an excessive production of information, beyond our capacity to consume or control, and that manual intervention has found a new role as a bridge between information and material. The process of realising digital form at the building scale has been based on a deliberately reduced pipeline between the digital and the physical, with a heightened authority bestowed upon the craftsman as the interpreter.

The same can be said of the resurgence of interest in the behaviours of materials. The initial exuberance of the ability to project digital forms into the physical has given way to a new-found respect for materials as important voices in this process, and developments are now concerned with back-propagating materiality – or at least its geometrified interpretations – into the digital tool set.

The value of generative design on the architectural side, and mass customisation, its closely related fabrication counterpart, does not seem to be particularly in the efficiencies afforded to the architects' studio, nor the ability to produce interesting patterns of form. These benefits could presumably be achieved through other means, with considerably more directness, freedom and tactility. The benefit is to project execution – to provide economies in fabrication, allow trade-offs between economies of information and component generation. To the

Digital models are increasingly incorporating materials simulation and aspects of process to provide effective tools for predicting system behaviours during installation. Top: Digital contract model with overlaid shop drawing submittals, MIT Stata Center (Gehry, Cambridge, Massachussetts, 2004). Bottom: A custom mesh simulation tool used in the design of the Gehry Retrospective installation, Guggenheim Museum (2000).

The forces of technology and economics have as yet by no means been universally favourable to architecture as a profession, nor necessarily to builders, owners or consumers of design. Yet there is a resurgence of interest in design as an economic differentiator, which has unfolded parallel to the evolution of design technologies, that appears as a counterforce to the ongoing commoditisation of both tools and practice.

extent that this phenomenon is of concern to design, it is to expand the opportunities of buildable form, to extend the reach of design intent deeper into the building delivery process, and bring economies of making within the set of formal trade-offs available within the scope of parameters available for design synthesis.

Predicting and Building the Future

Gehry Technologies has staked a somewhat unusual position in the spectrum of emerging building practice. We have found ourselves in the position of tool-makers, in order to fill tactical gaps necessary for new models of practice. Our experience suggests that there is a viable role for practitioners to engage directly in the business of technology innovation. The availability of computationally sophisticated talent in practice, and the increasing number of firms – both small and large – whose work is pushing the envelope of 'conventional practice' through digital means, suggests that other firms have much to contribute, and much to gain, in advancing the common pool of technology available to practise. To date, this course of action has been limited by the high barriers to entry into the technology and innovation market, combined with a perception that opening a firm's internally developed expertise to the larger audience represents a leak of intellectual property and technological differentiation to competitors. In short, the business case that will incentivise firms to share innovation with the wider community is missing. Our ambitions for the near future include developing business models for the productisation and distribution of technologies that lower the barriers to entry and incentivise a wider range of firms to contribute to the network of available technologies.

The forces of technology and economics have as yet by no means been universally favourable to architecture as a profession, nor necessarily to builders, owners or consumers of design. Yet there is a resurgence of interest in design as an economic differentiator, which has unfolded parallel to the evolution of design technologies, that appears as a counterforce to the ongoing commoditisation of both tools and practice. The questions of reach, opportunity and responsibility for participants that engage around projects is very much in play, and the economic pressures of differentiation and efficiency are sounding a mandate for innovation that digital methods are available to serve. The potential of process reconfiguration to reposition design as again central to building is large, and the opportunity for designers in taking on this challenge squarely seems open-ended. AD

Generative algorithms used to develop panel-layout strategies, based on rules provided by the fabricator, A Zahner Company (Gehry Experience Music project, Seattle, 2000).

Calculus-Based Form: An Interview with Greg Lynn

Greg Lynn, Alessi Tea & Coffee towers, 2003

Greg Lynn's name has become synonymous with digital architecture. The guest-editor of the seminal issue of Δ *Folding in Architecture* (1993; revised edition, Wiley-Academy 2004), Lynn pioneered a curvilinear approach when computerised technologies were only a marginal part of the discussion. Here, in an interview with Ingeborg M Rocker, Lynn speaks candidly and enthusiastically about his own journey through software – from appropriation of standardised packages to scripting customised tools.

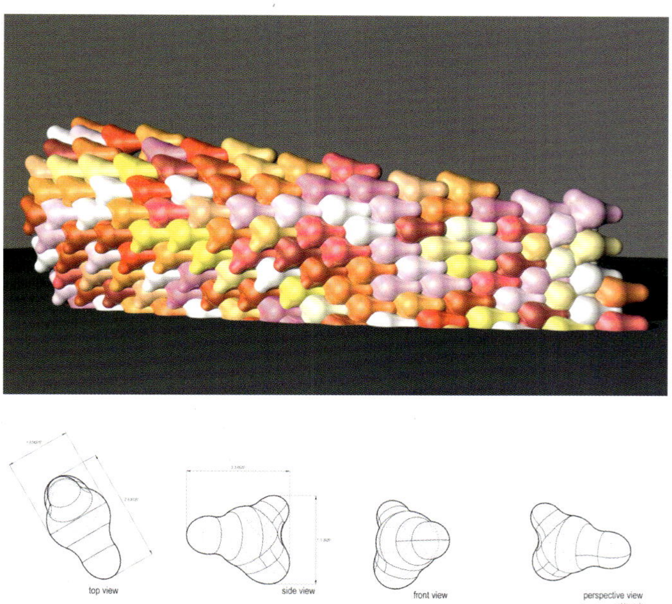

Greg Lynn, Slavin House, Venice, California, due for completion 2007
The continuity of the upper and lower levels of the house is organised around void lightwells. These consist of a series of bricks which – based on one and the same parametric design model – can vary in size, form and colour.

The arrival of interactive animation software – previously only used in Hollywood's movie industry or by car manufacturers – caused a dramatic change in the design and discourse of architecture during the early 1990s.[1] Most notably, architectural forms moved away from the fragmented, polygonal and rectilinear towards the smooth, continuous curvilinear, spectacularly subverting both the Modernist box and its Deconstructionist remains.

Greg Lynn, who had at the time just established his architectural firm FORM (1992) was one of the advocates of this dramatic change, and his projects – for example, the Korean Presbyterian Church, New York (1999), the competition for the Eyebeam Museum of Art and Technology, New York (2001), the Embryological House (1999), the Alessi Tea & Coffee towers (2003), the transformation of the Kleiburg Block in Bijlmermeer, the Netherlands (2006) and, most recently, the Slavin House in Venice, California (due for completion 2007) – have informed the current generation of architects.

Equally, Lynn's writings, including his issue of Δ *Folding in Architecture* (1993),[2] *Folds, Bodies & Blobs: Collected Essays* (1998),[3] *Animate Form* (1999),[4] *Architecture for an Embryologic Housing*[5] and *Intricacy* (2003),[6] changed the direction of architectural discourse, providing the intellectual framework for the appropriations of software exploring and challenging architectural form.

This interview traces how during the 1990s Lynn's work at first explored interactive prepackaged software, before more recently moving into the scripting of customised software tools and production environments, retaining the focus on the impact of calculus-based software and computer-supported modes of production on architectural form.

Software: New Media for Architectural Explorations

FORM was launched in 1992 with the aim of developing an expertise – or even vocabulary – to discuss questions of form. According to Lynn:

'I felt like the field was losing its claims and discourse on form. So I decided to throw down a gauntlet for myself and claim "form".'

Lynn inherited the obsession with form from his teacher and mentor Peter Eisenman, who since the early 1970s had worked mostly on process-driven explorations of form. Despite many similarities, Lynn's FORM tried to depart from Eisenman's modes of enquiry:

'I have always tried to get out of the process-driven bubble within which I found myself. I regret to say it hasn't really worked, as I still struggle to situate my work outside of the 1980s theoretical model of justifying shapes by processes of analytic transformation.'

For the development of new modes of enquiry, presentation and production, the digital medium became constitutive:

'It is always more interesting to begin with an inventory of what machines want to do to us before we start asking what we desire from the machines.'

Thus the modes of operation of a chosen software rather than the modes of operation of the digital machine started to become interesting to architects: development was no longer based on the history and theory of architecture, nor on past modes of architectural design and production, but rather on the technological regimes of computational design devices. Software, as the new media for the investigation and generation of form, changed how architects thought and designed.

'I think the medium of software is different to the medium of drafting equipment like compasses, maylines and adjustable triangles. I used to love drawing with pen and ink on Mylar, and I remember as a student at Princeton discovering a German-manufactured spline made of a rubber strip and aluminium discs. I still have several of them at different sizes. When I started using MicroStation[7] back in the late 1980s it was because it had elements called splines. I remember drawing for hundreds of hours in a small apartment using the rubber spline and adjustable triangles to produce the Sears Tower drawings. These were the last drafted documents I personally ever produced as the digital tools were so much more robust and exciting for me.'

Lynn's exemplary approach with regard to this change in the profession used computer software as new media in which, and through which, so far unknown calculus-based formal and geometric explorations could take place.

'I really wanted to explore the software medium at a basic as well as a deeper level, and I have always started with the first principles of the software and its geometry engines. Too many people understand the computer in terms of facilitating expression or in terms of a pseudo-scientific system when it is more simply just another design medium.'

Thus it was the MicroStation computer-aided design (CAD) software – which at the time enabled the modelling of roadways and earthworks using 'splines' – rather than the computer's genuine operations that not only introduced alternative modes of generating and producing form, but also highlighted the constitutive role of media in architectural thinking and design.

Animated Form

Shortly after, Lynn began to explore the potential of animation software such as Alias and, later, Maya, to generate form.

'I found that animation packages had similar geometric entities and calculus-based geometric models because animators wanted to use keypoints that could be infinitesimally interpolated, as this is the nature of keyframe animation. There were lots of interesting formal and procedural by-products of this temporal and spatial sensibility in the digital medium of Hollywood animation tools.

'The entire time I have been using CAD software back and forth with these things. Robert Aish noticed how many architects were using tools like Maya, and its procedural scripting language of expressions, to build custom modelling tools, and so he began to develop a procedural scripting package in MicroStation.'

Lynn's approach, rather counterintuitive to the planning of architecture, searched for the unanticipatable – the happy accidents. Playful experimentation – chance – replaced determined planning.

'I started to learn the software by experimenting, but after a happy accident it only makes sense that you practise, master and integrate the unanticipated result into a technique. I love the moment when I discover some new potential in software, but once I find it I try to turn this into a technique.'

Lynn uses intuition in the sense described by Henri Bergson:[8] According to Lynn: 'Intuition is the moment when the principles and techniques of a discipline are so integrated that one is able to extrapolate, develop and extend them as an invention or innovation. Intuition requires rigour and knowledge. Too often it is understood as the inverse of rigour and knowledge, and this is a complete misunderstanding of the term.'

His success lies in the exhaustive exploration and integration of all of the principles he discovers accidentally. Only the rigorous use of interactive software allows him to arrive at a point where results can be anticipated without prescribing them logically. Such exploration of interactive software has changed not only modes of design, but, perhaps even more significantly, concepts of form and space.

'Throughout the history of architecture, aesthetics and construction have been based on fixed points with exact coordinates that are defined relative to an absolute-zero position. Our discussions have, then, not surprisingly focused on proportions of whole numbers and whole number series – on forms that can be idealised and reduced to these mathematical principles and the resulting symbolic value of whole numbers.

'I realised that contemporary software could be animated because the geometric engines such packages were using were calculus based. You could move an object and then interpolate a whole collection of variables into infinitesimally smaller steps. The points in space were fluid due to the calculus relationships of variables, and this was giving form and shape to the models. I initially, in Animate FORM, focused my thinking on the revolution in motion, and only later realised that the real revolution was in the use of a 300-year-old invention: calculus.'

More recently, Lynn has been less interested in the justification or embodiment of force and movement, but rather in the mathematics and geometry of calculus-based curvature.

Calculus-Based Form

In this context, parts-to-whole questions (which suggest that the whole is more than the sum of its parts) seem to Lynn much more germane and provocative than questions of dynamic perception and literal motion, as the latter smack to him of the Gestalt psychology of the turn of the last century, and their architectural correlative is too focused on individuated interactivity rather than cultural and civic issues.

'Architecture has a disciplinary history and responsibility to express parts-to-whole relationships and hierarchy. At first, because we were amateurs, we didn't express this and instead buildings were proposed as seamless monolithic hulking masses. To ignore the history and richness of assembly is to miss the real impact of calculus.'

Departing from his force-informed 'blobs' of the 1990s, Lynn's Embryological House, the Kleiburg housing project in the Netherlands and the 50,000 Tea & Coffee towers for Alessi are all parametric designs that explore parts-to-whole relations.

Greg Lynn, Kleiburg housing project, Bijlmermeer, the Netherlands, 2006
For the existing 500-unit social housing block, built in the early 1970s on the outskirts of Amsterdam, Lynn's design proposes a diversity in both social and architectural arrangement through the reduction of public space, the division of the block into manageable neighbourhoods of 10 units, and the design of unit neighbourhoods with distinct identities. A series of more than 150 parametrically designed, uniquely shaped vertical steel trusses organises the building through a semitransparent stainless-steel fabric cladding.

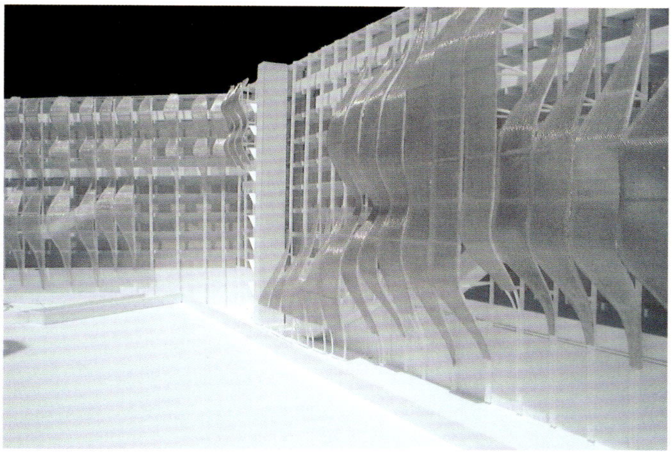

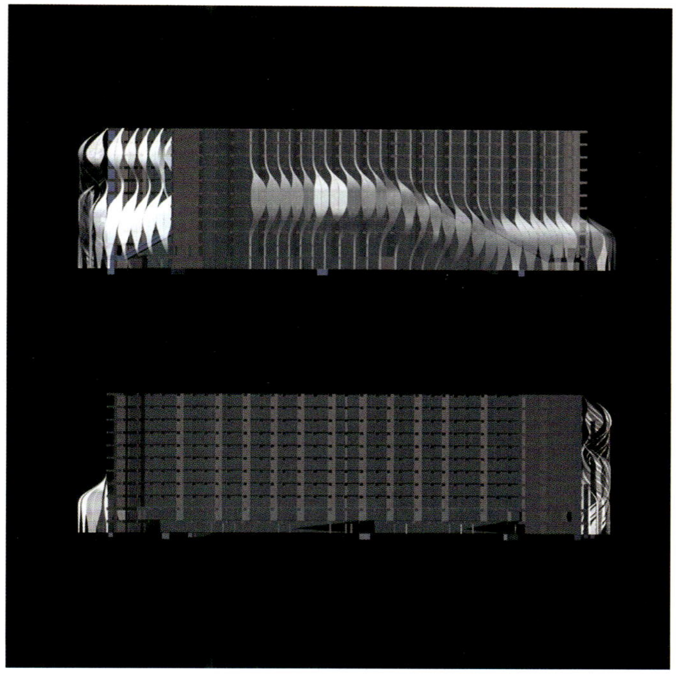

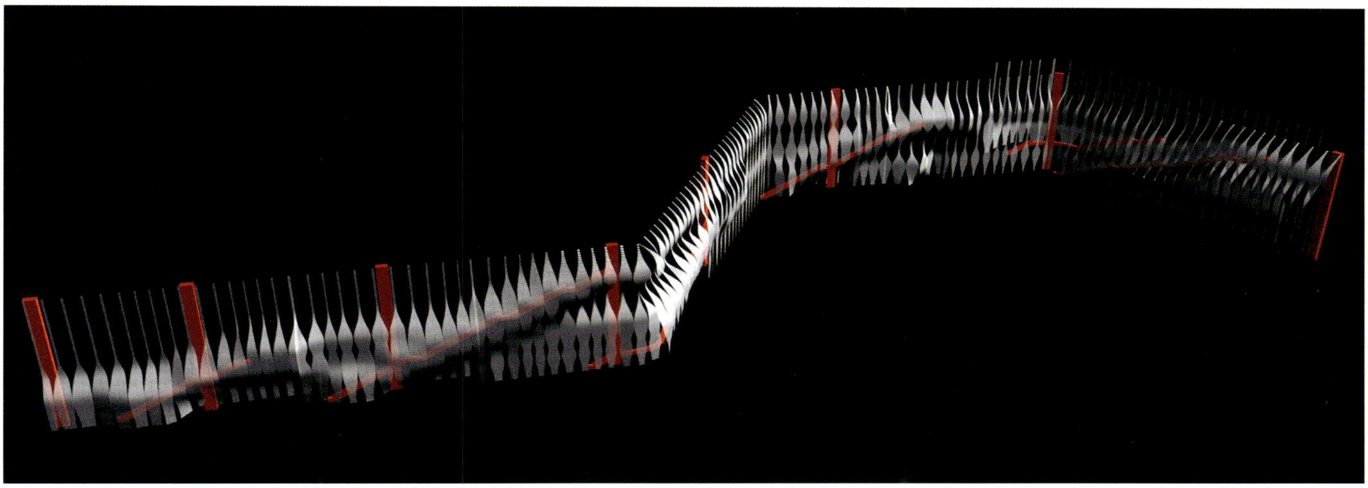

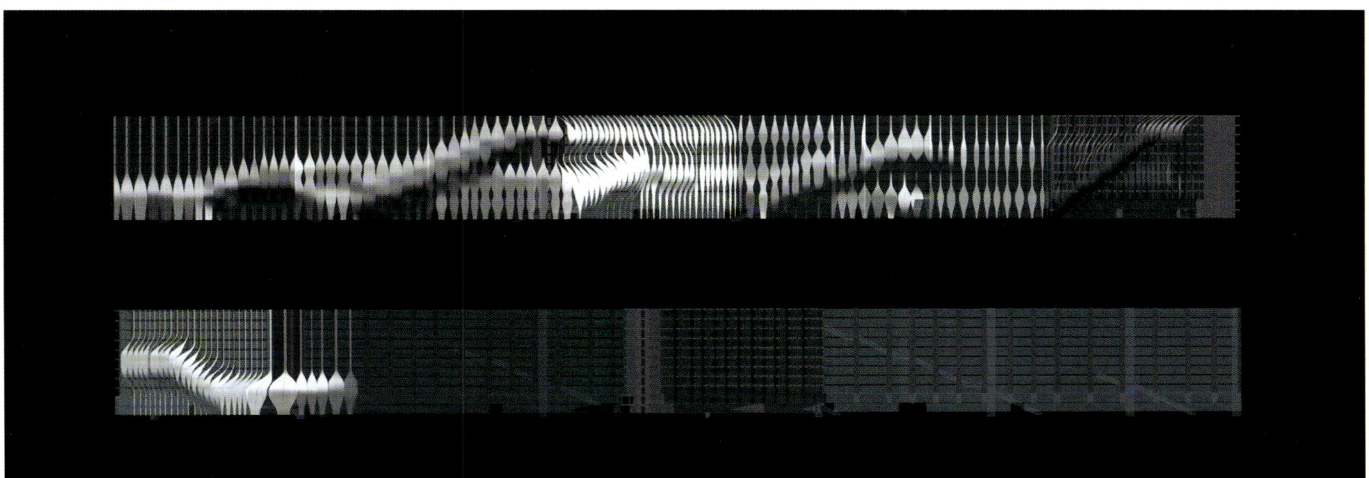

'Architecture is different to many other design fields because 1) practically it is about the assembly of a large constellation of elements into a whole that has an interior and an exterior that are continuous in terms of design, and 2) its design history is based on the continuity and hierarchy between interior and exterior and parts and whole, thus the discourse of facades, detailing, modularity, proportion, symmetry, and so on ... The relationship between parts and whole is essential to the evaluation of quality, meaning and experience of any architectural design.

'Parametric tools – that is, tools that blend the hierarchy of parts and whole – are extremely powerful for an architect because of this. Unfortunately, the initial response to parametrics was an abdication of the problem of the design of the whole in favour of the programming of the component. The use of parametric software is all about the design task shifting from either top-down or bottom-up to the territory of parts-to-whole fusion. I shy away from words like "feedback" and "synergy" between parts and whole because so far the experimental architects have just jumped from top-down determination of parts to bottom-up determination of wholes ... I find this theoretically naive and it avoids the most interesting thing about parametrics, and that is the ability to fuse the hierarchy of parts and whole to produce a deeply modulated whole as well as infinitesimal variation among parts.

'This is common from the scale of the 112 structural trusses of the Bijlmermeer facade to the 50,000 Alessi teapots, which are designed as a whole family. Parametric modelling is used in projects such as these to make the relation between parts and whole more complexly fused while maintaining design distinction across scale and hierarchy.'

Lynn describes the Embryological House as a strategy for the invention of domestic space that engages contemporary issues of variation, customisation and continuity, flexible manufacturing and assembly. A rigorous system of geometrical limits liberates an exfoliation of endless variations.

'I design not just one or two of the Embryological House instances. It is shocking how few architects get this, because they are so used to thinking of design as a once-and-for-all problem and not serially. Most architects want to understand the Embryological House experiment as a search for an ideal house – as if the whole collection of houses was a conceit to then select the best one. They are all equivalent. I love them all equally as if they were my children. The design problem was not the house, but the series, the entire infinitesimally extensive and intensive group.'

At the prototyping stage of the Embryological House, Lynn developed six instances exhibiting a unique range of domestic, spatial, functional, aesthetic and lifestyle constraints. In the project description he emphasises that:

'There is no ideal or original Embryological House, as every instance is perfect in its mutations. The formal perfection does not lie in the unspecified, banal and generic primitive, but in a combination of the unique, intricate variations of each instance and the continuous similarity of its relatives. The variations in specific house designs are sponsored by the subsistence of a

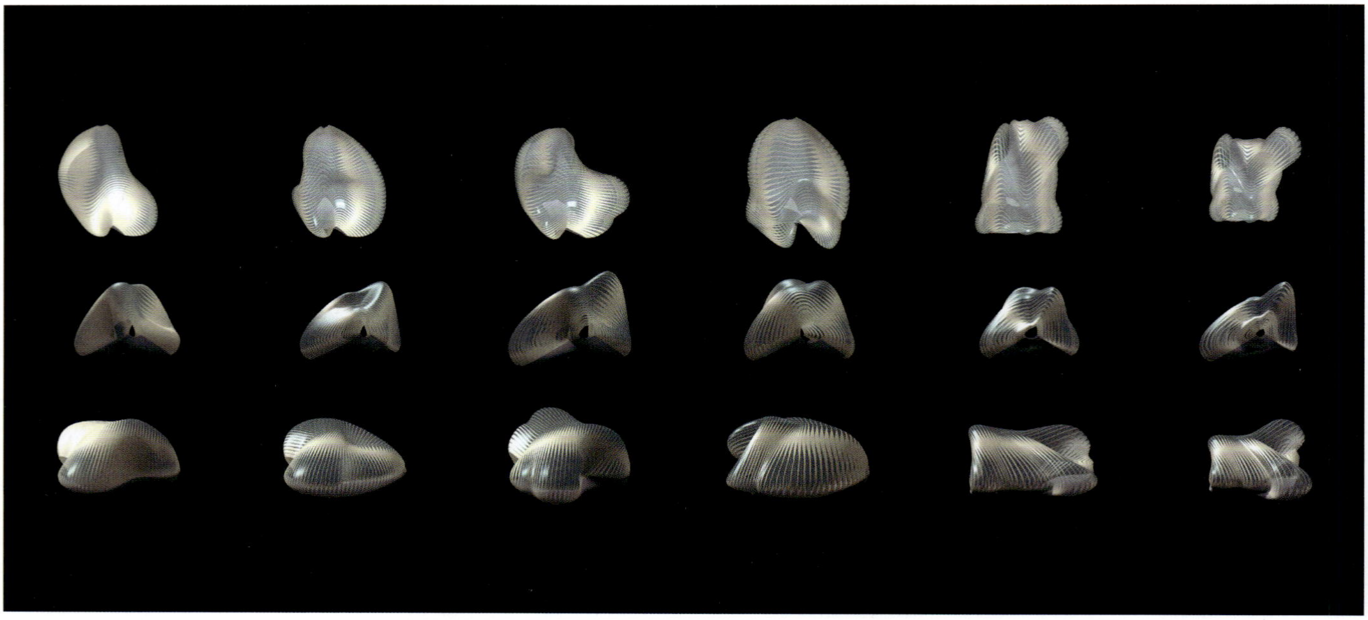

Greg Lynn, Embryological House, 1999
The Embryological House is a series of one-of-a-kind houses that are customised by Greg Lynn FORM for individual clients. The houses are adaptable to a full range of sites and climates. The minimum requirement for any site is a 30.5-metre (100-foot) diameter clear area of less than 30-degree slope for the house and its surrounding gardens, designed by Jeff Kipnis.

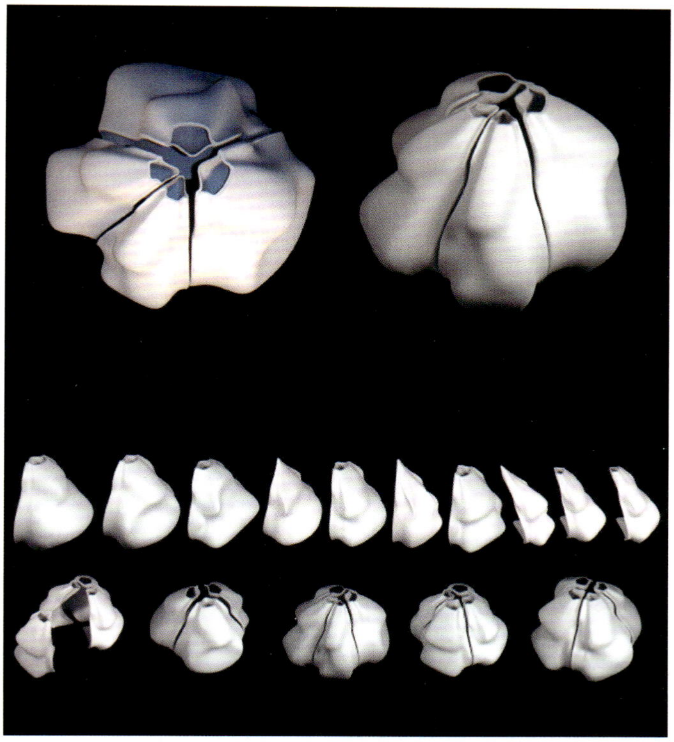

Greg Lynn, Alessi Tea & Coffee towers, 2003
The Tea & Coffee towers are an ensemble of mass-produced one-of-a-kind objects. The set is designed so that there are three modules of container: large- and medium-sized pots for hot water, coffee, tea and milk, and small containers for cream, sugar and lemon juice. These containers share the same form at their edges so that they can be combined in various radial arrangements. The pots are designed by combining nine differently shaped curves. The vessels are formed of thin metal titanium sheets using heat and pressure.

generic envelope of potential shape, alignment, adjacency and size between a fixed collection of elements. This marks a shift from a Modernist mechanical kit-of-parts design and construction technique to a more vital, evolving, biological model of embryological design and construction.'

Each of Lynn's parametric designs, like the product design for Alessi, represents one possible version of an infinite set of possibilities. The Tea & Coffee towers are an ensemble of mass-produced one-of-a-kind objects. Each of the containers shares the same form at its edges so that all can be combined in various radial arrangements, resulting in millions of possible unique settings.

Different design fields and production methods merge: 'The vessels are formed of thin metal titanium sheets using heat and pressure. Their surface retains the fine scale detail of the machined tool. The recently deregulated manufacturing process was invented for stealth aeroplane fabrication because of the quality of surface detail and the accuracy of wall thickness.

'The super-formed titanium follows the same general principles as vacuum-formed plastic. The design was refined at Greg Lynn FORM by CNC manufacturing of wood and composite formwork and testing through the vacuum-forming of plastic. Like plastic manufacturing, the super-formed metals introduce – unprecedented to the sensuous possibilities of form – a new variety of shapes through a single tool process and, finally, a degree of detail previously possible only with casting. The material itself makes for an incredibly lightweight and strong container appropriate to the military aerospace methods of its manufacture.'

And the differences between the various design fields also vanish as special-effects software, aerospace software and architectural design and engineering software begin to converge into fewer packages that do more and more.

'I find that the world of product design grasps this concept much more easily, that the design problems of a series, rather than of a single design, is the issue today. Identity, signature and meaning tend to move through series rather than single objects. Calculus, by the way, is the mathematics for defining these kinds of ensembles.'

Thus Lynn shares the found principles of calculus-based designs in his close collaborations with architects and designers from other fields.

From the Appropriation of Standardised Software to Scripting Customised Tools

Expertise and knowledge, rather than playful experimentation, here become increasingly important.

'I think the era of the happy accident is over in architectural design using computer-based design mediums, and now is the time for more depth and expertise in design. I see lots of people moving into programming with little or no design ambition or skill, and I would not advocate for another round of happy accidents and amateurism like we experienced in the 1990s (of which I was certainly a card-carrying member). Designers need to have an in-depth understanding and the ability to customise and manipulate their medium.'

Lynn's expertise with the digital medium has been less bound to a singular software, or software plug-in development, than to the integration of various existing software packages with hardware such as CNC routers, laser-cutters or 3-D rapid prototyping facilities. Lynn characterises this work as a 'loose and rather quasi-masonic project of software development' – an expertise he freely shares with others 'through teaching, lecturing or collaborating. This is not an altruism, but a desire to change the field for my own selfish reasons as well as to expand the possibilities for construction in general and to reap these benefits. There is a financial gain here for me, but the primary desire is to change the world. This is no different to Gehry Technologies,[9] which has to be a profitable business, but I suspect Frank's primary desire is also to change the world and the way architecture and construction work so that the new world he lives in is more amenable to the way he works creatively.

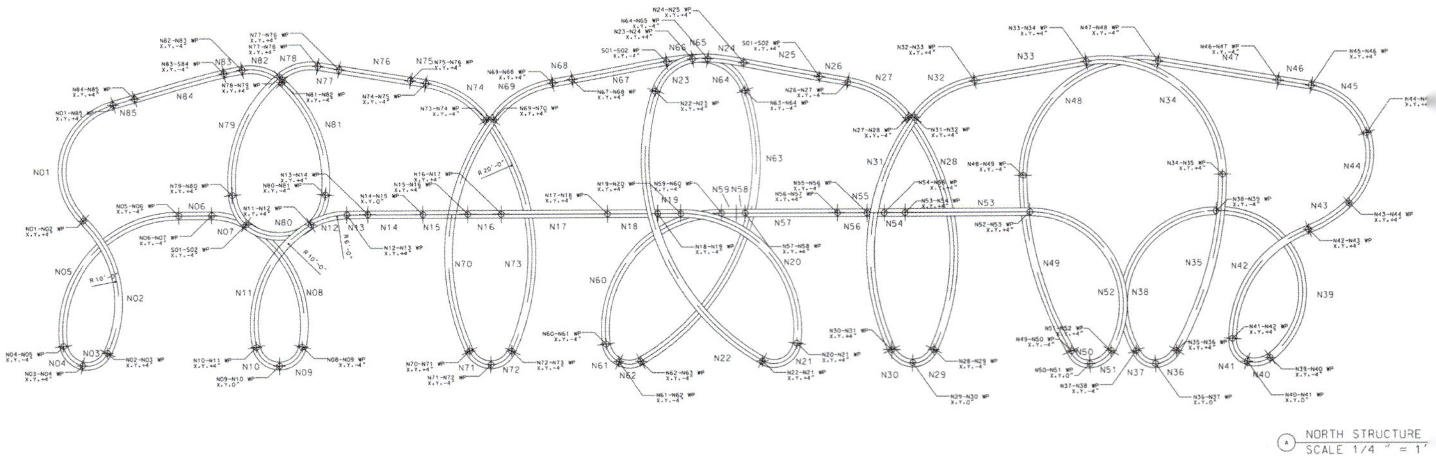

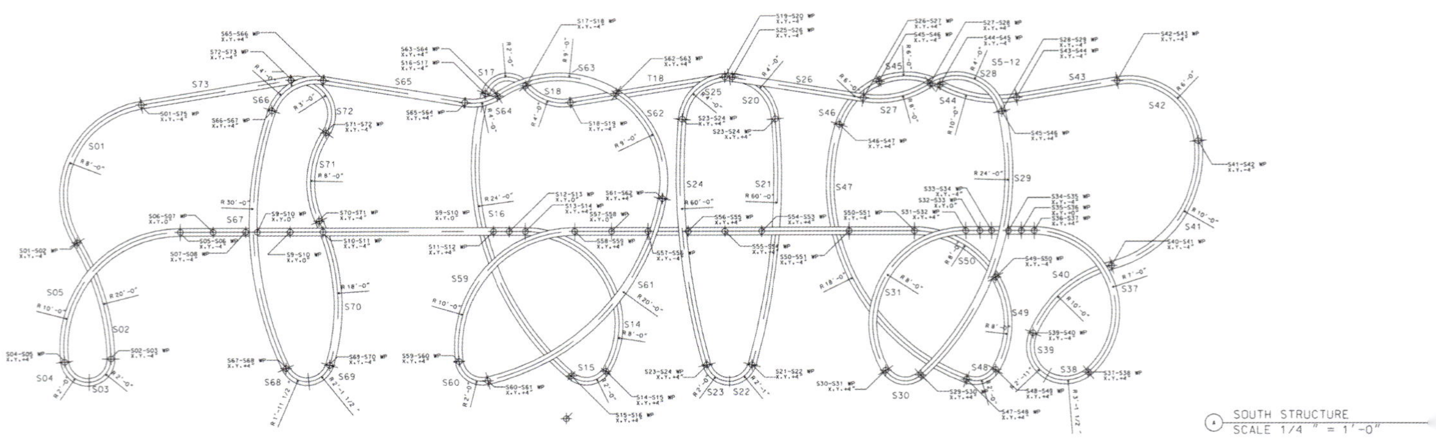

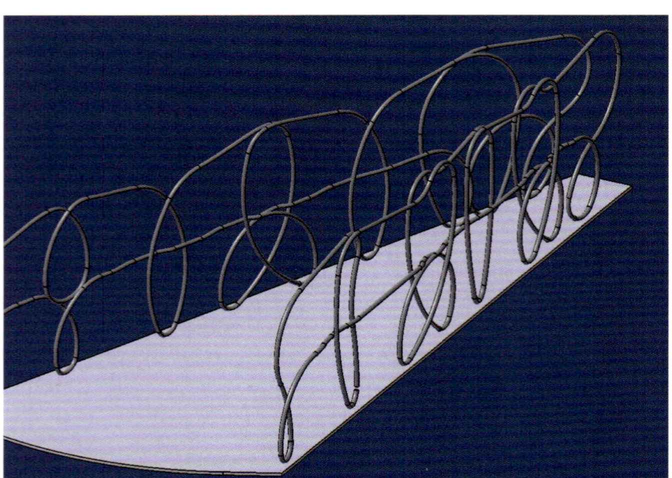

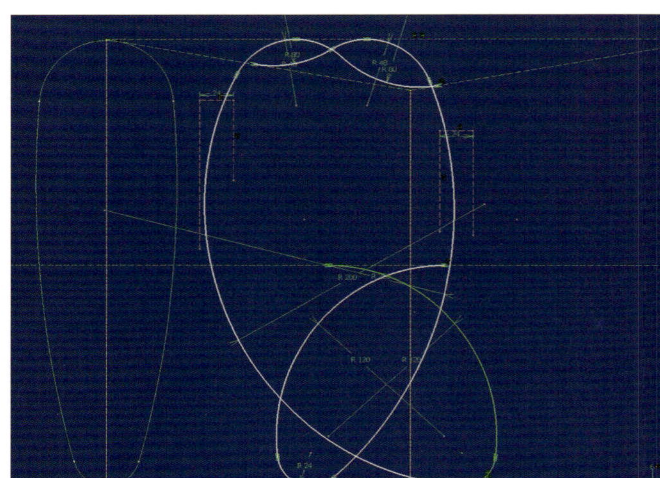

Greg Lynn, Slavin House, Venice, California, due for completion 2007
The Slavin House has been developed using MicroStation software. The house folds inside and outside rooms into a singular porous environment that occupies the entire triangular site. A single-storey occupiable structural truss defines the mass of the house, composed of only two continuous extruded and radially bent steel tubes, braided and looped through one another, which function simultaneously as horizontal and vertical members: beams and piloti. Each element of the house does more than one thing at a time: material and surface continuities make volumes both voids and solids, inside and outside, continuous fillets and radial tangents enable the curvilinear basket structure to both support and create hollow courts. This flowing continuity of upper and lower levels, of roof and ground, and of voided hollow structural baskets and mass, engenders a new kind of porous domestic space that folds together indoor and outdoor spaces, structural frame, void lightwells, solid figures, a translucent bounding envelope and an undulating ground plane into a suspended mixture.

So Lynn's focus on the customisation of his design tools is marked by three key issues: the convergence of software, the shift to a calculus-based medium instead of a modular medium of fractional dimensions and, finally, the history of holism.

However, faced with a growing practice and larger, more complex building commissions, Lynn has now turned away from standardised software packages and is instead concentrating on the development of customised tools.

'We do some scripting and programming in MicroStation Generative Components, but this involves sending people in the office to training sessions with Robert Aish as well as emailing him back and forth for specific tasks and having him come to the office every six to nine months. We started using Gehry Technologies software and have found the parametrics very robust, and we are programming and writing custom design tools with this software more and more. For discrete tasks we use this software all the time now.

'For the design of my house, Slavin House, we are doing the entire project in this package to test the limits of the software. It is very impressive and pretty easy to jump into making custom tools and doing parametric modelling. We also have people in the office training with Dennis Shelden and Christian Ceccato over at Gehry Technologies and so we impose on them less for support. However, I am also collaborating with Frank on a project, so we are over at his office all the time: there are many more layers of collaboration than only the software, thus the use of Gehry Technologies software is very provocative at many levels and is having a pretty significant effect on my work.'

Design Matters

So Lynn's focus on the customisation of his design tools is marked by three key issues: the convergence of software, the shift to a calculus-based medium instead of a modular medium of fractional dimensions and, finally, the history of holism. Nevertheless, for Lynn, both the appropriation of existing code and the writing of new code are merely means to an end: the architect's desire to realise a design idea. Often, even unnoticed, new design and manufacturing strategies are invented – through the architect's rigorous realisation of design – which may or may not include the writing and rewriting of code.

Regardless of his fascination with the appropriation and customisation of existing software, for Lynn it is still 'less important for the individual architect to learn how to develop his or her own software tools, to learn how to write code, than to learn how to design'. AD

Notes

1 Particularly notable was the introduction of Alias and Softimage. The Toronto-based firm Alias was founded in 1983, and created an easy-to-use software package to produce realistic 3-D video animation for the advertising industry and postproduction houses. Universal Studios was one of its earliest clients, followed by General Motors (GM) in 1985. At GM, Alias was used to incorporate NURBS (non-uniform rational basis spline) technology into the company's existing spline-based CAD system. Based on cardinal splines rather than polygonal lines, Alias/1 was producing uniquely smooth lines or surfaces. By 1989, many cars, like those of BMW, Honda and Volvo, were being designed using 3-D software created by Alias. In 1996, Alias and Wavefront have been merged to form AliasWavefront.

Softimage was founded in 1986 by the Canadian film-maker Daniel Langlois, who wanted to create animated movies. His vision was the creation of 3-D animation software not only for, but by, artists. Softimage developed rapidly. Most of its customers are production studios, such as Industrial Light and Magic, Digital Domain, Sega, Nintendo and Sony, who have used the software mainly to create animation for feature films such as *Jurassic Park*, *Titanic*, *The Matrix* and *Star Wars*, or for games like Super Mario 64, Tekken, Virtual Fighter, Wave Race and NBA Live.

2 Greg Lynn, *AD Folding in Architecture*, Wiley-Academy, 1993; revised edition 2004.

3 Greg Lynn, *Folds, Bodies & Blobs*, Princeton Architectural Press (New York), 1999.

4 Greg Lynn, *Animate Form*, Princeton Architectural Press (New York), 1999.

5 Greg Lynn, *Architecture for an Embryologic Housing*, Birkhäuser (Basel and Cambridge), 2003.

6 Greg Lynn, Claudia Gould and Tom Friedman, *Intricacy*, Distributed Art Pub Inc (New York), 2003.

7 MicroStation was originally developed by Bentley Systems in the 1980s for the engineering and architecture fields: it was first used primarily for creating construction drawings, but developed quickly adding advanced modelling and rendering features, including Boolean solids, ray-tracing, and keyframe animation to its features. MicroStation furthermore provides specialised environments for architecture, civil engineering, mapping or plant design among others.

8 The French philosopher Henri Bergson (1859–1941) argued that intuition is more profound than intellect. His writings *Creative Evolution* (1907) and *Matter and Memory* (1896) attempted to integrate the findings of biological science with a theory of consciousness, challenging the mechanistic view of nature.

9 Gehry Technologies, formed in 2002 by the R&D group of Frank O Gehry and Associates, writes and rewrites its own software programs based on CATIA, a design software originally developed for the aerospace industry by Dassault Systemes of France, with the aim of facilitating the design and production of architecture. Several years ago James Glymph, a senior partner at Gehry's firm, began developing individual software tools to facilitate the construction of Gehry's increasingly complicated designs. Contractors used the software to produce exact measurements of the steel, wood and other materials needed in the projects. Gehry Technologies also assists other architectural firms, offering consulting services, research and development, and technology products, including Digital Project, a suite of software applications based on the CATIA V5 modelling engine.

Contributors

Karl Chu is the principal of METAXY, an architectural studio that engages in the research and development of genetic architecture. He is the director of the Institute for Genetic Architecture at the GSAPP, Columbia University. He currently teaches at Columbia, Pratt Institute and ESARQ, Universitat Internacional de Catalunya, Barcelona, where he is the co-director of the Genetic Architecture programme.

Evan Douglis is the principal of Evan Douglis Studio, an architecture and interdisciplinary design firm committed to self-generative systems, membrane technology, contemporary fabrication techniques and multimedia installations as applied to a range of projects. His work was showcased in *10x10_2* (Phaidon Press, 2005). He was one of 10 international design firms selected by *Architectural Record* as part of its December 2005 Design Vanguard Competition profile. More recently, he was selected as one of eight international designers to participate as a fellow in the 2006 residency programme 'Brick Project: Ceramics and Architecture' at the European Ceramic Work Centre in the Netherlands. He was a finalist nominee for the 2006 James Beard Foundation – Restaurant Design Awards, and received a Merit Design Award for the 2006 International FEIDAD Competitin. He is currently the Chair of the Undergraduate Department at Pratt Institute in New York.

Pia Ednie-Brown is a senior lecturer at RMIT University in the architecture programme and at the Spatial Information Architecture Laboratory (SIAL). Her research practice, onomatopoeia, negotiates multiple research nodes, including interactive installations, animation, sculpture, creative writing and theoretical analysis. Her research is oriented towards articulating new paradigms of composition, incorporating concerns for embodied knowing and radical empiricism, emergence theory and computation, politics and aesthetics.

Haresh Lalvani is a professor at the School of Architecture, Pratt Institute, where he is also co-director (with William Katavolos) of the Center for Experimental Structures. He received a PhD in architecture from the University of Pennsylvania. He has received awards from NYSTAR, the Graham Foundation, the National Endowment for the Arts and the National Institute for Architectural Education, and received the Pioneers' Award from the Space Structures Research Centre, University of Surrey, UK, for his contributions to space structures. He is credited with numerous discoveries in morphology and is the originator of Genomic Architecture based on the morphological genome he has been mapping over the years.

John Lobell received his architecture degrees from the University of Pennsylvania, and is a professor of architecture at Pratt Institute. He is the author of *Between Silence and Light: Spirit in the Architecture of Louis I Kahn* (Shambhala, 1979), and is currently addressing the implications of quantum theory for architecture.

Greg Lynn is principal of Greg Lynn FORM. In addition to being a studio professor at UCLA, he is the Davenport visiting professor at Yale University and a professor at the University of Applied Arts in Vienna. He was previously a professor at the ETH in Zurich and Columbia University. His architectural designs have received numerous awards and his work is regularly exhibited internationally. He is a member of United Architects, with whom he participated in the site design competition for Ground Zero. He writes and lectures widely on architectural design and theory. He is the author of *Folds, Bodies, Blobs: Collected Essays* (La Lettre Volée, 1998), *Animate Form* (Princeton Architectural Press, 1999) and *Embryological House* (Princeton Architectural Press, forthcoming).

Malcolm McCullough is the author of *Digital Ground: Architecture, Pervasive Computing and Environmental Knowing* (MIT Press, 2004) and *Abstracting Craft: The Practiced Digital Hand* (MIT Press, 1996). He is associate professor of architecture at the Taubman College of Architecture and Urban Planning at the University of Michigan, and previously served on the design faculty at Carnegie Mellon and at Harvard.

CEB Reas is an artist employing ideas explored in conceptual and minimal artworks as focused through the contemporary lens of software. He teaches in the Design|Media Arts department at UCLA. His classes provide a foundation for thinking about computers as a medium for artistic exploration and set a structure for advanced enquiry into culture, technology and aesthetics. With Ben Fry, he has created Processing, a programming language and environment for generating images, animation and sound.

Ingeborg M Rocker received her Diploma of Engineering from the Technische Universität in Aachen, Germany. In 1995 she graduated with an MSAAD from Columbia University, where her research concentrated on computer-generated design. She worked at Eisenman Architects as a project architect and designer from 1996 to 1999. Between 1999 and 2005 she worked at Princeton University on her PhD 'Evolving Structures: the Architecture of the Digital Medium', and received her MA in 2003. She has also worked with the leading German media theoretician Friedrich Kittler at the Humboldt University in Berlin, and has taught and co-taught at Columbia, Princeton and the University of Pennsylvania. Since 2005 she has been an assistant professor at Harvard's Graduate School of Design. She is the author of *Re-coded: Studio Rocker* (Aedes Berlin, 2005).

Dennis Shelden is a founder and chief technology officer of Gehry Technologies, a building industry technology company formed in 2001 by the R&D team of Frank Gehry Partners. He joined Gehry Partners in 1997 and became director of the firm's computation efforts in 2000. Prior to this he worked at firms including Ove Arup & Partners, Consultants' Computation Bureau and Cyra Systems. He lectures and conducts research in building industry process advancement and in design computation and cognition, and has been a visiting faculty member at the Southern California Institute of Architecture and MIT. He holds a BSc in art and design, an MSc in civil and environmental engineering, and a PhD in computation and architectural design from MIT.

Mike Silver holds a masters in building design from Columbia University, and is a LeFevre '29 research fellow for the Knowlton School of Architecture in Columbus, Ohio, a Sanders Fellow at the University of Michigan, former director of digital media at the Yale School of Architecture and a studio instructor at Harvard's Graduate School of Design. He is also the author of numerous books and articles including *Pamphlet Architecture 19: Reading, Drawing, Building* (Princeton Architectural Press, 1996) and AD *Mapping in the Age of Digital Media* (March/April 2003). He currently directs a multidisciplinary design laboratory based in New York. Current work explores technologies such as LIDAR, CFD (computational fluid dynamics) simulation, computer programming (Automason Ver 1.0) and a variety of new robotic fabrication tools including numerically controlled wire-EDM and digital foam shaping. Silver currently teaches advanced design at Pratt Institute.

Stephen Wolfram is a scientist, author and business leader. He is the creator of the software system Mathematica, the author of the highly acclaimed book *A New Kind of Science* (Wolfram Media, 2002) and the founder and CEO of Wolfram Research.

Contents

98+

106+

Unified Design: Collaborative Working at Arup Associates

Designs for headquarters for British Waterways, Apsley, Hertfordshire
Black-and-white model of the building's concept design.

Global telecommunication networks and the emergence of a new digital tool base have informed the reshaping of design practice worldwide. As discussed in detail in the next issue of AD, *Collective Intelligence in Design* (no 5, vol 76, 2006), ever-evolving groups of designers, engineers, material scientists, manufacturers, contractors and even financiers are now working together across time zones and organisations. Though these current shifts have certainly facilitated a greater fluidity of exchange between disciplines, working across the professional setting is not a wholly new phenomenon. For over four decades, London-based Arup Associates have collaborated in design as a team of architects and engineers, sitting within the greater corporate framework of the Arup Group. Declan O'Carroll, a principal at Arup Associates, tells Helen Castle how Arup Associates are now launching the Unified Design Unit that is set to recast Ove Arup's ethos of totality in design for the 21st century.

Arup Associates is based in a Regency terrace on the south side of Fitzroy Square, designed by the Adam brothers. It is one of a number of buildings that form Arup and Partners' London 'campus' in Fitzrovia on the west side of Tottenham Court Road (there are premises in adjacent Fitzoy Street, Maple Place, Howland Street and Whitfield Street, as well as Tottenham Court Road itself). Fitzroy Square is surprisingly quiet for central London: pedestrianised on all four sides, it has no through traffic bar the odd passer-by scuttling through on his or her way to the nearby hospital; the central square is shaded with handsome plane trees. The classical, Portland stone facade of 38 Fitzroy Square, though, has little bearing on what goes on inside. On walking through the main entrance to the left one is drawn back across the house's front into a modern, wooden-floored lobby that spans its width. Once through the security turnstile at reception, the building is given over almost entirely to floors of open-plan studio space with the circulation pushed over to the right-hand side. Any sense of the original domestic Georgian interior has been entirely extracted; clusters of young designers sit at work stations or gather in small meeting rooms for project discussions in a quiet hubbub of concentrated activity.

One senses that the discrepancy between inside and outside is a condition that Arup Associates has grown accustomed to. The global recognition of Arup as a name is so strong that it is almost inevitable that Arup Associates are often bundled together with the engineering group's wider activities. Conversely their design skills mean that they can all too simplistically be regarded as the architectural side of Arup. The practice came about in 1963 as a parallel partnership between architect Philip Dowson and founding engineer Ove Arup. Over the ensuing decades, it has remained true to Ove Arup's aspirations for collaboration between the professions and wholeness in architecture. In its practice brochure, Arup Associates invokes Ove Arup's vision:

'"Total Architecture" implies that all relevant design decisions have been considered together and have been integrated into a whole by a well-organised team. This is an ideal worth striving for, for artistic wholeness or excellence depends upon it.'

Today the practice continues Ove Arup's pan-disciplinary ethos, having extended its reach from architecture and structural engineering to environmental engineering, cost consultancy, urban design and product design. A hundred-strong group – a sizeable practice in design terms – it also manages 'to punch above its weight in terms of visibility'[1] within the greater organisation of Arup, which is now 7,500 globally. There is no doubt that this perpetual need to both continually dodge misconceptions and explain themselves has worked in Arup Associates' favour, instilling them with not only a strong sense of identity – defined in relief not only by what they are not, but also by what they offer

The collaborative atmosphere at Arup Associates.

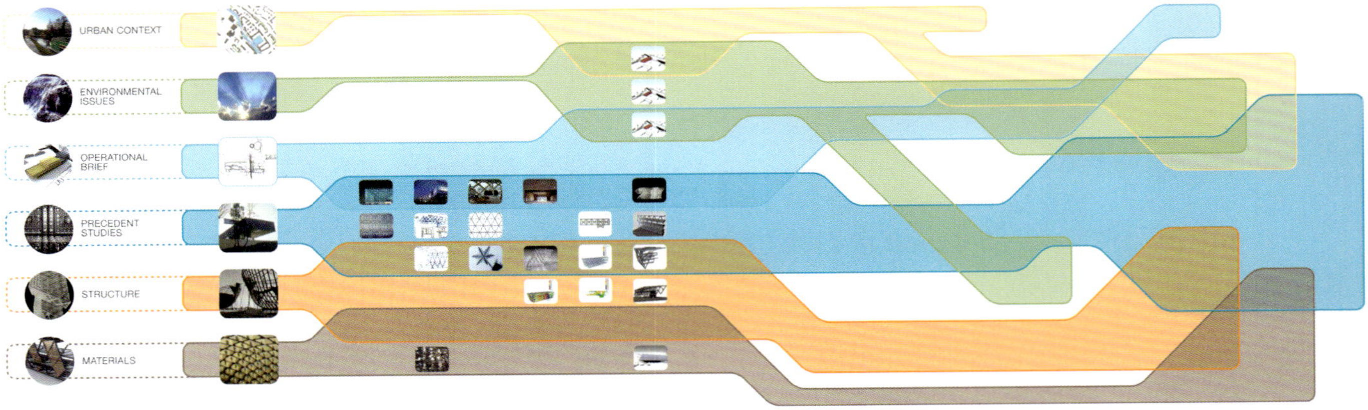

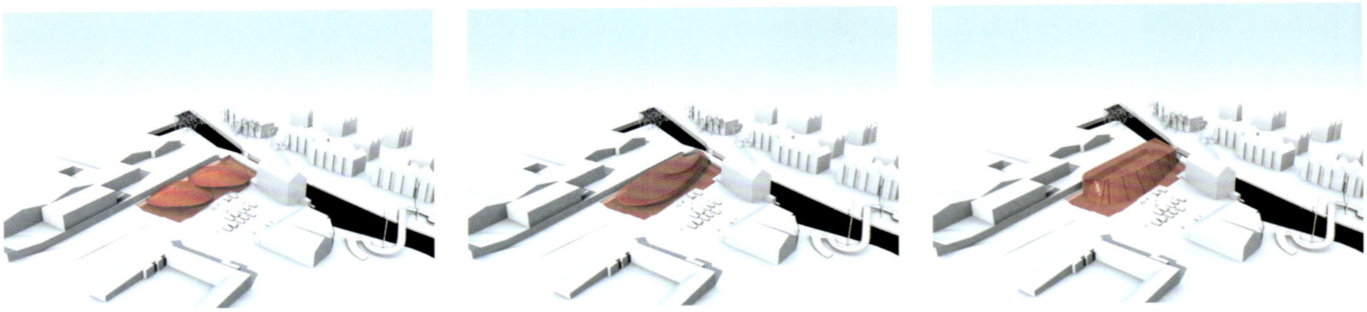

The new offices for British Waterways offered Arup Associates the opportunity of developing the sort of 'alternative creative framework' that Declan O'Carroll is advocating in the Unified Design Unit. From the initial stages onwards, the design was fitted to the circumstances of the proposal rather than working to a prescribed style or remit.
Top: Design evolution mapping developed by Arup Associates in order to sift and synthesise the data provided by a diverse range of engineers and other consultants, such as the Rossmore Group, maximising the potential spatial performance and occupational use of the British Waterways headquarters.
Above: Forms developed by the environmental engineers at Arup Associates in order to experiment with means of producing the optimum envelope orientated to the building's microclimate.

in terms of their distinct philosophy.

Declan O'Carroll, the principal who is leading the initiative to establish the new research and design unit within the practice, is very aware of Arup Associates' lineage; he has worked in the practice since graduating in architecture from Manchester, and was first spotted by Richard Frewer from Arup Associates when Frewer was sitting on a panel at the Royal Society of Arts awarding student travel scholarships. Energetic, enthusiastic and articulate, O'Carroll is passionate about the pertinence of the firm's philosophy for contemporary architecture and engineering. He holds true to the practice's belief in a humane, 'life-enhancing architecture' and one that is driven by intellectual goals rather than the vicissitudes of design fashions. A reformer working from the inside, he is a member of a relatively young leadership team including Jonathan Rose, Mike Beaven, Dipesh Patel and Rob Saunders, all in their late 30s and early 40s, who are keen to see Arup Associates evolve for today's challenges.

The evolution that O'Carroll himself has in mind with the founding of a new unit within the practice is focused on creative techniques and methods and on the forging of a new generation of collaborative partnerships. This is intended to not only revolutionise the manner in which architecture and the built environment is produced, but also to reap the rewards of drawing on specialist knowledge bases at the earliest stages of a design's inception. It effectively redefines what it previously meant to be multidisciplinary: a paradigm shift that maximises the power of collective creativity.

O'Carroll puts the origins of the company's multidisciplinary approach in its historic context: 'Arup Associates pioneered a step change in the 1960s with the creation of a unique single studio bringing together the core architecture and engineering disciplines. This was a direct response to challenges posed by the increasingly complex highly serviced buildings at the end of the 20th century. The emphasis was on the coordination and integration of the building parts, seamlessly brought together and assembled to create a

Arup Associates and Simon Patterson, Plantation Lane, London, 2005
By cutting this alleyway through British Land's new office development at Fenchurch Street, in the City, Arup Associates were able to create a public art space with an enlivening focus for the immediate area.

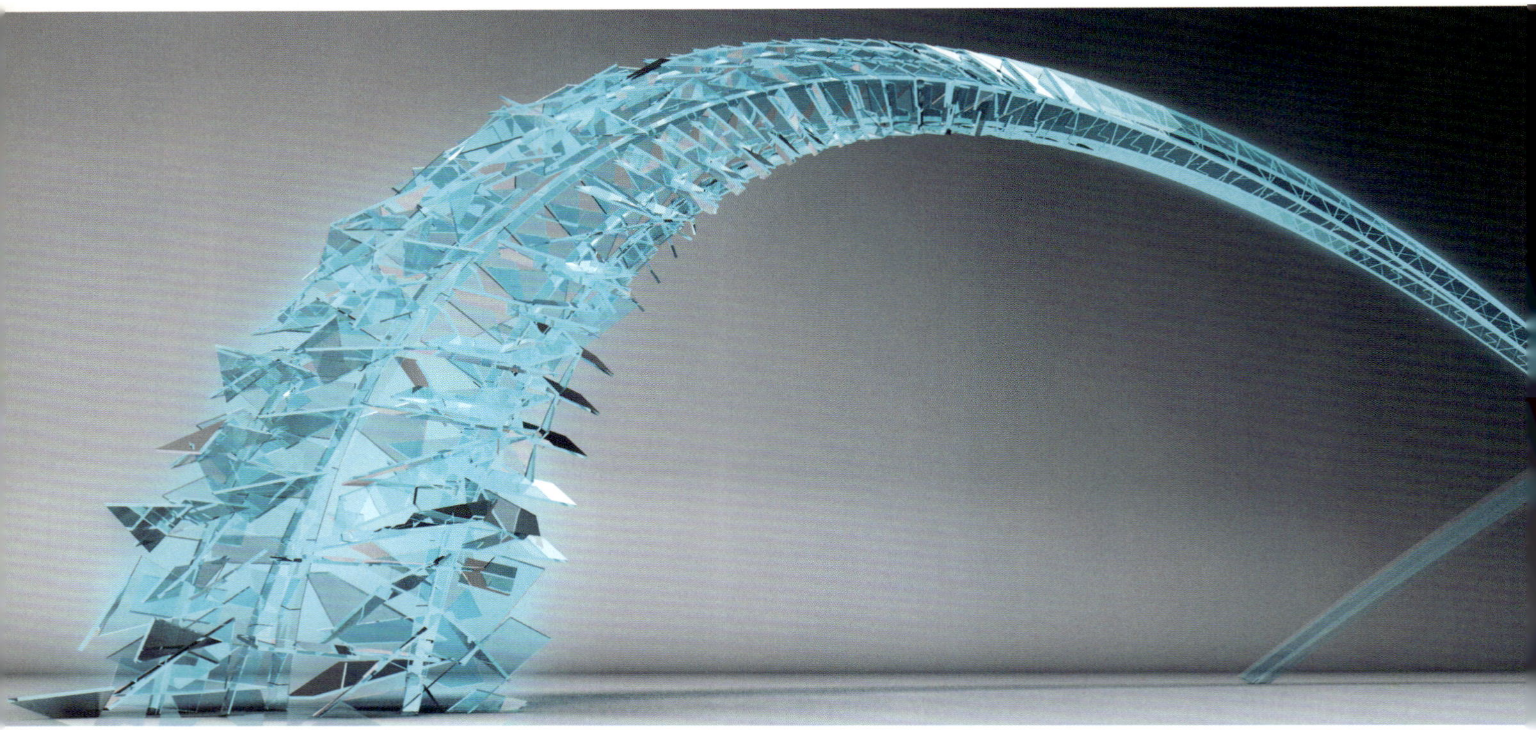

Arup Associates and Simon Patterson, concept illustration for Rocket Junction, Liverpool
This new gateway feature for the east of the city is a pivot to the area's regeneration.

whole.'[2] Rather than being interested in applying different professional skills to a building that is a sum of parts, O'Carroll is interested much more in finding a means of working that aspires to 'unify the Whole'.[3]

In order to uncover the totality of the whole, O'Carroll is proposing research and experiment in architecture and engineering that is centred on real buildings and their inhabitants rather than the novelty of forms or visual impact. Sensing that there is 'a depressing malaise within the architectural community', he believes that 'the substantial questions of how architecture is of "present use" have been sidelined'.[4] Architects are all too often delivering a design solution dictated by a house style, which the client is buying into as if it is off the peg regardless of context or use; if they are purchasing a Gehry building, they require it to have all the signature flourishes and forms. 'The paradox of "signature style" does not address the complexities of contemporary living,' says O'Carroll. 'The *bricolage* of our built environment is inextricably linked to our sense of self and acts as a key influence in the quality of our whole-life experience. It is natural, therefore, to explore radical alternatives, to invent and develop new creative methodologies that respond to a complex world.'[5]

Whereas the structural and environmental engineers are all too often brought in to clear up after the architects, it is O'Carroll's desire to realise the potential of cross-disciplinary input at the earliest stages of design. He cites the example of the headquarters that Arup Associates are designing for British Waterways to accommodate 120 staff on a brownfield site at Apsley, between Hemel Hempstead and Watford. Previous to establishing a conceptual design, they are developing three or four different options for the client that adopt distinct methodologies with varying drivers. They are, for instance, working with the Rossmore Group, behavioural and occupational psychologists who consult in performance improvement and have worked extensively with London Underground, on a spatial template for the occupation of the building. This is visualised by the Arup software team, who are working out of the basement in 38 Fitzroy Square, creating programs that will transfer Rossmore's data into a visual three-dimensional medium that will help establish whether the client will, in fact, require the 1,000 square metres (10,764 square feet) of open-plan office space that the developers have told them they need.

Simultaneously, the environmental engineers at Arup are developing solutions that produce the optimum envelope orientated to its macro-climate. And naturally, they are developing architectural solutions with bubble diagrams and site analysis, taking into account sight lines and aspect. 'Orthodox models of creativity, with their singular focus on the visual,

have disillusioned the public,' comments O'Carroll. 'There is a clear need to develop an alternative creative framework: a flexible model for creativity that informs all design output with a sense of integrity, but which is liberated from any prescribed style. The language of any proposal is then particular to its circumstances, so that physical form and material evolve from a natural synthesis.'[6]

This is a deliberate attempt on behalf of Arup Associates to challenge themselves and unearth characteristics that can be visualised for the client. Rather than presenting clients with a priori solutions, they are sifting and synthesising the conceptual designs with them, pushing towards a compelling holistic solution.

British Waterways is not Declan O'Carroll's first foray into collaboration with parties outside Arup. As project principal, he played an instrumental role in the engagement of Turner-nominated artist Simon Patterson at Plantation Lane: the alleyway Arup Associates persuaded British Land to cut through their Plantation Place and Plantation South development at Fenchurch Street in EC3, and transform into a public art space.[7] The enlivening and humanising effect of this insertion of pavement text and lunar images on LED screens on this corner of the City is very much in evidence. It represents an almost seamless stitching of artistic and architectural skills, as Jay Merrick has described in the *Independent*: 'There is an engrossing subtlety to the way the new lane and the artwork have been arranged ... For a start, the lane is not flat – it arcs very slightly, and its width varies. These "moves", coupled with the way the screen has been positioned, mean that the view from either end of Plantation Lane becomes dynamic: there's a gentle skewing of both the vertical and horizontal planes ... You're looking at a collage of art, and old and new architecture, that also allows historical incident a place in this carefully arranged postmodern visual cut-up.'[8]

Arup Associates have also involved artists in the massing strategy for their mixed-used residential scheme in Chatham, Kent, and at Rocket Junction in Liverpool they are again working with Simon Patterson, this time on a new gateway feature to the Edge Lane corridor that will provide a major piece of public art for the city's eastern approach.

Despite the very apparent design benefits of Arup Associates' highly collaborative way of working, it is undisputable that it throws up obstacles for everyday commercial practice. There may be a thrust towards the multidisciplinary in academia and among smaller boutique firms, but Arup Associates remain an anomaly among the bigger, established practitioners. Clients have to acquire the Associates' professional services as a team, which means they have to be convinced at the outset that they want to take the entire package

Arup Campus, Solihull, 2000
Left: This building for Arup brought together existing offices from Birmingham and Coventry, providing an energy-efficient and flexible space for 350 people. It outwardly expresses its sustainable features in its use of natural construction materials. It is a demonstration of Arup Associates' belief in the long-term investment in the working environment.

Druk White Lotus School, Western Himalayas, North India
Below: This ongoing project that Arup Associates developed as part of an initiative of the Drukpa Trust has enabled the company to develop a long-term living community scheme that is appropriate both to the local vernacular and sustainable use.

(environmental and structural engineering as well architectural design). This also negates conventional commercial control mechanisms in which project managers conspire to 'divide and rule' over the professional parties engaged on a scheme.

The Arup Associates' set-up, purely because it lies outside the norm, can all too easily be perceived as challenging. It certainly requires a special sort of enlightened client. Clients not only have to be able to recognise the advantages of Arup Associates' joined-up thinking, but also be in it for the long haul rather than the short term and thus seeking measurable qualities from their architecture; Arup Associates have a programme of revisiting their buildings and assessing their performance. It necessitates an overt desire on the part of clients to create a high-quality environment over the instant gratification of an attention-grabbing image or form, or the lowest price per square metre. It is ideal for companies who are, in effect, investors in people, their staff's working environment – and the broader environment beyond.

Arup Associates are well versed in building quality office space and company headquarters, as demonstrated by BT Brentwood (2000), Arup Campus in Solihull (2000) and The Square Stockley Park in Middlesex (1999).

Plantation Place, which Arup Associates completed for the property developers British Land in 2005, with its natural ventilation, engaging spatial layout and openable windows has proved a more attractive prospect for tenants than Foster's iconic Gherkin which was completed in 2004, but which has been more difficult to let. It is also an approach that could now prove timely. After the initial push towards flexible working and outsourcing, companies are now coming to realise the benefits of enriching the working environments of their staff with IT companies like Microsoft leading the way not only in terms of the financial packages they are offering to retain their staff, but also on site amenities.[9] 'Enlightened clients,' believes O'Carroll, 'recognise the power of design, and wish to challenge the usual binary client–designer relationships. In this way new alliances are fostered that remove the traditional discipline boundaries.'

As well as being outside the game in terms of their organisational and working strategies, the fact that Arup Associates do not chase trends or put on conspicuous displays of architectural design means that they do not 'have a voice readily received by the press'.[10] For instance, though a project like Plantation Lane has attracted national and architectural media attention, it is an artistic collaborative effort in place-making rather than for its architectural design.[11] Discussion of the architectural quality remains implied rather than explicit. One of the most highly recognised of their international projects in recent years is the Druk White Lotus School in the Western Himalayas of North India.[12] An initiative led by the Drukpa Trust, a UK registered charity under the patronage of the Dalai Lama, the school, for 750 pupils, has a very simple architecture of robust materials drawing on the vernacular design of local monasteries. It is organised as an ongoing nonprofit scheme, and Arup selects graduates to send on a programme there for six months at a time. The expertise here lies in optimising sustainable resources and drawing on local knowledge for the design of the detailing and the symbolic aspect of the architecture. It is the environmental and human aspect of the scheme that has brought it to the world's attention, rather than flamboyant architectonics.

There is no doubt that with the launch of the new Unified Design Unit, Arup Associates is taking a valuable 'opportunity to redefine' its 'ambitions'.[13] From a design perspective, the emphasis on the creation of new generative processes that harness the skills of other knowledge bases is courageous, exciting and generous, as it gives over much fought-over ground in the conceptual stages to other specialists. It is a brave recognition by O'Carroll and his team that conventional architectural design as it stands is 'not a thorough investigation'[14] and needs to question its point of departure and the very premises on which it is built. The fact that this research is being applied and taken up in a practice setting, where it becomes directly relevant feeding into future projects, is both invaluable and proof that Arup Associates is prepared to continue in what it believes in, even when this requires going against the grain of conventional business and practice models. 'Our challange' says O'Carroll, 'is re-designing people back to into our design culture'. Δ

Helen Castle is Editor of Architectural Design and Executive Commissioning Editor of the Wiley-Academy architecture list at John Wiley & Sons.

Notes

1. In conversation with Declan O'Carroll, 27 April 2006.
2. Notes by Declan O'Carroll on 'Arup Associates' New Research and Design Unit', sent by email April 2006.
3. Ibid.
4. Ibid.
5. Ibid.
6. Ibid.
7. Jay Merrick, Declan O'Carroll and Simon Patterson, 'Public Art as Civic Space', Thursday 20 October, 2005. The Gallery, 77 Cowcross Street, London EC1M 6BP, and Paul Brislin (ed), *Plantation Lane: Time and Tide*, RIBA Enterprises (London), 2005.
8. Jay Merrick, *Independent*, 3 November 2004.
9. Diane Bass, 'Microsoft spends more to keep staff', *International Herald Tribune*, Friday 19 May 2006.
10. Declan O'Carroll, 27 April 2006.
11. Jay Merrick, *Independent*, 3 November 2004; Rob Gregory, *Architectural Review*, January 2005.
12. In 2003, Arup and Partners and Arup Associates won British Consultants and Construction Bureau – International Expertise Awards, sponsored by *The Times*, for the project; the firm also won three awards with the building from World Architecture in 2002; Jonathan Glancey also nominated it best international building of the year in his column in The *Guardian*, 'From Buddhists to Golfers', 16 December 2002.
13. Notes by Declan O'Carroll on 'Arup Associates' New Research and Design Unit', sent by e-mail April 2006.
14. Ibid.

Colors Restaurant

Jim Walrod and Dine Murphy Wood, Colors restaurant, Greenwich Village, New York, 2006
A row of stylised steel columns marches down the centre of Colors, dividing the bar near the entrance from banquette seating on the north wall and providing inspiration for the early 20th-century industrial decor.

One of the few good things to come out of the World Trade Center disaster was the Restaurant Opportunities Center of New York (ROC-NY), a nonprofit organisation formed after 11 September to provide ongoing support to displaced workers and families of victims from the centre's Windows on the World restaurant. Now ROC-NY has 700 members, is working to improve conditions for restaurant workers all over the city, and is helping displaced workers from all the World Trade Center restaurants open cooperatively owned restaurants of their own. Jayne Merkel describes the first, the ambitious Colors, which has 58 owners from 24 countries, most of whom once worked at the enormous Windows on the World at the top of the famous twin towers.

Dimly lit Colors, in rich browns and deep greys, is anything but colourful. Its name was chosen, before it was designed, to suggest the owners' palette of ethnicities. And its deep, narrow, completely enclosed 280-square-metre (3,000-square-foot) space is the antithesis of the 4,650-square-metre (50,000-square-foot), almost square one that was surrounded by 'Windows on the World' (or at least overlooking Manhattan). The original, sleek, daring modern interiors by Warren Plattner had been replaced in 1993 by a busy, chaotic, multicoloured scheme by Hardy Holzman Pfeiffer. Colors bears no resemblance to either.

It could, however, be mistaken for an eating place at the 1939 New York World's Fair. It is subtle, solid, dense and, apparently, aged, because designer Jim Walrod and the architects at Dine Murphy Wood took their cues from the 1920s commercial building in which the restaurant is located, in Greenwich Village, near the Cooper Union and the Public Theater on Lafayette Street, close to Astor Place.

'A row of tall steel columns marching down the centre of the space provided the only inspiration,' Walrod says, adding that the cooperative's international ownership and the industrial character of the space all seemed to recall the 1939 World's Fair with its global theme and buildings inspired by ocean liners of the time. Colors' brown columns have vertical dowels with curved tops and bottoms protruding from their surfaces, like flutings in reverse. These heavy stylised forms resemble those often found in projects from the Works Projects Administration (WPA) of the 1930s, 'the only really socialistic enterprise in American history,' as Walrod puts it. As at Colors, the goal of that programme, which produced not only works of art but also bridges, viaducts and dams, was to put people to work creating useful, well-designed things.

Colors' interior certainly does have the feel of that idealistic era – dark, solid, modern in an unselfconscious, industrial sort of a way although, of course, to create such an atmosphere in the 21st century required a heightened consciousness and appreciation of the design of the period when industrial materials were celebrated artistically. The lozenge-shaped dowels found on the columns are repeated, at various scales, on the mirrored bar and the wall that separates it from the dining area along one side.

A glistening corrugated 'safety glass' wall screens a private dining space in the rear, allowing glimpses in and out while casting an amber glow that is repeated in new light fixtures designed to look old in the banquettes along the south wall. The intimate banquettes are

Cosy banquettes along the north wall are upholstered with the same grey mohair used in old Packard automobiles. The banquettes are tucked under an enclosed catwalk fire escape and divided by maps in black-steel silhouettes on translucent amber glass.

The wide world from which the owners of Colors originate appears in the mural behind diners, providing a subtle glow and the illusion of space beyond the confines of the long, narrow, completely enclosed typical New York City restaurant.

cleverly tucked under a catwalk that houses a fire escape for the entire mixed-use building in the high-ceilinged space. Tubular Edison light bulbs and amber glass cylinders set on the dark steel fixtures approximate candlelight while maintaining the tamed industrial character of the rest of the space.

Partitions between the banquettes are made of water-jet-cut amber glass with black-steel silhouettes of the globe floating on top of them. And the global theme is expressed more emphatically in a colourful mural on the south wall where David Higginbotham, a decorative painter, has reproduced a 1974 map of the world that extends across three bays. The greens, reds, ochres and dark blues of WPA posters are etched in paint on the back of a mirror and then covered with clear corrugated glass, so the imagery is both emphatic and slightly elusive.

The gracefully curved yet solid chairs and tables with their round, black-steel, stepped pedestal bases are both popular items from the 1930s which, remarkably, were available from Chairmasters, Inc, a small furniture company located in the Bronx. The chairs have brown leather seats and backs upholstered in grey mohair fabric designed in the 1930s for Packard automobiles. 'These were really lucky finds,' says Walrod, who used to have a gallery with modern 'antiques'. The ceiling fixtures – globes with bands around the centre – came from a dealer he remembered who had owned them for 10 years.

Striated marble walls, brown-and-white in the entry area, black-and-white in the rear, have aerial maps etched into them, carrying the global place-making theme even further – ever so subtly. If the owners can bring the same subtlety to the cooking as they have to the design, for these restaurant workers the tragedy will have a silver lining. The dishes on the menu were inspired by the workers' favourite family recipes from all 24 countries, re-created by executive chef Raymond Mohan from Patria and the Park Avenue Café. The waiters' uniforms were designed by Cynthia Rowley. And all this was accomplished for little more than $1 million, partly because the designers worked *pro bono*. The restaurant has been a labour of love and resolve.

David Higginbotham's glowing mural on the south wall depicts a map of the world to reinforce the international theme. The various countries are painted in greens, reds, ochres and dark blues etched in paint on the back of a mirror and then covered with clear corrugated glass. Glowing pilasters between each section supplement light from recessed coves and ceiling fixtures.

Jordan Mozer & Associates: New American Narratives

Hudson Club, Chicago, Illinois, 1997
Based in Chicago, JMA has created several high-profile local restaurants including the Hudson Club, which continued the firm's tradition of playing with references from American design. Partially inspired by Norman Bel Geddes' futuristic 1929 design of an aeroplane, the design draws on Art Deco, yet distorts elements such as portholes to give the impression of the speed of flight

Jordan Mozer is a designer of surprising contradictions. Having pursued a specifically American form of storytelling through his designs for the likes of Bellagio in Las Vegas and the Hudson Club in Chicago, he despises the impulse towards homogeneity in the US. He begins all designs with a service plan, yet pursues the expressionistic potential of architecture. **Howard Watson** provides insights into the work of a designer who has proved as successful in Germany as in his hometown of Chicago.

Over the last 20 years, the Chicago-based practice Jordan Mozer & Associates (JMA), has explored specifically American narratives by drawing on geographical and cultural locality for the creation of highly idiosyncratic and successful restaurant, bar and retail interiors. With the recent completion of an acclaimed hotel in Germany and two new restaurant buildings that have shocked the American suburbs, the practice's highly intuitive and narrative approach is now making an impact both overseas and in the realm of the newbuild. It has also drawn up daring plans for a curvaceous new retail city in the desert. Curiously enough, it all started with a pet pig (more of which later).

Perhaps narrative architecture could be seen as a dead end in terms of classification – it is easy to argue that all buildings, no matter how prosaic, introduce some form of narrative even if the story is dissipated by the repetition of form or is confused by incoherent embellishment. However, the work of Jordan Mozer can be meaningfully determined as narrative, and he does not shy away from explaining both his influences and the resultant designs in the form of a story, even explicitly referring to his wish to create 'a once upon a time feeling'. Mozer's approach certainly bears comparison to the ideas that were being established almost simultaneously by Nigel Coates and Narrative Architecture Today (NATO) in London. Coates created NATO with a group of his students in 1983 when their work was deemed not 'architectural' by the Architectural Association (AA), and they went on to espouse a multidisciplinary approach whereupon seemingly divergent stories or cultural references are placed together in a new context. Mozer himself is a multidisciplinarian artist/designer/architect who was frustrated by his teachers' proscriptive mantra as to what constitutes architecture and, like Coates, he clearly enjoys pushing boundaries through cultural juxtaposition. Mozer, though, is an interested admirer rather than a conscious co-conspirator of Coates (listing him alongside the likes of Ron Arad and Frank Gehry as architects to whose work he is attracted), and the designs that result from their narrative approaches are very different.

If a label has to be prescribed, Mozer's is more likely to read 'New American' rather than 'old NATO'. The designer and his practice have created a specifically American-influenced form of storytelling through the built form, and his association with some of the major players of American culture, such as the film-maker George Lucas, restaurateur Richard Melman, Disney and hotelier Steve Wynn, are testament to this. This roll call of famous collaborators could infer that Mozer is knee-deep in the blandness and superficiality of commercial American culture, but the opposite is true. He revels in the heterogeneity of American society, and is an animated enemy of emotionally superficial content and the reduction of the range of influences on the built environment.

Mozer was initially drawn to sculpture and art, studying at the Art Institute of Chicago, and also studied writing at the University of Wisconsin. It was at Wisconsin in 1977 that he had a 'road to Damascus' moment when his roommate, an art history student, drew his attention to the similarity between his paintings and the buildings of Gaudí 'I decided then and there to go to architecture school as I saw that it was possible to be expressive – like sculpture – in buildings, and I didn't understand that before.'[1] Following degrees in both architecture and product design at the University of Illinois, he formed his own Chicago practice at a young age, becoming involved in restaurant design and linking up with George Lucas for a scheme to experiment with the possibilities of the shopping mall experience. Recession put paid to that idea, but the early 1990s brought success with designs for the Vivere restaurant in Chicago and, most significantly, the commission for the Cypress Club restaurant in San Francisco. Shortly after the Cypress Club project, architect Jeff Carloss joined Mozer and both the structure and ethos of JMA, which is now a mid-size practice with about 18 employees, were established.

Entering a Mozer-designed space such as the Cypress Club is to walk into an apparently surreal, filmic fantasy that begins with the approach to the facade as a prologue, followed by suggestions of the story through the unusual doorway and handle, before the interior envelops the customer in a multilayered world that has side-stepped accepted logic and proportion. Mozer cites Jorge Luis Borges as well as the surrealists as a major influence: 'There's a lot of structure to Borges that he messes with. He does it so well that you don't see the structure.' Similarly, though Mozer's work may seem fantastical, it is deeply rooted in an understanding of how spaces work in both a narrative and functional manner. The design always begins with a service plan to find the optimum functionality of the space before any creative ideas are thoroughly discussed.

It is crucial to Mozer's work that it is environmentally responsive rather than formulaic. He ties his practice's approach to his love of magic realism: 'In Gabriel Garcia Márquez's work, there's a mystery to it, an unfolding that references backwards and forwards all the time. He is writing for the Americas, he's writing for a blend of Europe, Africa and the indigenous peoples of the Americas. He is founded in *the place*. This is a very important thing for me, that each project is founded in *the place*. What I absolutely hate is how things have become homogenised. So much of Bond Street is the same as Rodeo Drive. So many hotels are homogenised. Márquez has a relationship between where he's from and where the story is set. He takes the reality of the Europeans, our sense of time, our sense of relationships, our expectations, but he also infuses the story with the reality of the indigenous people and the African people, their sense of time, their sense of legends, which make fantasy seem possible. There's a contained logic and dimension to what he's doing.'

Márquez's approach to storytelling was to be mirrored by Mozer's approach to designing the Cypress Club, which established his ability to develop a specifically West Coast – and suitably filmic – narrative that remains very distinct from East Coast counterparts.

Restaurateur John Cunin's Cypress Club venture was anchored to the rise of a new American cuisine in California, with an emphasis on fresh, local and seasonal produce that would match the burgeoning sophistication of the local wines coming out of Napa and Sonoma. Mozer says: 'We were looking for a way to represent this new American food culture. We were wondering what's American. Our architecture, especially in San Francisco, borrows tremendously from European architectural culture. John didn't want to follow the tradition. So we started to look at postwar American culture, which was very distinct from European culture, as here it was a time of optimism.' Mozer wished to reinterpret the soft, round futurism of late 1940s and early 1950s American car design and to take elements from the classic San Francisco diners of the same postwar period, particularly their non-European, 1.8-metre (6-foot) high wainscots, but he also played on the intimacy and mythology of European café society. Cunin and Mozer were also drawn to the paintings of Thomas Hart Benton, who captured the American landscape and the frontier mentality with what Mozer describes as 'a soft realism that was a little bit bigger than life'.

However, Mozer needed a device through which to reinterpret these forms and match the new American cuisine. It is here that the pig comes in. Mozer was inspired by the happily curvaceous shapes formed by his pet pig Clemente (named after the painter Francesco Clemente) as it sat in front of the fire. He decided to create a 'fat space', full of pudgy, organic shapes, hog-bellied beams, round lights and curving walls that expressed the natural bounty of the local produce as well as the rounded forms of Benton's paintings and the futurist cars of the 1950s. Mozer's wish to make sure that every element of the space carried through this curved motif led him to create many of the fixtures and fittings for the space, which is something he continues to do for each project. With the success of the Cypress Club, the principles were in place for JMA to focus on intelligent, bespoke and unusual designs that are rooted in their locale.

The Cypress Club heralded a decade of high-profile restaurant designs in the States, including the Hudson Club in Chicago, and Mozer's involvement with Disney in Orlando and Steve Wynn's Bellagio hotel and casino in Las Vegas. Mozer's work may be highly distinctive, but its signature curves and the way he inveigles comprehendible references make them unthreatening and inclusive. His designs may be shocking, but people still enjoy being seated in the centre of the narrative. 'On one hand we want the mythology that we usually recognise at some point – the story of the building and of the neighbourhood, or of the kind of space it is – to be legible. We want people to be comfortable, but we want to contrast with it things that don't quite fit the story ... We don't want to hurt anyone, but we want to surprise them and excite them, and we want to create a little bit of mystery.' Mozer is inspired by the blend of cultures that exist within American society. However, instead of responding to this with blandness or a reduction to the average, he takes risks, drawing out the unusual and fantastical to deliver narratives that fit within that heritage.

Despite espousing a ground-breaking American-narrative style and having been involved with the kind of high-profile American commercialism that can bring a European architectural cognoscente out in hives, Mozer has been able to translate his principles for a European audience. In recent years, his work has been received with tremendous enthusiasm in Germany, where he has designed bars, restaurants and stores, as well a children's museum for Volkswagen. When asked why he feels his work has found such acclaim in Germany, he says it may be because 'German buildings are so rational. Because what we do is missing there.' He sees a similarity between Chicago following the 1871 fire and many German cities following the Second World War, where devastation led to the rapid rebuilding of urban areas. 'As a child growing up in Chicago, all these Modernist buildings, all the high-rises, felt sterile to me and they made me unhappy. In Chicago, I wanted to try to create spaces that were more comfortable. There is the same problem in Germany with some of their Modernism – stripped down, inexpensive and soulless. I'm not an anti-Modernist, but I'm interested in appropriate Modernism. What is sometimes missing in Germany is the details, those layers of information and some of the warmth that used to be there before it was bombed out.'

East, his 2005 award-winning hotel in Hamburg, shows his adeptness at ensuring that his designs form a cohesive narrative with a particular environment. It is made up of a former foundry building, now housing a restaurant and four bars, and a purpose-built guest-room block centred on a sunken courtyard. The main dining space is a cathedral-like, 12-metre (39-foot) high space surrounded by the rising levels of bars, and features a monumental, sculptured wall of windows and huge carved pillars – it is a surreal, organic space which, like Mozer's youthful paintings, immediately brings to mind the work of Gaudí. The origins of the building are evident in the exposed brickwork and in

JMA's bespoke, metal and resin castings of everything from furnishings to candlesticks. The castings are inspired by the foundry origins of the building, but the design is also influenced by an Eastern recognition of spirituality.

As in East, the practice's work often has a central focus – Mozer refers to it as a 'doughnut plan' – where there is a ring of seating or facilities cusped around a lower, central hole. This gives a space focus, intimacy and inclusiveness and furthers the possibilities of the narrative. And it is taken to its extreme in Gamba Ristorante, JMA's intriguing newbuild in Merrillville, Indiana, which seems to coil up from the earth. The firm's other newly built restaurant is Copper Bleu on the outskirts of Minneapolis. Set alongside the anonymous new buildings of a strip-mall development, it has left passers-by stunned and has become an immediate local sensation. Yet its curving all-copper facades and its twisting, rising and undulating roof are directly drawn from the surrounding landscape, while elements of its courtyard garden and interior evoke memories of the local Midwestern passion for life in the wild outdoors. Like Gamba Ristorante and the design for the GGP City in the Southwestern US, Copper Bleu shows the extent of JMA's ambition to populate the American landscape with locally inspired narrative forms that revel in the heterogeneity of the culture. ⅅ

Howard Watson is a freelance journalist and author of *Bar Style: Hotels and Members' Clubs* (2005), *Hotel Revolution: 21st-Century Hotel Design* (2005) and *The Design Mix: Bars, Cocktails and Style* (2006), all published by Wiley-Academy.

Note

1 All quotations are from a series of conversations between Jordan Mozer and Howard Watson.

Gamba Ristorante, Merrillville, Indiana, 2006
The practice has recently stepped into the world of newbuild restaurants, taking the opportunity created by the expanding American suburbs to design startling, brick- and metal-clad, curving buildings that draw upon the American landscape.

Cypress Club, San Francisco, California, 1992
The Cypress Club restaurant was a major early success for Jordan Mozer & Associates and established many of the working and ideological principles that have sustained the practice's development. The interior, full of bulbous forms and curvaceous, handcrafted fittings, borders on the surreal, but it is an extension of motifs of true American (rather than European colonial) design. Mozer ensures that his designs are drawn from their physical and cultural locality, and reinterprets references that are established in the regional collective consciousness. At the Cypress Club, these include the curving fenders and headlight fittings of futurist car design from the 1950s, the 2-metre (6-foot) high wainscots and colour schemes of San Francisco diners from the same period, and jazz, represented by Mozer's painted interpretation of a Count Basie tune. Inspired by the curved forms of a pig, he made almost all the elements rounded, picking up on the fresh produce theme of the Californian menu while also offering a soft, comforting experience.

East, Hamburg, Germany, 2005
East, which won a European Hotel Design Award in 2005, features a 250-cover restaurant, four bars and hotel guest rooms situated in two buildings – a renovated foundry and a new block (the latter designed prior to JMA's involvement) – cusped around a central courtyard. The main dining area, sunken so its floor is at cellar level, is dominated by organically inspired, white sculptured plasterwork pillars and a three-storey wall – called the 'Hive' – with angled contours of plaster surrounding cut-out, internal windows. Four 8.5-metre (28-foot) high glass doors, leading out to the garden courtyard, constitute one side of the restaurant. Almost all of the interior design features of East have been specially created by JMA. Inspired by the building's former use as an iron foundry, many elements have been made from cast materials, including aluminium-magnesium-alloy three-legged tables and bar stools. The restaurant chairs and additional bar stools are made from a colour-integrated, fibreglass-and-Kevlar-reinforced resin that has been hand-finished to create a satin sheen. The design is also imbued with an Eastern, philosophical appreciation of the spiritual perfection of natural forms, which marries with the oriental influence on East's food and cocktails.

Copper Bleu, Minneapolis, Minnesota, 2006
Prior to development as a shopping centre, the land around the Copper Bleu restaurant site was rolling farmland with deciduous forest and prairie grasses. Mozer says that the owner, Scott Winer, wanted to buck the trend towards chain restaurants in the American suburbs, envisaging a dining experience that was rooted in local Midwestern, mid-century restaurant archetypes, but with modern, sophisticated and global influences. Evoking the local Dakota County prairie landscape and the outdoor cabin culture, the restaurant is made up of two undulating copper-clad buildings that wrap around a sunken terraced patio surrounded by evergreens. The interior extends the organic theme with wood, soft textiles and glass, while the ceiling is a wave of Douglas fir beams hung with chandeliers made up of around 30,000 incandescent test tubes.

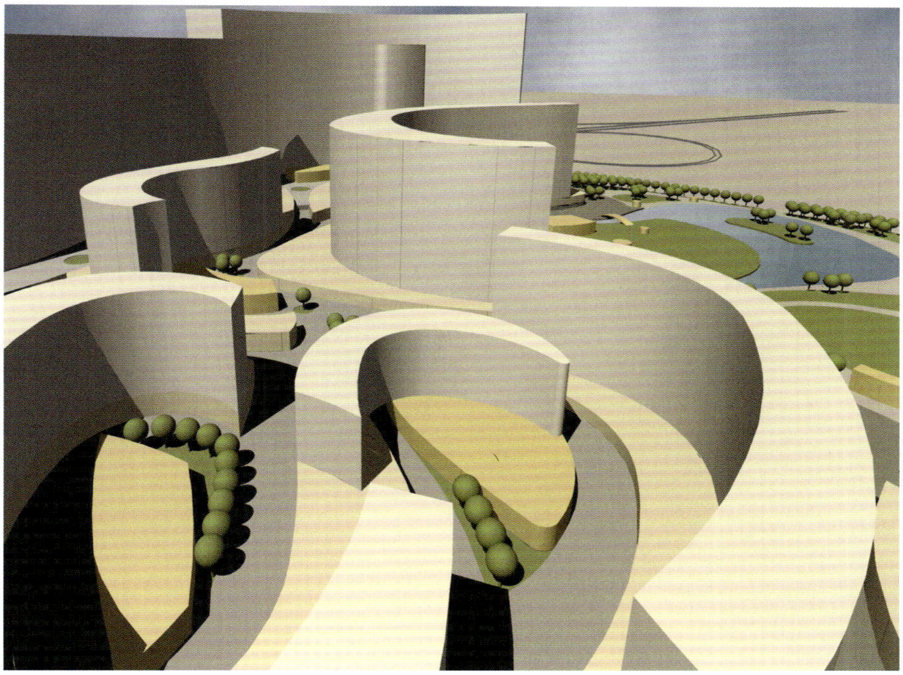

GGP City, Arizona, 2005
JMA's signature of enveloping curvaceous forms is taken to the extreme in a design for a retail city for General Growth Properties in Arizona. Once again, there is a specifically American, filmic narrative to the design, establishing the idea of a bold new future in a frontier, desert setting. Jordan Mozer is acutely aware that he has a social responsibility to the visitors to his retail and restaurant enterprises. This city design suggests that he could carry through his narrative, experiential ideals into the arena of permanent place-making.

Resumé

Jordan Mozer and Associates

1991
Vivere restaurant, Chicago

1992
Cypress Club restaurant, San Francisco

1993
Stars restaurant, Frankfurt
Surf 'n' Turf restaurant, Matsuyama, Japan
The Tempest restaurant, Houston

1994
Américas restaurant, Houston

1995
Mad 61 & Fred's restaurants at Barney's, New York
Iridium restaurant, New York

1996
Cheesecake Factory restaurant, Chicago

1997
Hudson Club restaurant & wine bar, Chicago
Coco Pazzo Café, Chicago
H2O Plus Office and Lab, Chicago
Rolling Stones tour conceptual studies

1997–8
Bellagio Hotel bars, restaurants & stores, Las Vegas

1998
Absolut Mozer for Absolut Design Series
Disney Quest entertainment centre, Orlando
Mythos restaurant at Universal Studios, Orlando
Venetian Hotel stores, Las Vegas
Outer Circle Products office & factory, Chicago

1999
XS restaurant & entertainment centre, Orlando
Allegro Hotel, Chicago

2000
Children's Museum, Cylinder Restaurant & store for Volkswagen's Autostadt, Wolfsburg
Trend Hotel Expo, Hanover
Lebensart Exhibition, Berlin

2001
Nectar Lounge at Bellagio Hotel, Las Vegas

2002–03
Karstadt department store prototype, Dusseldorf

2003
'Now's the Time' sculpture at Bellagio Hotel, Las Vegas
Royal Hotel, Miami
Herzblut café & club, Hamburg
Asprey & Garrard store, London

2003–04
Mikado, Anna Mae & Porthouse restaurants at Beau Rivage Resort, Las Vegas

2004
'Music Paintings', Jordan Mozer watercolour exhibition, Carl Hammer Gallery, Chicago
Wow Bao restaurant, Chicago
Canter's Deli at Treasure Island, Las Vegas
Bangkok Joe restaurant, Washington DC
Marsh Grocery store prototype

2005
East Hotel, Hamburg (Best Interior Design, European Hotel Design Awards 2005; Best Hotel Design finalist, Gold Key Awards 2005)
GGP City, Arizona

2006
Copper Bleu restaurant, Minneapolis
Gamba Ristorante, Merrillville

Jordan Mozer and Associates: Jordan Mozer (left) and Jeff Carloss (right). In 2006 they were joined by a new partner, architect Tom Rossiter.

House in Keremma

On the Brittany coast in northern France, Lacaton Vassal has built a home on the shore. **Jeremy Melvin** describes how the house's seemingly precarious sandy site celebrates nature for not being 'entirely benign', while also underlining architecture's ability to adapt the environment to human use.

Lacaton Vassal, House in Keremma, Brittany, France, 2005
View through the central block. When opened, the house allows wind and sound to permeate throughout.

Interior of the western block. It, too, opens to the sheltered precinct, though its internal spaces create their own relationship with the exterior.

Ever since they commissioned and chose the site of a traditional wattle-and-stick house in the desert of Niger, Anne Lacaton and Jean Philippe Vassal have been fascinated by the challenge of making a home from almost nothing other than imagination and its interaction with the qualities of a site. The house in Niger has no more than a circular wattle wall enclosing a simple domed hut, adjoining a rectangular wattle roof resting on nine posts, all resting on a sand bank. Their celebrated house at Cap Ferret, near Bordeaux, embracing a tree on a wooded sand dune, shows how building on sand has remained a feature of their work since their return to France, and even as they began to explore the aesthetic and volumetric possibilities of industrially produced components. The house at Keremma, near Roscoff on the northern coast of Brittany, continues the theme.

Its site has the typical qualities of a sandy seafront. Two strips run between dry land and the sea, one pure beach and the other a protective sand dune that is stabilised by vegetation. All this takes up only a few dozen metres, but the dune, though low, is high enough to make the sea invisible from the site. Instead, its presence is apparent through sound, wind and the rolling waves. In this interstitial zone between sea and where biblical lore might suggest constructing a house, sight alone is not enough; its true character only becomes apparent when all the senses combine to stimulate the imagination into suspending conventional perception, and so to open up new possibilities.

To Lacaton, these very particular qualities of nature are never entirely benign, and architecture is the discipline that adapts them to human use. Whether on the edge of desert or ocean, architecture starts by using what shelter occurs naturally and adding whatever is necessary to tame, but not exclude, the elements. Here the house, divided into three separated volumes, is pushed to the northern and eastern limits of the site, where a group of trees affords some protection. This arrangement presents a convex face to the north, defending the precinct from inclement weather, while offering a concave face to the south to create an intimate and protected exterior space that receives the southern sun. Occupation of the house emphasises this particular characteristic. When empty the three volumes are solid and separated, but when the house is inhabited the walls slide open, linking the three parts into a single curving suntrap, with minimal barriers dividing the interior spaces from the outdoor court.

All three blocks have the same dimensions of 13 x 7.6 metres (42.7 x 24.9 feet) on plan, and a double pitched roof reaching 5.6 metres (18.4 feet) high. This gives it a volume that is pretty close to the typical image of a house that a child might have, but what keeps this reference at an abstract level, and provides one means of differentiating the blocks from each other, is the nature of the cladding. Other means of expressing the differences between blocks are the internal organisation and their manner of closing. Were it not for the artful positioning and careful detailing, these three volumes might be mistaken for a trio of basic barns, individually adapted to particular needs. Each has its own internal character and a particular relationship with the exterior, which follows logically from that character.

At some subliminal level, the overall composition might have some reference to the traditional *parti* of a main block flanked by a pair of wings around a *cour d'honneur*, and in keeping with this the central volume is the heart of the complex. A living room/kitchen occupies almost the entire volume up to the roof, though a pair of sliding screens can divide two sleeping spaces adjacent to the bathroom according to the number of occupants. Solid walls slide back to reveal the interiors, and from most of the interior one is aware of the total volume, though from the outside glass screens interrupt and reflect some views, creating a richness of

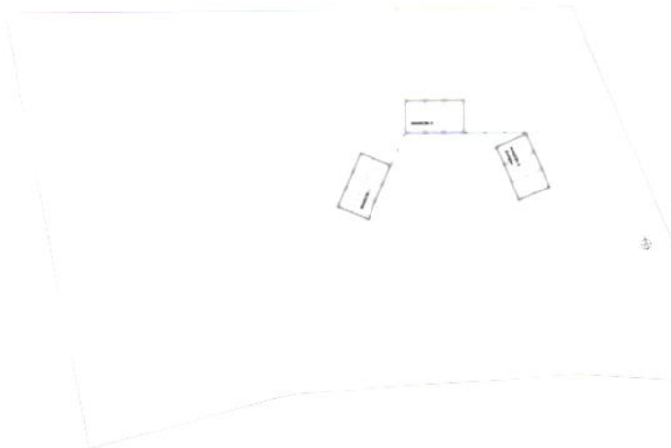

Site plan. Divided into three parts, the house provides shelter, but does not exclude the elements.

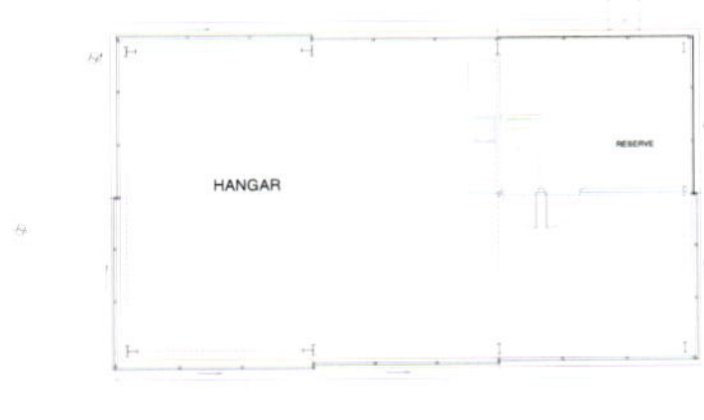

Plan of the eastern block, which provides covered space for games and storage.

Plan of the western block. With plenty of sleeping accommodation, the block is divided into separate spaces, each of which has its own relationship to the exterior.

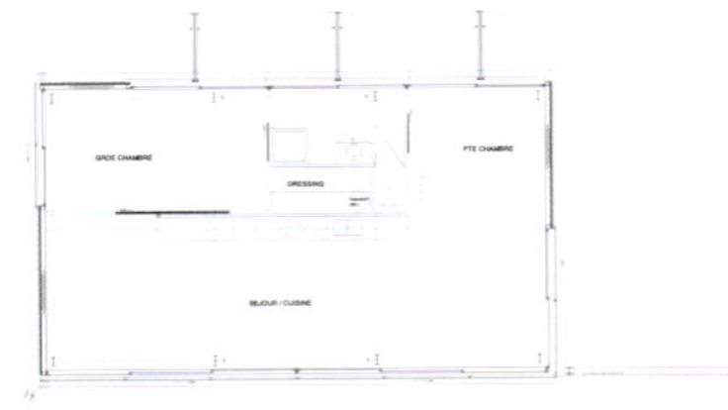

Plan of the central block, essentially a large, single volume with subtle means of differentiating the different activities and areas from one other.

Under a transparent roof and on a sandy floor, the east block allows outdoor games to continue even in a wet, northern European summer.

It is possible to sense the ocean between the blocks.

The Brittany coastline divides land from sea with clear thin strips of beach and wooded dune.

transparency and opacity that responds to the human need for occasional privacy as well as a sense of depth and space. In a landscape where sound, wind and smell seem to merge into each other and to roll like low clouds over the topography and between the foliage, the house begins to imply, if not impose, a sense of structure and order that complements nature's own structure of the dune as a means of protecting land from sea. Here nature and architectural space interact, not in opposition, but changing each other's characters in a continuous flow.

The second building, to the west, is divided into smaller spaces. It has a floor with five or six beds for children inserted into the roof, while at ground level are a living room, a kitchen, three large bedrooms and a large bathroom. As a logical extension of dividing the volume into smaller, defined spaces, every room has a particular character, and this is reinforced by giving each a unique view to the outside. Reflecting the division of the inside, the relationship between interior and exterior is treated as a series of discrete events.

Most fluid of all in function and its lack of distinction between inside and out is the third block, to the east. The architects describe it as a 'hangar', a large shed clad in transparent polycarbonate. Apart from an opaque enclosure with a shower and storage space it is entirely open, and the floor is compacted sand like the ground outside. This emphasises its ambiguous status between inside and out, with the architects suggesting that it is outdoors without the inconveniences, especially when its walls open to allow the continuity of ground surface to become apparent and only the vertical posts interrupt the flow of people and air. Here games can be played when it rains, hammocks can be set up for summer nights, or meals served on sunny winter days, and plants placed for protection from frost.

Overall, the design provides a graphic illustration of Lacaton's characterisation of architecture as the means to make nature habitable, but not to exclude it. As well as responding to nature, it also responds to the variations in family life: its division means that it can be occupied by a couple, with or without children, grandchildren and guests, and different generations can entertain themselves without disturbing each other, though always aware of a ghostly presence – the sea. ⌂

'House in Keremma' is also featured in Jeremy Melvin's book *Country Houses Today* (2006), in the Interior Angles series published by Wiley-Academy.

The group of volumes subtly delineates inhabited space from nature.

Islington Square, Manchester

With its bold gables, Islington Square is a conspicuous presence in New Islington, the area of east Manchester that is currently being developed to take the place of the dilapidated Cardroom Estate. Bruce Stewart explains how, rather than being an exercise in wilful pattern-making, the form of the facade and the interior planning of this unique scheme have come about as the result of FAT's lengthy consultation process with the housing residents.

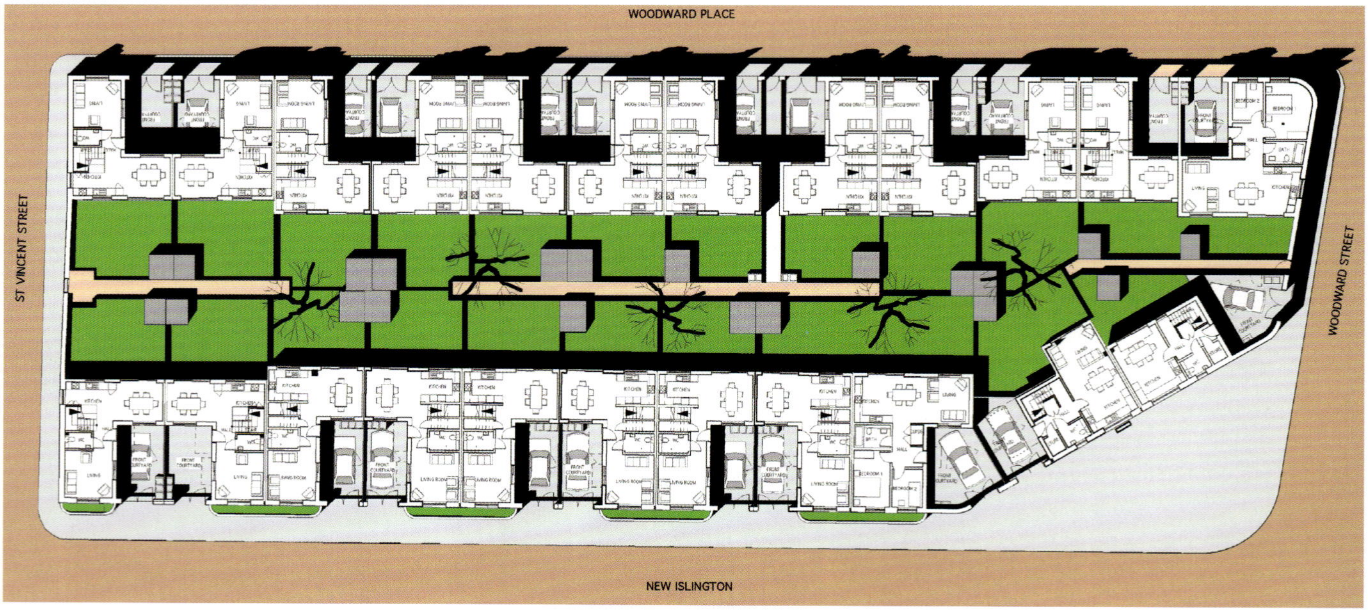

FAT, Islington Square, New Islington, Manchester, 2006
The layout of the block allows each of the houses to have a private, off-road parking space and a rear garden – essential to the new residents' ideas of what a home should have. All of this is then protected by the enclosing wall.

As part of the extensive New Islington redevelopment project in Manchester, Islington Square is one of the first of the affordable housing elements here to reach completion. The relatively modest development, consisting of 23 houses with a combination of two- and three-bedroom units alongside flats for the disabled, is unusual due to the very direct working relationship the architects, Fashion Architecture Taste (FAT), had with the prospective residents. From the outset, the residents had a very distinct voice in the decision-making process for the scheme. The subject of a RIBA competition in 2003, the entrants' proposals were not only judged by a jury of their peers, but by the people who would actually be the end users of the housing, who had very firm ideas about what they wanted.

The New Islington Millennium Community project is a partnership that includes the developers Urban Splash, regeneration agency English Partnerships, urban regeneration company New East Manchester Ltd and Manchester City Council. Its vast urban renewal project, over 12 hectares (29 acres), was master-planned by Will Alsop, and replaces the Cardroom Estate – a run-down and depopulated 1970s housing estate in the east of Manchester. The registered social landlord of the development is the Manchester Methodist Housing Group. There are over 20 individual plots for development by a wide range of architects, which will hopefully bring back life to what was a once desolate area of the city.

Such a range and mix of architects and designers echoes one of the primary tenets of the idea behind this millennium community: that a viable community is a mix – a mix of tenures, age groups, incomes and building types. However, a major problem has been that while for private developers, and in terms of creating higher densities, well-designed blocks of apartments are often seen as the most obvious and easiest solution, the Islington Square residents who chose to be involved in

The scale of the scheme is very much in keeping with the traditional brick terrace that is part of Manchester's industrial heritage.

Each of the individual houses has been given a distinct identity by the treatment of the gable facing onto the street. The polychromatic brickwork and the possibility of a small balcony not only define each house, but the block as a whole.

the new project were not unhappy with the traditional terrace or semi-detached typology, and in fact insisted that the new housing reflect their notions of home and security.

The community was asked what they wanted from the new development, and responses included both front and back gardens, two storeys, a pitched roof, safe parking, a greengrocer, baker, butcher, chippy, Indian takeaway, pub, personal security, property security, a footie pitch, and somewhere for the kids.

Residents' main concerns included a perceived lack of private outdoor space with flats, the materials that might be used (what would the housing look like), and a desire to reduce the amount of communal outdoor space, seen as just extra space for marauding gangs to congregate in. Thus the challenge for FAT was how to combine these quite traditional, yet valid, aspirations with the concerns currently facing all house builders – sustainability, increasing densities to maximise land use, and the notion of 'added value' for the end user. A further challenge was how to integrate the seemingly modest aspirations of the new tenants with the more 'slick' metropolitan architecture of sites being developed elsewhere as part of the regeneration of New Islington.

In order to help the residents explain their desires for and fears about the new housing scheme, the team at FAT undertook an exhaustive preliminary research programme that included several visits to the existing homes of residents to see how the space that was to be used as a model for the new scheme was inhabited. What were the requirements for daily life, and how could they be better provided for in the new homes? For example, central to any home is the daily ritual of cooking and eating. Although most of the existing homes had no separate dining room, in many a table and chairs had been placed in the living area, cramping the space for both eating and for relaxation. But, reducing the space in the living area was seen by residents as secondary to eating at the table.

Throughout the consultation process, the residents were adamant in their resistance to modern design, perhaps a legacy of the poor housing of the 1960s and 1970s where tower blocks and prefabrication that were once held up as ideal solutions are now seen by many as the cause of the current social problems. In order to broaden their horizons, a group of the residents joined the FAT team on a trip to the Netherlands to look at the recent developments in social housing there. Among the places visited were Borneo Sporenburg, master-planned by West 8, and Ypenburg, an old airport now being used as land for housing. However, although this helped the residents to see the wider design possibilities, they remained firm in their notions of what a family home should be, and it became clear that their ideas of a front door at ground level, gardens front and rear, and so on, were unshakable.

FAT's solution combines the desires and wishes of the residents with the firm's own idiosyncratic design perspective. Formed in 1995 as a research laboratory, the practice has undergone a number of personnel changes, but the driving ethos remains the same. FAT sees architecture as much more than a reductive process based on narrow, Modernist references. Using explicit, figurative imagery, its work could be seen as whimsical and devoid of serious concern about how architecture impacts on daily life. But this is most definitely not how the practice would describe its projects. Though the architects do react against the 'less is more' aesthetic, it is in a very carefully thought out manner. All their built projects are very context specific, using reference points from the particular environment of each. In a very assertive, graphic manner they hope to provide an alternative to the often sterile legacy of Modernism. Although this could be seen as a latent Postmodern methodology, their work is not a simple regurgitation and pastiche: it shows a concern for its impact on the environment and on those who will use the end product, setting up a dialogue between the nature of the building and the user. Thus, at Islington Square, the intensive working relationship with the residents has produced a very individual city block.

The L-shaped plan of the new houses considers the way in which the homes

ISLINGTON SQUARE	G 0-29%	F 30-39%	E 40%	D 41-49%	C 50-59%	B 60-69%	A 70-100%
QUALITATIVE							
Space-Interior							A
Space-Exterior						B	
Location						B	
Community					C		
QUANTITATIVE							
Construction Cost						B	
Cost-rental/purchase						B	
Cost in use						B	
Sustainability							A
AESTHETICS							
Good Design?							A
Appeal						B	
Innovative?					C		

This table is based on an analytical method of success in contributing to a solution to housing need. The criteria are: Quality of life – does the project maintain or improve good basic standards? Quantitative factors – has the budget achieved the best it can? Aesthetics – does the building work visually?

The Islington Square housing, while very different to its existing neighbours, will have to compete with the varied architectural styles of the rest of the New Islington development.

In their previous homes, the residents had gone to a lot of trouble to personalise their spaces, as in this example of DIY, proving that the adage 'an Englishman's home is his castle' is very much a truism.

were previously used by residents and tries to clarify and expand upon the way the spaces can be used. By keeping the number of walls to a minimum, the ground floor is freed up to provide an open-plan kitchen/dining/living arrangement that accommodates domestic rituals such as eating and cooking without compromising the need for space to relax. The nature of the plan thus creates space for daily life. The ground floor also includes a good-sized WC and storage space, which means it is flexible: for example, should at some point in time the occupier become unable to manage stairs, then the living area can easily be adapted to a bedroom with accessible bathroom space – very much part of the homes-for-life initiatives currently being talked about.

When combined in pairs, the L-shape plan again fulfils the desires of the residents by forming a terrace, so that each house now has a courtyard to the front, providing a private, almost defensible space. This can also be used for off-street parking, bike storage or as a buffer from the street.

On the first floor the generous landing could be used as a study area, for example. The bedroom and bathroom arrangement is a very standard layout, but again very much in keeping with what the end users wanted.

The external spaces of the development were yet another area for intense discussion between the architects and residents. The initial proposal for the layout of the gardens, with an alleyway bisecting them, was firmly rejected, perceived as a security threat since the space this would create would not be under constant observation by the residents. A compromise was reached with shorter passageways with key access.

In terms of construction, the concerns of the residents were again taken on board. For them, a house must look like a house, thus load-bearing masonry with internal blockwork was chosen for the scheme. This choice of materials gives the block a very solid presence and it is hoped that it will age well (perhaps better than some other technologies currently

While the layout of the ground floor allows for a more adaptable living space, the first floor maintains a more traditional form, though the landing could be used as a study area, for example.

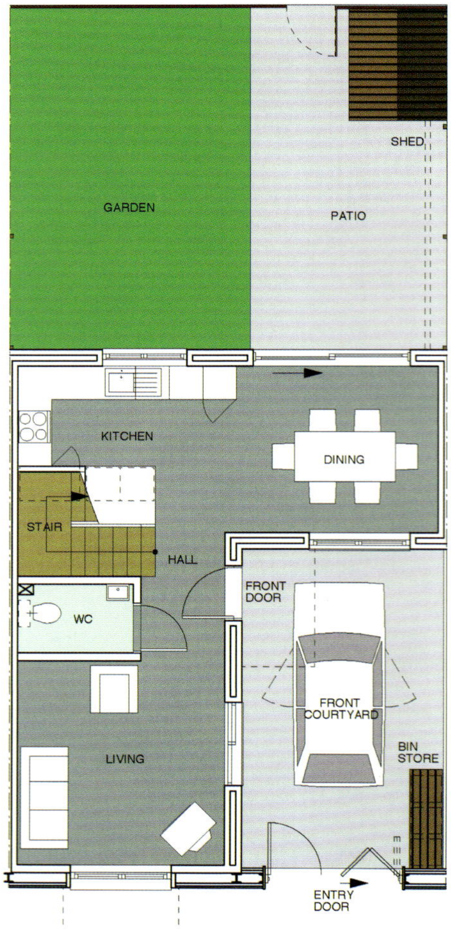

ground-floor plan

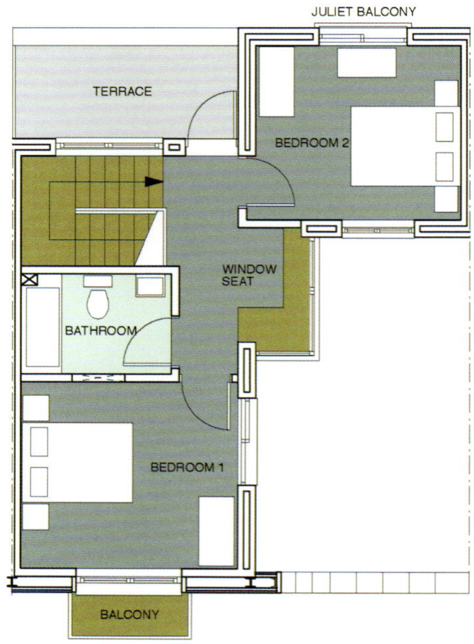

first-floor plan

being investigated in the affordable/social housing arena). The use of these materials alongside design decisions such as higher than normal ceiling heights, using micro UHP combined heat and power systems (which recycle their own excess energy) and good daylighting, have combined to give the scheme an 'Eco- Homes' rating of excellent.

Of all the features of the project, it is the encircling wall which protects and announces the scheme that is the most arresting. This polychromatic device at once declares the presence of the houses while allowing the residents shelter from neighbouring development. With the position of Islington Square on the periphery of the New Islington development, FAT wanted to give the scheme a very definite identity, not only in the context of the range of other architectural languages that are/will be employed across the entire 12-hectare (29-acre) site, but also in terms of empowering the residents of the project. They will be able to view their block from various vistas around the whole development and be able to recognise their own homes, for not only does the wall mark the urban block, but each gable end has an individual profile, arrived at after discussions between the architects and residents. Added to this is a small 'catalogue' of personal options for each household to choose from: for example, whether or not to add a small balcony. In this way, the potential for blank uniformity leading to anonymity for the residents, often associated with affordable/social housing, has been avoided.

Perhaps because FAT's work is as yet not very well known, at first glance the dramatic enclosing wall could be misread as strange, if not wilful, pattern-making. But the aims of this element – to announce and protect – have certainly been achieved, and the philosophy that architecture should be symbolic and rhetorical with meaning for its users can now reach a wider audience and, hopefully, stimulate some interesting debate. AD

Bruce Stewart is currently researching and writing *The Architects' Navigation Guide to New Housing*, to be published in early 2007 by Wiley-Academy. He trained as an architect and is currently a college teacher at the Bartlett School of Architecture, UCL London.

McLean's Nuggets

Outer Spaces

What have man's explorations of outer space delivered for humanity? One common answer is the nonstick marvel that is Teflon (see frying pans, PTFE and ETFE), which is true, but not the whole picture. The whole picture may be the image of Earth taken by William A Anders during the *Apollo 8* mission in December 1968, 'Earthrise', a hitherto unseen yet much-imagined world view of spaceship Earth. Described as one of the most important environmental images ever taken, it is often reproduced incorrectly as a horizontal landscape with the photographer routed to the moon. In reality this orbiting manned camera had no such fixed horizons. Like Antoine de Saint-Exupery's North African flying adventures during the nascent years of the aeroplane, this era-defining image of the world is at once a technological delight, while affording us new perspectives on the physical entity of Earth and its homeostatic cybernetic feedback-control system (AKA James Lovelock's Gaia).

'Earthrise' taken by William A Anders during the *Apollo 8* mission, 1968.

The competitive space race of the US and the former Soviet Union has not been the purely militaristic research and development of intergalactic weaponry initially imagined, but a very expensive zero-gravity research facility for what Buckminster Fuller called 'Livingry' (human life advantaging), as opposed to weaponry (human life disadvantaging). Nothing seems to focus minds like war and associated technological superiority, and we benefit from the huge advances in material sciences and information technology, but at a terrible cost. Livingry needs not the acuity of battle to operate, but the impetus for new modes, methods and methodologies for the development of human comfort and welfare.

The break-up of the former Soviet Union led to huge budget cuts in its various space programmes, but this failed to curtail the inventive potential of the Star City residents who, in 1999, unsuccessfully tested the elegant, but environmentally ambiguous, Znamya. Znamya was a 25-metre (82-foot) diameter space mirror designed to project a 5- to 7-kilometre (3- to 4.5-mile) diameter spot of souped-up 'lunalight' on the Earth in some of the former Soviet Union's sun-starved outposts. More recently announced by the Russian news agency TASS (November 2005), Nikolai Sevastyanov (head of Russian space corporation Energia) has stated their ambition to start mining for the nonradioactive isotope helium-3 on the surface of the moon (more specifically the Sea of Tranquillity) by 2020. While there are only a couple of tonnes of the stuff on Earth, the moon contains an estimated 500 million tonnes. Sevastyanov, quoted in the *Independent* newspaper, claimed that 'ten tonnes of helium-3 would be enough to meet the yearly energy needs of Russia'. I can hear the lunar bulldozers now. Meanwhile, at the NASA Institute for Advanced Concepts (NIAC), a small group of space-agency funded scientists continues to explore and exploit space-grade technology for the terrestrial customer.

Togged up

Building fabric is a widely used term to denote what a building is made of, but rarely describes a Semperian view of constructed building fabric. Why is this? We invest heavily in the commodity of performance in electronics, cars and clothing, but with buildings only the regulations will do. Human comfort is defined by U and R values, and now by 'airtightness', which does not sound very humanly comfortable at all. With clothing we do not accept poor technical performance unless the sartorial gain is worth it. In the field of technical textiles and engineered fabrics we expect the fabric to breathe yet maintain waterproofing, we can expect the fabric to 'wick' the moisture from our skin when we sweat, and we may also expect excellent thermal comfort (in building terms) in a slim cross-sectional area. To this end, companies such as Actis (based in France) are manufacturing and promoting thermal blankets to take the place of mineral wools or rigid foam insulations. Tri-Iso Super 10, also known as MLI (multi-layered insulation), is one such product. Another company, Aspen Aerogels, has just started to manufacture an Aerogel blanket for use in space suits, winter sports apparel and, tentatively, in building and construction. These thin translucent blankets have excellent thermal-insulation properties and good sound absorption, and can suppress infrared radiation and resist fire. Why does architecture not wholeheartedly embrace the clothing analogy and wrap up warm for the winter? Architect Adam Kalkin has proposed such apparel for a disaster-relief research project to be undertaken at Pingry High School in New Jersey, where his shipping container courtyard will gradually be clothed in thermal blankets, designed, fabricated and tested by the students over the course of one year. Experimenting with heat, coolth, shade, storage and waterproofing with a variety of fabrics and fabrication methods, the removable (functioning) layers are building jackets, coats, hats, scarves and tea cosies. In October 2006, the Institute for Nanotechnology is holding a conference in London – 'New Technologies and Smart Textiles for Industry and Fashion II' – to explore the future use of nano-coated fibres and fabrics in the fashion industry. Why the fashion industry does not specifically include architecture we can only guess, but it is surely the fault of the architect. If the 'designer' (generic description) were able to generically design, our physical environment would be much improved one supposes. Unfettered by the explicit demands of 'good design' (whatever that is), we may all be able to get on with 'performance-related fashion' ... I'm talking about some kind of loose-fit (technologically, not sartorially) combination of physical framework and appropriate (textile-based) clothing for site-specific, time-dependent climatic and social conditions.

A Tyvek-wrapped house in New Jersey.

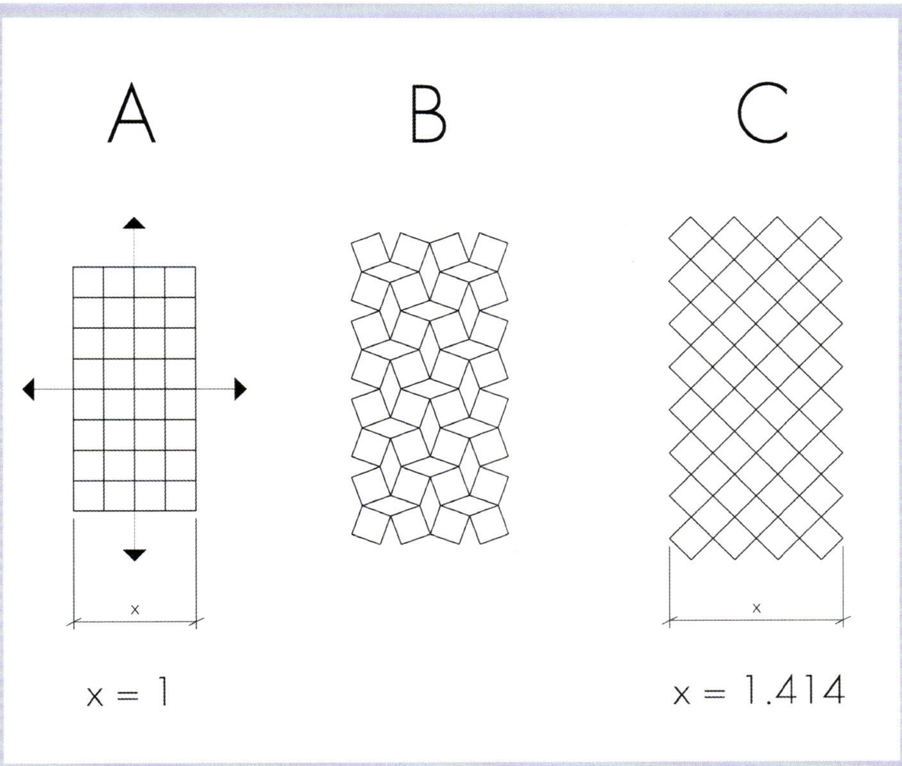

The principles of an auxetic expanding grid.

Auxetics: Expanding and Expanding
Who could resist writing about something called a negative Poisson's ratio? Far from a fish deficit issue, a negative Poisson's ratio is the chief property of a type of material or structure called auxetic. The word 'auxetic' has been attributed to Professor Ken Evans (head of the School of Engineering and Computing at the University of Exeter), and was first used to describe materials in *Nature* 353,124 (1991). It originates from the Greek *auxin*, or *auxegis* (to expand). Auxetic materials exhibit a curious effect whereby, as opposed to getting thinner when stretched (think of chewing gum), their width actually increases as their length increases. Likewise, when compressed their cross-sectional area decreases also. These types of material properties are not new, but have not until recently been identified as a material group. Another pioneer in this field is Roderick Lake of the University of Wisconsin (http://silver.neep.wisc.edu/~lakes/toPoisson.html). As well as this excellent web resource, Lake has also created auxetic polymeric foams by altering the hexagonal (close-packing) geometry through compression, causing a kind of inverted hexagon. The applications for these types of materials are extensive as, unlike many materials, auxetic structures happily transform from flat to synclastic and anticlastic (double-curved) without the material distortion (stretch) that other substrates suffer from. Auxetic materials can resist cracking and do not dent easily, because an impact causes the material to thicken at the impact point, the opposite of what usually happens when a material is weakened by the 'stretch' of a sudden force. Auxetic fibres are being explored for use in the composites industry (stiffening when stretched); and think how well the auxetic principle works when a structure is subject to the shear (twisting) forces of a building, a car or aeroplane. Add to that the auxetic (difficult to remove) bolt fixing/rivet and bullet-resisting apparel, and a wholly different approach to a branch of material science becomes possible. Also striking is the scalability of this technology. Lake is working at the micro scale, Evans at the nano, which leaves the macroscale for the designer, as we can simply enjoy the physical mechanics of these 'counterintuitive', 'anti-rubber', 'dilatational', 'optimised topology' materials. ᗡ

'McLean's Nuggets' is an ongoing technical series inspired by Will McLean and Samantha Hardingham's enthusiasm for back issues of ᗡ, as explicitly explored in Hardingham's ᗡ issue *The 1970s is Here and Now* (March/April 2005).

Will McLean is joint coordinator of technical studies in the Department of Architecture at the University of Westminster with Pete Silver. Together they have recently completed a new book entitled *Fabrication: The Designer's Guide* (Elsevier, 2006).

The Crown Liquor Saloon, Belfast

Jane Peyton, the author of *Pub Scene*, raises her glass and writes a eulogy in celebration of one of Britain's finest 19th-century gin palaces: The Crown Liquor Saloon, which remained a 'dowager' in Belfast during the troubles.

Visitors to the Crown Liquor Saloon are transported back in time, not just by the original Victorian tiling, woodwork and mosaics, but also by the lighting fixtures that still use gas to illuminate the pub.

Polychromatic ceramic tiles on the facade make the pub a Belfast landmark.

Visitors can drink in private away from prying eyes in one of 10 snugs.

Masterpiece is an overused word, but in the case of the Crown Liquor Saloon in Belfast city centre it is accurate. In a beauty pageant of Victorian gin palaces, the Crown is certainly queen. Such is the priceless decoration of this public house owned by the National Trust; and its status as one of the most unique pubs in the world is recognised by tourists who visit the city specifically to enjoy a drink in this one-of-a-kind watering hole.

So what is so special about the Crown Liquor Saloon? Well, for a start it is remarkable that this dowager has survived intact because it is situated directly opposite the Europa Hotel, which had the unfortunate experience of being bombed several times during late 20th-century terrorist campaigns. With a facade covered by a riot of polychromatic ceramic tiles and decorated with classical columns and pilasters, porthole and stained-glass windows, and a mosaic entryway, one might sense that this is no ordinary boozer.

The term 'stepping back in time' may be another cliché, but that is what it feels like on entry to the Crown, not least because it is still lit by original gas lamps and the natural light that streams in through stained-glass windows. Discretion and the class system were entrenched concepts in Victorian times, and the Crown Liquor Saloon still boasts a design feature that arose from those rules of 19th-century society. That is the snug, or drinking box, and the Crown has 10 of them, different-shaped carved-wood and stained-glass units entered by their own doors and screened from prying eyes or the hoi polloi. Each snug has a table and bench seating, and an antique bell system that still works. These snugs remain much in demand for secret rendezvous, private conversations and quiet lunches, and for the sheer novelty value of having a private room within a public house.

The concept of minimalism has no place at the Crown Liquor Saloon and there is something new to notice during each visit. The actual bar is a long red granite-topped fixture faced with yellow ceramic patterned tiles and divided by mahogany mirrored screens. A heated brass footrest runs along its base. Behind the bar is a hardwood cabinet that is decorated with coloured mosaic words proclaiming the pub's former distinction of being a 'High Class

The pub may look like a baroque church, but the features on the right are drinking snugs, not confessional boxes!

Whiskey Importer-Special Wines' and contains huge wooden casks with polished brass taps. The ceiling is decorated with yellow, gold and red plasterwork and supported by carved wooden columns with Corinthian capitals; the walls are brocaded, pilasters are tiled, windows are stained and everywhere you look glass is painted or etched with shells, fleurs-de-lis, fairies and pineapples. More is more is the concept here, and it works beautifully because the pub is constantly busy with customers who come to admire the extraordinary surroundings.

For some people, the Crown Liquor Saloon might remind them of a church interior – particularly with the stained glass, the mosaic floor and the snugs with their distinct resemblance to confessional boxes. Perhaps this is to be expected because the skilled craftsmen who created the pub were Italians moonlighting from building Catholic churches in Northern Ireland.

But despite its status as a National Trust heritage property, this is no museum where visitors murmur reverentially. The craftsmanship is so stunning it encourages strangers to talk to each other and that is, to use the Irish phrase, the start of a good *craic* – what all pubs aspire to. ᗡ

Jane Peyton is author of *Looking Up in London*, *Looking Up in Edinburgh* and *Fabulous Food Shops*, all published by Wiley-Academy. Her latest book on pub design, *Pub Scene*, was published by Wiley-Academy in February 2006. See www.wiley.com and www.pub-scene.com for further details.

Subscribe Now

As an influential and prestigious architectural publication, *Architectural Design* has an almost unrivalled reputation worldwide. Published bimonthly, it successfully combines the currency and topicality of a newsstand journal with the editorial rigour and design qualities of a book. Consistently at the forefront of cultural thought and design since the 1960s, it has time and again proved provocative and inspirational – inspiring theoretical, creative and technological advances. Prominent in the 1980s and 1990s for the part it played in Postmodernism and then in Deconstruction, in the 2000s AD has leveraged a depth and level of scrutiny not currently offered elsewhere in the design press. Topics pursued question the outcomes of technical innovations as well as the far-reaching social, cultural and environmental challenges that present themselves today in a period of increasing global uncertainty. AD

SUBSCRIPTION RATES 2006
Institutional Rate (Print only or Online only): UK£175/US$290
Institutional Rate (Combined Print and Online): UK£193/US£320
Personal Rate (Print only): UK £99/US$155
Discount Student* Rate (Print only): UK£70/US$110

*Proof of studentship will be required when placing an order. Prices reflect rates for a 2006 subscription and are subject to change without notice.

TO SUBSCRIBE
Phone your credit card order:
+44 (0)1243 843 828

Fax your credit card order to:
+44 (0)1243 770 432

Email your credit card order to:
cs-journals@wiley.co.uk

Post your credit card or cheque order to:
John Wiley & Sons Ltd.
Journals Administration Department
1 Oldlands Way
Bognor Regis
West Sussex PO22 9SA
UK

Please include your postal delivery address with your order.

All AD volumes are available individually.
To place an order please write to:
John Wiley & Sons Ltd
Customer Services
1 Oldlands Way
Bognor Regis
West Sussex PO22 9SA

Please quote the ISBN number of the issue(s) you are ordering.

AD is available to purchase on both a subscription basis and as individual volumes

○ I wish to subscribe to AD *Architectural Design* at the **Institutional rate of (Print only or Online only** ***(delete as applicable)*** **£175/us$290.**

○ I wish to subscribe to AD *Architectural Design* at the **Institutional rate of (Combined Print and Online) £193/us$320.**

○ I wish to subscribe to AD *Architectural Design* at the **Personal rate of £99/us$155.**

○ I wish to subscribe to AD *Architectural Design* at the **Student rate of £70/us$110.**

○ AD *Architectural Design* is available to individuals on either a calendar year or rolling annual basis; Institutional subscriptions are only available on a calendar year basis. Tick this box if you would like your Personal or Student subscription on a rolling annual basis.

Payment enclosed by Cheque/Money order/Drafts.

Value/Currency £/US$ ____

○ Please charge £/US$ ____ to my credit card.

Account number:

Expiry date:

Card: Visa/Amex/Mastercard/Eurocard *(delete as applicable)*

Cardholder's signature

Cardholder's name

Address

Post/Zip Code

Recipient's name

Address

Post/Zip Code

I would like to buy the following issues at £22.99 each:

○ AD 182 *Programming Cultures: Art and Architecture in the Age of Software*, Mike Silver
○ AD 181 *The New Europe*, Valentina Croci
○ AD 180 *Techniques and Technologies in Morphogenetic Design*, Michael Hensel, Achim Menges + Michael Weinstock
○ AD 179 *Manmade Modular Megastructures*, Ian Abley + Jonathan Schwinge
○ AD 178 *Sensing the 21st-Century City*, Brian McGrath + Grahame Shane
○ AD 177 *The New Mix*, Sara Caples and Everardo Jefferson
○ AD 176 *Design Through Making*, Bob Sheil
○ AD 175 *Food + The City*, Karen A Franck
○ AD 174 *The 1970s Is Here and Now*, Samantha Hardingham
○ AD 173 *4dspace: Interactive Architecture*, Lucy Bullivant
○ AD 172 *Islam + Architecture*, Sabiha Foster
○ AD 171 *Back To School*, Michael Chadwick
○ AD 170 *The Challenge of Suburbia*, Ilka + Andreas Ruby
○ AD 169 *Emergence*, Michael Hensel, Achim Menges + Michael Weinstock
○ AD 168 *Extreme Sites*, Deborah Gans + Claire Weisz
○ AD 167 *Property Development*, David Sokol
○ AD 166 *Club Culture*, Eleanor Curtis
○ AD 165 *Urban Flashes Asia*, Nicholas Boyarsky + Peter Lang
○ AD 164 *Home Front: New Developments in Housing*, Lucy Bullivant
○ AD 163 *Art + Architecture*, Ivan Margolius
○ AD 162 *Surface Consciousness*, Mark Taylor
○ AD 161 *Off the Radar*, Brian Carter + Annette LeCuyer
○ AD 160 *Food + Architecture*, Karen A Franck
○ AD 159 *Versioning in Architecture*, SHoP